SAFEGUARDING **CHILDREN** AND **YOUNG PEOPLE**

SAFEGUARDING **CHILDREN** AND **YOUNG PEOPLE**

A Guide for Nurses and Midwives

Catherine Powell

Open University Press

Open University Press
McGraw-Hill Education
McGraw-Hill House
Shoppenhangers Road
Maidenhead
Berkshire
England
SL6 2QL

email: enquiries@openup.co.uk
world wide web: www.openup.co.uk

and Two Penn Plaza, New York, NY 10121-2289, USA

A catalogue record of this book is available from the British Library.
ISBN 10 0335 220282 (pb) 0335 220290 (hb)
ISBN 13 9780335220281 (pb) 9780335220298 (hb)

Library of Congress Cataloging-in-Publication Data
CIP data applied for

Typeset by BookEns Ltd, Royston, Herts.
Printed and bound in Poland EU by OZGraf S.A.
www.polskabook.pl

The McGraw·Hill Companies

For Jonathan and Edward Powell –
two wonderful children.

CONTENTS

PREFACE

There are many reasons to believe that it is a good time to be a child growing up in the United Kingdom (UK). Along with almost every country in the world, the UK is a signatory to the United Nations Convention on the Rights of the Child 1989. We now have a Children's Commissioner and a Children's Minister to advocate for children and young people in England, Wales, Scotland and Northern Ireland. The rights of children and young people to be full participants in society, with a voice to be heard and to be reckoned with are increasingly being recognised. Improvements in standards of living and advances in the care and treatment of children, young people and expectant mothers have led to today's children enjoying better health and more positive outcomes than in any previous generation. Nurses, midwives, health visitors and school nurses have made a major contribution, alongside others, in achieving this laudable state of affairs.

However, as we celebrate the overall improvements in the health and well-being of our children and young people it is important to recognise that for a significant minority of families, life is far from idyllic. There remain major inequalities in the health and life chances of those children who are born into disadvantaged groups. This is reflected in the higher rates of infant mortality, reduced life expectancy and higher levels of illness and disability among the poorest groups in our society. New challenges for child health such as those relating to childhood obesity, mental health, sexual health and emotional well-being require the development of new approaches to ensure that children and young people have a healthy and productive future into adulthood. Furthermore, it is now widely understood that approximately ten per cent of all children and young people will suffer some form of child abuse or neglect during their childhood (National

Commission of Inquiry into the Prevention of Child Abuse 1996). As child health improves and new treatments are developed for previously fatal or life-limiting conditions, the morbidity and mortality from child maltreatment,[1] an essentially *preventable* event, feature ever more strongly as a key public health issue of our time. Child abuse and neglect thus needs to be on the agenda of all nurses and midwives who work with children, young people and their families. Furthermore, the potential of their unique role needs to be recognised within the wider safeguarding workforce.

Nurses and midwives provide a far reaching, universal and non-stigmatising service centred on the protection and support of the health of individuals, families and communities (NMC 2004a). This factor is an important aspect of the uniqueness of their contribution. Arguably however, while many nurses and midwives are in an ideal position to prevent, identify and respond to child maltreatment, they may not currently have a clear understanding of the theory and practice of safeguarding children. It is often said that safeguarding children is 'everybody's business' and this book, which is based on education, practice and research in the field, has fundamentally been written for *all* nursing and midwifery students and *all* qualified staff. This inclusiveness recognises that children and young people are accessing health care in ever diverse settings and, in addition, that those practising essentially with adults may find themselves in situations where health problems or disability impacts on their patient or client's ability to parent. Furthermore, nurses and midwives may also encounter practice situations where unresolved issues from childhood, such as sexual abuse, are continuing to have a major detrimental effect on an individual's health and well-being in adulthood. Prevention is uppermost, but where this is not possible a timely and appropriate response to suspected child maltreatment can have a major, even life-saving, outcome.

The book is written with a profound awareness that child maltreatment and its sequelae touch the lives of many individuals and their families. It is a matter that requires utmost sensitivity. For those who may like to be guided, or to guide others, towards additional sources of help and support outside of their organisations, details of a number of organisations and helplines are provided in the appendix. Professor Sir David Hall argued that, despite the difficulties, child protection work could be 'rewarding' (D. Hall 2003). This is a view that I share and my hope is that in providing knowledge for practice this book will help others in our caring profession take that view too and that, as a result, the major contribution that *all* nurses and midwives can make in safeguarding and promoting the welfare of children is finally realised. And the time is right to do so.

How to use this book

One of the key aims in writing this book is to ensure that it is easy to read and accessible. Essentially it is a book that can be 'dipped into' but it is probably best to read the chapters sequentially. Each chapter sets out the content and a number of *learning outcomes* that can be achieved. Within the text are some *case examples*. Whilst these are fictional they are drawn from real-life cases. Their brevity is deliberate and reflects the reality of practice whereby initial concerns need to be contextualised and tested out against a backdrop of uncertainty. The reader may like to consider what else they would need to know about the case and how they would go about finding that information before making a judgement that a child may be at risk of, or suffering from, harm. Without exception, all the cases are worthy of further assessment and enquiry. There are also some interspersed *points for reflection* which are designed to encourage practitioners to think about their own practice context and to seek local sources of information, help and support. Practitioners may also like to consider how reflective activities can help them to develop specific competencies in safeguarding practice and how they may demonstrate this learning and development within their professional portfolio.

The chapters conclude with bullet-pointed *messages for practice* and a short list of *recommended reading*. Full references are given at the end of the book and here the aim has been to draw largely on British works that are easily accessed in the library or, in many cases, downloaded from the internet.

Children and young people's safeguarding policy in the United Kingdom

At the end of the 1990s central government devolved some of its key functions to the governments and offices of Wales, Scotland and Northern Ireland. This has meant that children's policy has become more of a discrete function of each of the four countries of the UK. In England safeguarding policy is now the responsibility of the Department for Education and Skills; in Wales the Welsh Assembly Government take the lead; in Scotland it is the Scottish Executive and in Northern Ireland it is the Department of Health, Social Services and Public Safety. This presents a problem to anyone wishing to author a book on safeguarding practice in the UK, given that government guidance provides the overall framework. However, to reference four sets of guidance, associated legislation and supporting documents would be somewhat clumsy and repetitive. Whilst this book largely features the English system, where it seems appropriate reference is given to policy (and research) from one or more of the other countries of the UK. Practitioners looking for their key overarching safeguarding policy guidance are directed as follows:

England

HM Government (2006) *Working Together to Safeguard Children: A Guide to Inter-agency Working to Safeguard and Promote the Welfare of Children.* London: Department for Education and Skills.

Wales

All Wales Area Child Protection Committees (2005) *All Wales Child Protection Procedures*. Cardiff: Wales Child Protection Review Group.

Scotland

Scottish Executive (2004) *Protecting Children and Young People: Framework for Standards*. Edinburgh: Scottish Executive.

Northern Ireland

DHSSPS (Department of Health, Social Services and Public Safety) (2003) *Co-operating to Safeguard Children*. Belfast, Northern Ireland: DHSSPS.

In addition, it should be noted that broader children's policy, in which safeguarding policy is embedded, is developing rapidly in each country. It is suggested therefore that readers 'bookmark' their country's lead department's website in order to keep abreast of developments and to develop their practice accordingly.

LIST OF ABBREVIATIONS

ACPC	Area Child Protection Committee
BMA	British Medical Association
CAFCASS	children and family court advisory and support service
CAMHS	Child and Adolescent Mental Health Services
CDOP	Child Death Overview Panel
CDRM	Child Death Review Meetings
CEOP	Child Exploitation and On-line Protection
CFHI	child friendly healthcare initiative
CPC	Child Protection Committee
CSCI	Commission for Social Care Inspection
CVS	court video surveillance
DfES	Department for Education and Skills
DH	Department of Health
DHSS	Department of Health and Social Security
DHSSPS	Department of Health, Social Services and Public Safety
EPO	Emergency Protection Order
FGM	female genital mutilation
FII	fabricated or induced illness
FTT	failure to thrive
GCP	graded care profile
GP	general practitioner
ICT	information and communication technology
LGA	Local Government Association
LSCBs	Local Safeguarding Children Boards
MAPPA	multi-agency public protection arrangements
MSbP	Munchausen Syndrome by Proxy
NCIPCA	National Commission of Inquiry into the Prevention of Child Abuse
NICE	National Institute for Clinical Excellence
NMC	Nursing and Midwifery Council

NSCAN	National Safeguarding Children Association for Nurses
NSF	*National Service Framework for Children, Young People and Maternity Services in England*
NSPCC	National Society for the Prevention of Cruelty to Children
NWGCPD	National Working Group on Child Protection and Disability
ONS	Office for National Statistics
PCT	primary care trust
RCN	Royal College of Nursing
RCPH	Royal College of Paediatrics and Child Health
SCPHN	Specialist Community Public Health Nurse
SHA	Strategic Health Authority
SIDS	Sudden Infant Death Syndrome
SUDI	Sudden Unexpected Death in Infancy
UNCRC	United Nations Convention on the Rights of the Child
UNICEF	United Nations Children's Fund
WCPSRG	Welsh Child Protection Systematic Review Group
WHO	World Health Organisation

chapter **one**

INTRODUCTION: WHY A SAFEGUARDING CHILDREN GUIDE FOR NURSES MIDWIVES?

Learning outcomes

This chapter will help you to:

- define safeguarding and associated concepts;
- debate the importance of the universality of the nursing and midwifery professions to safeguarding practice;
- compare and contrast the core attributes of safeguarding with the defining attributes of nursing;
- understand the need to promote and protect the best interests of the child.

Introduction

The provision of care to families where issues of possible or actual child maltreatment have been raised is probably one of the most difficult and challenging areas of contemporary practice that nurses and midwives will encounter. Experience suggests that there are three key elements that will help practitioners face such challenges and make a confident, valuable and unique contribution to safeguarding children and promoting their welfare. These elements are:

- a sound knowledge base;
- accessibility of supportive advice and clinical supervision; and
- engagement in integrated working with other children's services.

Clearly this book cannot provide all of the above. However, what it does aim to do is to provide knowledge for practice in a way that serves to encourage nurses and midwives to be proactive in supporting children and young people to achieve optimum health and well-being and to ensure a timely and professional response to any concerns.

Points for reflection
Have you ever come off duty with a feeling that all was not well with a child, young person or their family?
Or wondered whether an expectant mother would be able to provide for the needs of her newborn baby?
Or whether an adult you are caring for has health or social problems that may interfere with their ability to parent?
Have you felt able to take action to share your concerns?
This book will help you to develop your knowledge and skills in safeguarding children, explain how the actions that may be taken by nurses and midwives can protect children and young people from harm, and how you can seek local support.

Next steps
As you progress through the book make a note of the actions and pathways that you may follow in ensuring the safety and well-being of a child or young person who you may recognise to be at risk of, or suffering from, significant harm. This should include noting which guidance informs your actions and who else is likely to be involved.

This opening chapter introduces the concept of safeguarding children and young people. The chapter includes a review of the

Victoria Climbié case and the subsequent developments in policy that have sought to improve the lives and life chances of all children. The overarching aim of safeguarding work is to make sure that children and young people are able to reach their potential and enter adulthood successfully and, with appropriate support, knowledge and understanding, nurses and midwives can make a significant contribution to achieving this. The core attributes of these professions and those of safeguarding are discussed and seen to be symbiotic. The chapter closes with an outline of the remainder of the book.

What is 'safeguarding'?

Interestingly, it would appear that 'safeguarding' is a term that has increasingly replaced the notion of 'protecting children' when referring to the prevention of, and response to, child abuse and neglect. Recent statutory reconfiguration of the 'Area Child Protection Committee' (ACPC) to the 'Local Safeguarding Children Board' (LSCB) in England and Wales under the auspices of the Children Act 2004 illustrates the case in point. Safeguarding is best thought of as an umbrella term for a number of different, but related, actions that ensure the well-being of children and young people, all of which may be encompassed within the professional activities of nurses and midwives.

A basic definition of safeguarding is provided in a joint inspectorate review of services for children, young people and their families: here it is suggested that at its simplest safeguarding means 'keeping children safe from harm such as illness, abuse or injury' (Commission for Social Care Inspection et al. 2005: 5). However, this definition says little about how this can be achieved. The recent Government guidance for England, *Working Together to Safeguard Children,* opens by emphasising that safeguarding children and young people is primarily accomplished through good parenting: 'Good parenting involves caring for children's basic needs, keeping them safe, showing them warmth and love and providing the stimulation needed for their development and to help them achieve their potential, within a stable environment where they experience consistent guidance and boundaries' (HM Government 2006a: 1).

The guidance also recognises that parenting can be challenging and that parents may require support and help. It notes that early engagement and partnership with professionals is of key importance. Furthermore, the guidance suggests that where parents seek help from the wide range of services available to families this should be seen as a sign of responsibility not of failure. The need for competent professional judgement, based on a sound assessment of the needs of the child or young person and the parents' capacity to respond to these needs is made clear at the outset. The guidance notes that the requirement for any compulsory intervention in family life should be seen as 'exceptional' (p. 2). This is important because it supports the notion that universal services, such as health and education, have a key role to play in early intervention and support to families experiencing difficulties. Other countries in the UK take a similar stance.

Safeguarding and promoting the welfare of children and young people is thus seen to encompass a number of separate, but interrelated activities (HM Government 2006a). These include: protecting children from maltreatment; preventing impairment of their health and development; and ensuring that they are safe and well cared for. The overarching aim of safeguarding work is to make sure that children and young people are able to reach their potential and enter adulthood successfully.

Child protection is clearly seen as an important part of safeguarding, but refers specifically to the actions undertaken to protect children who are at risk of, or suffering from, significant harm. Crucially, the guidance suggests that proactively safeguarding children and promoting their welfare will reduce the need for interventions to protect children. It thus appears that in comparison with previous child protection guidance there is considerably more emphasis on *promoting welfare* rather than simply recognising and responding to child abuse and neglect. This has important implications for nurses and midwives who are engaged primarily in preventative services as well as other, more specialist health services that care for children, young people and their families in a variety of settings. Nevertheless, in common with the previous editions of *Working Together* the emphasis on joint working between agencies and professionals remains, with the recognition that some of the most vulnerable children, especially those at risk of social exclusion, will need coordinated help from a number of agencies including health, education and children's social care.

The need for joint working and its perceived failings are often reflected in the public inquiries into headline child maltreatment tragedies. Perhaps most notably this includes the [then] Department of Health and Social Security's (DHSS) report into the death of Maria Colwell (DHSS 1974) and the London Borough of Brent's inquiry into the death of Jasmine Beckford, published in 1985. Both have been instrumental in the setting up of multi-agency child protection systems and the production of Government guidance and legislation to better protect children. The death of Victoria Climbié and Lord Laming's subsequent inquiry report, published in 2003, have been pivotal to new guidance and legislation. The new guidance and legislation not only seek to ensure better protection of children, but also to introduce and to develop wider policies to improve the outcomes for all children and young people, particularly those who are most disadvantaged. The timeline illustrated below, which has been adapted from Corby (2006), provides a quick overview of the key events that have influenced the development of policy and practice in this dynamic field.

1974	Maria Colwell inquiry (non-accidental injury) Formation of the child abuse prevention system
1975	Susan Auckland inquiry and Children Act
1974–80	Seventeen public inquiries into child abuse deaths
1980	Broadening of concerns (child abuse)
1981–85	Fifteen public inquiries into child abuse deaths
1984	Short report
1985	Jasmine Beckford inquiry MORI poll survey into child sexual abuse
1986–91	Twelve public inquiries into child abuse deaths
1986	Draft Working Together guidelines (child protection)
1987	Kimberley Carlile and Tyra Henry inquiries
1988	Cleveland inquiry and new *Working Together* guidelines
1989	Children Act
1991	*New Working Together* guidelines
1995	*Child Protection: Messages from Research*
1996	National Commission of Inquiry into the Prevention of Child Abuse
1999	New *Working Together to Safeguard Children*
2000	The framework for assessment of children in need and their families
2000	Safeguarding Children Involved in Prostitution
2002	Safeguarding Children in Whom Illness is Fabricated or Induced
2003	The Victoria Climbié inquiry: Report of an inquiry by Lord Laming
2003	*Every Child Matters* Green Paper
2004	The Chief Nursing Officer's Review into the nursing, midwifery and health visiting contribution to vulnerable children
2004	National Service Framework for Children, Young People and Maternity Services: Core Standards
2004	*Every Child Matters: Change for Children*
2004	Children Act
2005	Safeguarding Children: The Second Joint Chief Inspectors' Report on Arrangements to Safeguard Children
2006	New *Working Together to Safeguard Children*

Other 'headline' cases that have also been influential in contemporary policy development across the UK include the death of Lauren

Wright (Norfolk Health Authority 2002), Ainlee Walker (who was also known as Ainlee Labonte; Newham Area Child Protection Committee 2002) and Kennedy McFarlane (Hammond 2001; Scottish Executive 2002). However, the importance of the Victoria Climbié inquiry and its findings and recommendations are of particular significance to the nursing profession and are thus outlined in the following section.

The Victoria Climbié inquiry

The report of Lord Laming's inquiry into the death of Victoria Climbié makes disturbing reading (Laming 2003). The report contains vivid details of the appalling maltreatment suffered by this young girl and it clearly highlights 12 key occasions where opportunities to intervene to protect her were missed. Laming described the extent of failures in the system as 'lamentable' (p. 3). Nursing staff and their medical colleagues were among the numerous professionals from a range of agencies and organisations who were seen to have failed in their duty to protect Victoria. As Corby (2006) notes, the main recommendations of the report centre on strengthening inter-agency processes, record keeping and information sharing rather than developing the expertise of practitioners *per se*. Nevertheless, whilst Stevenson (2005b: 97) is clear that the 'gross deficits' highlighted in the report do not reflect usual practice in the UK, there are important messages for nurses, especially those working in hospital settings, and thus an outline of the case, drawn from the inquiry report, is given below.

Victoria's story

Victoria Climbié was born on the Ivory Coast on the 2 November 1991. She was said to be a lovable and intelligent child who, in 1998, was apparently taken by a great aunt to France, and subsequently to England with a view to obtaining a better education and more opportunities for the future. However, what followed was an almost unbelievable sequence of escalating violence and maltreatment that implicated both the great aunt (Marie-Therese Kouao) and a new partner (Carl Manning) as the perpetrators.

The physical abuse and neglect suffered by Victoria ultimately led to her death, aged 8 years and 3 months, on 25 February 2000. The post-mortem, undertaken by a Home Office pathologist, said to be the 'worse case [of child abuse] he had ever dealt with ... or heard of' (Laming 2003: 1), found 128 separate injuries on her body. It transpired that Victoria had been beaten with implements such as shoes, football boots, a coat hanger, a wooden cooking spoon and a bicycle chain. Furthermore, she was also said to have spent long periods of time tied up in a bin-bag, covered in urine and faeces and made to eat leftover food off a piece of plastic 'like a dog'. When Victoria was admitted to hospital in a moribund condition she was found to be bruised, deformed, hypothermic and malnourished. Kouao and Manning are currently both serving life sentences for her murder.

Whilst it is likely that Victoria was hidden from view for much of her last remaining days it transpired that during her time in England she was known to three housing authorities, four social services departments, two police service child protection teams and a National Society for the Prevention of Cruelty to Children (NSPCC) family centre. She was also admitted to two separate hospitals, the first time because of concerns about various cuts and marks on her face and hands and the second time following a scald to her face. The second admission spanned 13 days. Victoria was also seen at some point by a practice nurse, who undertook a 'new patient' review. In addition to the contact Victoria and her great aunt had with statutory agencies, she was seen from time to time by distant relatives and also members of the church. For a brief period of time Victoria was also cared for by a childminder. However, she did not, despite the given reasons for her coming to Europe, attend school whilst she was in England. What is notable about the contributions to the inquiry made by the 'lay people' who had contact with Victoria, is that they had evidently been concerned about her welfare and in some instances had taken action in contacting statutory agencies to share their concerns.

With the benefit of 'retrospectoscopy' (Alper 2005) it is clear that Victoria Climbié was a victim of severe physical abuse and neglect and the failure of so many agencies to protect her seems astonishing. But, as Corby (2006) has highlighted, much of the contact with agencies was centred on issues of homelessness and securing accommodation, rather than responding to any jointly held concerns about Victoria's safety and well-being. Nevertheless, the focus on the (very real) needs of adults has been documented previously as being a fundamental issue in failings to protect children (London Borough of Brent 1985; Cantrill 2005). In these instances the children and young people appear to take on an invisible quality in the shadow of the problems faced by their parents and carers.

The inquiry recognised that there were some reports of concern from professionals and others who knew Victoria during her short time in the country. She had been noted to be small and frail and had been seen to be inappropriately dressed. The possibilities of child maltreatment were raised by individual health professionals during both hospital admissions. However, as Laming notes:

> The concerns that medical and nursing staff at the hospital told me that they felt about Victoria never, in my view, crystallised into anything resembling a clear, well-thought-through picture of what they suspected had happened to her and that would have helped social services in determining how best to deal with her case.
>
> (Laming 2003: 274)

The contribution of the nursing staff, albeit given in hindsight to the inquiry, reflects important omissions and failures in the documentation and reporting of their espoused concerns. Basic social history data, such as where Victoria was at school, does not seem to have been collected (and specific enquiries should always be made of any school-aged child who is missing, or frequently absent, from education). It may be unfair to be judgemental, and to question professional practice, without knowing more about how well the nurses involved in the care of Victoria were prepared or supported in safeguarding practice. It can also be very difficult for nurses and midwives to challenge the clinical decisions made by other colleagues. Nevertheless, the above quote suggests fundamental principles of assessment and care-planning were not followed through. Because of their involvement with the family during Victoria's hospitalisation, several members of the nursing staff were called to give evidence to the inquiry panel.

Nursing evidence to the inquiry

In their evidence to the Laming inquiry nursing staff reported observing and discussing possible physical and behavioural indicators of abuse. These included seeing lesions that they later considered to be serious deliberate physical harm such as burns, belt marks and bites. As worrying were their reports of witnessing Victoria's demeanour in the presence of Kouao and Manning. This was described as a 'master and servant' relationship that they illustrated by describing how Victoria would stand to attention and change from being lively and vivacious to withdrawn and timid on their infrequent visits to the ward. On one occasion she was seen to 'wet herself' in their presence. Furthermore, unlike possibly every other child admitted to hospital in the UK, it was perhaps notable that Victoria's 'parents' brought her no treats during her relatively lengthy admission; nursing staff even provided her clothing.

The inquiry report suggests that 'failure of nursing staff to record their observations in the notes, and the consequent discrepancy between the levels of concern they expressed in their oral evidence and that reflected in the records made at the time, was a matter which arose with depressing regularity' (Laming 2003: 261). Laming argued that nurses have a vital contribution to make in recognising and reporting abuse and that this includes a fundamental responsibility to record suspicious injuries. I share this viewpoint and have previously expressed much the same sentiment, based on duties and responsibilities, to the children's nursing profession (Powell 1997). However, the scale of the challenge of ensuring that such a large and diverse workforce, with many competing priorities and responsibilities, attain competence in safeguarding children practice, as well as having the knowledge base to understand 'normal' childhood and family life should not be underestimated.

Inquiry recommendations

Not surprisingly the inquiry made a number of recommendations for health services, especially in relation to the need for good record keeping and documentation of concerns. In addition, the recommendations point to the need to ensure that difference of opinion is reconciled and that any actions or referrals are carefully documented and followed through. Discharge of a child from hospital back into the community is seen to be a pivotal point for ensuring continuity of care and follow-up, particularly if there are outstanding issues or concerns about a child. This may well be a point at which nursing and midwifery staff, who arguably have a greater degree of continuity of care for inpatients when compared with their medical colleagues, can intervene to ensure that it is safe to discharge a child from both a medical and a social perspective.

The Government response

The death of Victoria Climbié and the subsequent inquiry report were highly significant in the development of the *Every Child Matters: Change for Children* policy programme. This in turn incorporates the *National Service Framework for Children, Young People and Maternity Services* in England (NSF) (DH 2003; DH, DfES 2004b). The NSF, which also drew on lessons to be learnt from the Kennedy Report of the public inquiry into children's heart surgery in Bristol (Kennedy 2001), provides an important benchmark for the health and social care of children, young people and their families. Although the Kennedy and Laming reports were looking into disparate areas of care, a unifying theme was the call for professionals to centre their practice first and foremost on the needs and well-being of the child. The NSF, which is evidence-based, outlines 11 national standards for children's health and social care that form the basis on which service providers will be inspected and is of vital importance in guiding and developing nursing and midwifery practice. The central thrust of the NSF is that services should be high quality, personalised and centred on the needs of women and children. However, it also picks up on the themes of promoting health and tackling inequalities. Core Standard Five, which relates specifically to safeguarding children, is outlined below, although wider safeguarding practice provides an important thread throughout the whole document.

National Service Frameworks

In England the NSF Core Standard Five states that: 'All agencies work to prevent children suffering harm and to promote their welfare, provide them with the services they require to address their identified needs and safeguard children who are being or who are likely to be harmed' (DH, DfES 2004: 145). A number of markers of good practice are suggested. These place an emphasis on the local development of safeguarding policies, procedures and practices, including those concerned with recruiting and managing staff. Prevention is seen to be key with the focus on activities to make certain that children and young people achieve optimal outcomes. The NSF advocates actively involving children, young people and families in assessment processes and ensuring the accessibility of universal services, such as health, education and housing. Particular note is made of the increased likelihood of harm being suffered by children and young people with disabilities, an issue that is highlighted in Chapter 5 of this book.

The standard states categorically that all staff (whatever their level) should understand their roles and responsibilities in safeguarding and promoting the welfare of children and young people. It recognises that they will need both training and support to enable them to do so. The standard also states that senior management must take responsibility for the actions of its staff and that difference in professional opinion will need to be managed. Although a timescale of 10 years has been given for the achievement of the English NSF standards (i.e. working towards achievement by 2014), safeguarding is considered to be a priority. Indeed, the part played by hospital-centred failings in the development of the standards (Kennedy 2001; Laming 2003), led to the early publication of Standard Seven entitled '*Getting the Right Start: National Service Framework for Children: Standard for Hospital Services*' which, as the title implies, focuses on the care provided to children and young people in hospital (DH 2003). Many of the safeguarding messages contained in this standard were reinforced by the publication of the Core Standards document and, importantly, this included the notion of both individual and corporate responsibilities.

Similar proposals have been incorporated into the Welsh *National Service Framework for Children, Young People and Maternity Services*

(Welsh Assembly Government 2005). Chapter two of this document highlights core universal standards for all children and young people. Standard Six relates to safeguarding children:

> In every area, there are multi-agency and multi-disciplinary systems and services in place, in line with local Area Child Protection Committee (ACPC) procedures, which safeguard and promote children's welfare and development. These systems enable clear identification of risk, referral to the appropriate statutory agency with the duty to investigate and multi-agency participation in interventions to achieve the best possible outcome for children.
>
> (Welsh Assembly Government 2005: 21)

One of the strengths of the Welsh NSF is that it is matched by an impressive audit tool and some tight deadlines for achievement of its standards. Throughout the UK there is considerable activity currently to improve the lives and life chances of all children and young people. The tragic death of Victoria Climbié, and others who have died from child maltreatment, may have acted as an important catalyst for action, but the wider improvement for the well-being of all children and young people is, perhaps, a fitting legacy.

A safeguarding guide for nurses and midwives

An important driver for writing this book is a belief that the nursing and midwifery professions have not yet reached their potential in what they can uniquely offer the safeguarding agenda. Nor is there necessarily recognition by the professions and others as to what this 'unique contribution' may be. This may be due in part to the nursing and midwifery professions' own history of subservience to the dominant paradigm, but it is also likely to be a reflection of a crowded and adult-centric pre-registration curriculum and limited access to continuing professional development in safeguarding children's practice. Perhaps, more worryingly, Nayda (2004), who observed the child protection practice of registered nurses in Australia, describes 'systematic malpractice' whereby nurses defer decision-making in child abuse cases to medical staff and fail to meet the legal and ethical standards of client advocacy ascribed to contemporary practice.

Yet there are pivotal reasons why nursing and midwifery professionals can, and should, be key players in the field. These include: the *universality* of nursing and midwifery services for expectant and new parents, children, young people and families; the increasing recognition of *professional accountability* as the nursing and midwifery professions take independent lead roles in the provision of modern child- and family-centred health care services in a range of traditional and non-traditional settings; and the shared *core attributes* of the professions and of safeguarding philosophies. These themes, which will provide a thread throughout the text, are introduced below.

The universality of nursing and midwifery

The universality of nursing and midwifery services means that there are unparalleled opportunities for practitioners to play key roles in safeguarding children and promoting their welfare. Unlike many other professionals who engage in child protection work, the fact that *all* children, young people and their families will have contact with nurses and midwives, suggests that there will be important opportunities for the provision of preventative support and guidance as well as the early recognition, and where necessary referral, of concerns about possible or actual child maltreatment.

In the UK we expect that every pregnant woman will have access to, and engage with, high quality maternity services. It is also increasingly recognised that for the majority of women, pregnancy and childbirth are normal life events and that care of these women and their babies may be exclusively midwifery-led. Recent guidance for England (HM Government 2006a) acknowledges the importance of midwives in contributing to the identification and care of vulnerable women, especially those who are suffering from domestic violence, in itself an important risk factor for child maltreatment.

Children, young people and their families will continue to have access to nursing services throughout childhood. Specialist Community Public Health Nurses (SCPHNs) practising as health visitors, school nurses, family health nurses (in Scotland) and public health nurses (in Northern Ireland) provide a range of universal services based largely on promoting health and provision of support to individuals, families and communities. In comparison with other groups of nurses and midwives, SCPHNs have tended to play a more dominant role in traditional child protection practice, with a natural progression for some to specialise in lead roles as Named and Designated Professionals. However, recent intercollegiate guidance on the safeguarding roles and competence of health care staff (Royal College of Midwives et al. 2006) recognises that there will be other groups of nurses and midwives who will increasingly have the skills, knowledge and competence to undertake these leadership roles. This reflects the findings of *The Chief Nursing Officer's Review into the Nursing, Midwifery and Health Visiting Contribution to Vulnerable Children* (DH, DfES 2004a) which emphasises the responsibility for all nurses and midwives who work with children, young people and their families to engage in safeguarding children work.

Other nursing and midwifery professionals who will have contact with many children and young people include those working in General Practice and in National Health Service (NHS) Direct and Walk-in Centres. A further group will practise in more specialist or targeted services such as learning disability and child and adolescent mental health services (CAMHS). A significant number of children and young people will also access hospital-based services such as emergency departments and minor injury units, as well as various inpatient and outpatient settings. The inquiry into the death of Victoria Climbié, which is outlined earlier in this chapter, has been central in recent efforts to improve safeguarding practices within hospital settings and the inquiry's recommendations carry important messages for the nursing profession. In addition, it should be noted that because safeguarding children policy and legislation in the UK applies to all children and young people up to the age of 18 years (generally 16 years in Scotland), whether or not they are living independently, those nurses and midwives who are practising in what might be considered to be 'adult services' (e.g. gynaecology) will also have a contribution to make to safeguarding and promoting the welfare of young people cared for in these areas.

Furthermore, it is important to consider the broad range of services that nurses and midwives provide for adults who are *parents* or carers. In some circumstances, for example where parents have mental health problems, are misusing substances or have other health problems that prevent them from responding to their children's developmental needs, nurses and midwives will need to ensure that the welfare of children, including unborn babies, takes priority in any care-planning processes.

Case example

Lola, aged 21 years, was taken to the emergency department, having taken an overdose of benzodiazepines after an argument with a boyfriend. She is a single parent living with a 14-month-old daughter. What are the safeguarding issues?

The key safeguarding issue here is that in taking an overdose Lola has not considered the welfare of her child. Indeed, if she was alone with her daughter at the time of the overdose she has jeopardised her daughter's health and safety as well as her own – the outcome may well have been two fatalities.

Other concerns may arise from the effects on the child of having a depressed mother and her ability to provide the emotional warmth and stimulation essential for her daughter's development.

Is the argument with the boyfriend part of a spectrum of domestic abuse? If so there are clear links to the increased risk of all forms of child maltreatment.

Is Lola isolated from family and friends? Is she experiencing the effects of poverty and deprivation? Social exclusion is an important risk factor for child maltreatment.

Professional accountability

Nurses and midwives practise in a range of primary and acute care settings. A key unifying factor for the professions, wherever they practise, is the essential role of nurses and midwives in the assessment of health needs for the planning and delivery of care. As Fitzgerald (2002) notes, assessment is a continuous process that should carry on throughout the nurse/patient relationship. This is an important aspect of the increasing autonomy and independence of the profession. Nurses and midwives are expected to base their assessment on formal frameworks that seek to identify the impact of health needs on the daily lived experiences of the 'patient' and their 'family'. Many of these frameworks reflect the development of professional theory and practice since the 1970s and demonstrate that assessment should move beyond the purely physical, embracing psychological, socio-cultural and environmental factors.

Assessment frameworks support nurses and midwives in exercising a high degree of clinical judgement in deciding which actions need to be taken to meet the assessed health needs. Such decisions are made in partnership with the patient and/or their carers. However, what is crucial here is that registered nurses, midwives and SCPHNs are personally and professionally accountable for their practice. This means that they are responsible for their actions (and omissions) in spite of any instructions from other professionals. As we note in places throughout the text, the challenges of safeguarding children and young people can lead to differences of opinion within health care teams. It is thus important that nurses and midwives understand how to seek help to address dissonant viewpoints. The continuity of relationships with 'patients' and their families, together with the ability to engage in meaningful holistic assessment are important factors in ensuring the safety and well-being of children and young people.

In the UK, the Nursing and Midwifery Council (NMC) set the standards for the conduct, performance and ethics of the nurses, midwives and SCPHNs who are on the professional register (NMC 2004a). The purpose of the professional code is to inform the professions of what is required of them in exercising their professional accountability in practice. The document also serves to inform the public, other professionals and employers as to the standards expected of nurses, midwives and SCPHNs. Notably, practitioners must:

- 'Protect and support the health of individual patients and clients
- Protect and support the health of the wider community
- Act in such a way that justifies the trust and confidence the public have in you
- Uphold and enhance the good reputation of the professions.'

(NMC 2004a: 4)

In achieving the above, the professional code acts as an important guide to issues which may concern nurses and midwives in exercising their responsibilities in protecting children and young people. This includes guidance on confidentiality, consent and information sharing which may sometimes be perceived as actual or potential barriers to good safeguarding practice. Chapter 4, which outlines professional roles and responsibilities, revisits the code and explains how practitioners can act to safeguard children and young people, whilst keeping to the requirements of their professional regulatory body.

Core attributes

Nurses and midwives are thus autonomous professionals working with individuals, families and populations in a diversity of settings. The multiplicity of roles has led to difficulties in defining what it is that nursing and midwifery actually *is* and what it actually *does*. In the UK, the Royal College of Nursing (RCN) have undertaken extensive consultation in an effort to delineate the characteristics of contemporary nursing and midwifery (RCN 2003). One of the purposes of this work is to provide a tool to help to describe the professions to those who may have a rather narrow and stereotypical image of a subservient professional caring for sick people. In contrast to this image, albeit still recognising the essential caring role, key concepts that define modern nursing are said to include the notions of promoting health, prevention, minimising suffering, empowerment, partnership and holism. 'Partnership' is described as being with patients, their families and in collaboration with the wider multidisciplinary team. This work appears to build on the Government's ambitious plans for a new patient-centred NHS, which emphasises not only the crucial role of nurses and midwives in promoting health but also in reducing inequality (DH 2000a).

Attributes of modern nursing and midwifery have much in common with the core attributes of safeguarding, i.e. assessing need and working in partnership with individual children and young people, their families and multidisciplinary teams to promote physical and emotional well-being and ensure safety. Taken together with the profession's universality and accountability this arguably place nurses and midwives at the forefront of safeguarding practice.

This chapter has aimed to provide the rationale for a book on safeguarding specifically aimed at nurses and midwives. Thus far I have argued that this rests on the universality of the professions; the recognition of professional accountability; and the notion of promoting health and well-being as a core purpose of nursing and midwifery. In addition to the rationale already expressed for writing a book such as this, it is notable that it would be extremely unusual for a nurse or midwife not to come across a child protection issue in the course of their practice. This includes not just those nurses working primarily with children and young people, but also those working with vulnerable adults who are parents and carers. Indeed, I would go as far as suggesting that those who go through their careers without encountering a single case of child maltreatment either at work or in their local community may well have knowingly or unknowingly failed in their duty to protect children and young people. Clearly, this is difficult to accept.

Child abuse and neglect have a serious impact on health and development and the effects can last a lifetime. Indeed, there is increasing evidence of the links between childhood abuse and long-term health problems, including major causes of morbidity and premature death in adulthood (NCIPCA 1996; Felitti et al. 1998). The work of Perry (2002) in relation to the severe effects of early global neglect on neurological development has demonstrated the importance of social interaction, communication and touch for normal brain growth and development. Southall et al. (2003) note that maltreatment interferes with children's emotional and physical development and results in 'dysfunctional adults' (p. 102) who suffer from low self-esteem, emotional immaturity, poor coping strategies and mental health problems. For many, but not all, abused children, the effect of child maltreatment does not bode well for their future roles as parents. Inter-generational transmission and child maltreatment itself are both common and potentially preventable. The suggested scale of the problem provides a tentative evidence base on which to inform the development of the education, research and practice of nurses and midwives in this field.

The scale of the problem

In contrast with headline cases, fatal or grievous abuse is rare. Most cases of child maltreatment will be of a less dramatic nature, although as with Climbié, the challenge is that a child or young person who is at risk of, or suffering from, maltreatment will rarely be initially 'diagnosed' or 'labelled' as such. Yet, in his evidence to the Laming inquiry, Dr Chris Hobbs, one of the UK's leading medical experts on child maltreatment suggested that 'Maltreatment is the biggest cause of morbidity in children' (Laming 2003: 284). The inquiry report develops this proposition by comparing the likely prevalence of maltreatment with other common health problems in childhood. The suggestion, which may be surprising to some, is that the scale of maltreatment is probably greater than that of well recognised childhood health problems such as diabetes and asthma and should be approached with the same importance and care. This seems to echo Dubowitz and King (1995) who argue that child abuse and neglect, alongside other childhood psychosocial problems, may represent a 'new morbidity' in paediatrics that will increase proportionally in the work of professionals as overall improvements in child health are sustained. Hall and Sowden (2005) also recognise that serious, acute childhood illnesses have become less common, but suggest that the care and resources for modern paediatric problems such as psychosocial and behavioural disorders are inadequate.

Thus, the issue of ongoing assessment, which reflects a full social and developmental history, as well as a careful evaluation of the presenting signs and symptoms, becomes crucial. The notion of the 'lived daily experiences' of the child is an important facet of any assessment. This may mean that the nurse or midwife needs to draw information from external sources to inform their clinical judgement. The assessment should be balanced and include a consideration of the strengths and abilities of the parents as well as any risks to the child (Daniel 2005). In all cases the views or perspective of the child or young person should be taken into account. The *rights* of children and young people to be heard and to be protected from maltreatment, to be healthy, to be safe, to be well cared for and to have the opportunities to achieve their potential, form the underpinning philosophy of this text.

Underpinning philosophy

Child-centredness and children's rights theories are increasingly reflected in the philosophy of many professionals and groups whose personal and professional lives bring them into contact with children. Many will have been influenced (as I have been) by the commendable work of those authors who have promoted the importance of giving children a voice (e.g. Butler-Sloss 1988; Alderson, 1993; Newell, 1989; Archard, 1993, 2003). The children's rights movement is given global[1] recognition in the inception of the Convention of the Rights of the Child, adopted by the General Assembly of the United Nations on the

20 November 1989. The Convention, ratified by the UK in 1991, establishes the incontestable rights of children and young people (defined as those less than 18 years of age) and outlines the actions and responsibilities of governments in ensuring that all services for children are offered in a child-centred, rights-based framework. It proposes both welfare rights (such as food, health care, housing and education) and protective rights (from child maltreatment). Both sets of rights reflect safeguarding practice. The rights to protection are enshrined in Article 19 which states:

> State parties shall take all appropriate legislative, administrative, social and educational measures to protect the child from all forms of physical or mental violence, injury or abuse, neglect or negligent treatment, maltreatment or exploitation, including sexual abuse, while in the care of parent(s), legal guardian(s) or any other person who has care of the child.
>
> Such protective measures should, as appropriate, include effective procedures for the establishment of social programmes to provide necessary support for the child, and for those who have care of the child, as well as for other forms of prevention and for identification, reporting, referral, investigation, treatment and follow up of instances of child maltreatment described heretofore, and, as appropriate, for judicial involvement.
>
> (Article 19, Convention on the Rights of the Child)

A commitment to the Convention is reflected in recent legislation and policy for children in the UK. This may be exemplified by the appointment of Commissioners for Children to all four countries of the UK. However, there is still much to be achieved (e.g. Children's Rights Alliance for England 2005; Croke and Crowley 2006). As public servants nurses and midwives are 'agents of the state', they therefore have a duty to abide by its legislation and policy, including that for safeguarding children. The remainder of this book, which builds on the fundamental rights of the child to be safe from harm, helps them to do so.

Outline of the remaining chapters

Chapter 2 considers contemporary childhood in the UK and explores current challenges to health and well-being. In exploring the nature of childhood, the chapter also considers parenting, particularly in terms of an analysis of 'good-enough' parenting as a precursor to understanding concepts of safeguarding and child maltreatment. The issues of discipline and corporal punishment are also considered.

Chapter 3 outlines theories and definitions of child maltreatment, especially in relation to recent broadening of our understanding as to what may be considered to be abusive, and how this impacts on policy and practice. This links to a consideration of the epidemiology of maltreatment and the difficulties associated with measurement.

Chapter 4 concentrates on professional roles and responsibilities in the identification and referral of child maltreatment. The chapter draws on current policy in the UK, as this ultimately guides practice.

The next few chapters seek to provide an overview of safeguarding children in special circumstances, many of which will be familiar to nurses and midwives. Chapter 5 considers the needs of vulnerable children; including those who are disabled, victims of sexual exploitation (including 'on-line' abuse) or seeking asylum. It also covers the issue of domestic violence, particularly in relation to midwifery practice. Chapter 6 outlines the challenges to protecting children who are at risk of being, or are victims of, fabricated or induced illness.

A whole chapter – Chapter 7 – is devoted to a consideration of neglect and the challenges that it raises for nurses and midwives. The chapter will reflect back to Chapter 2's deliberation on what is meant by 'good-enough' parenting. Chapter 8 considers fatal abuse and the new processes being put in place to review all child deaths. The guidance on serious case reviews is also explained and the chapter highlights the significance of the involvement of health services in cases where children have died from their abuse. The final chapter looks at the way forward in safeguarding practice for nurses and midwives and celebrates the contribution that the professions can surely make.

Messages for practice

- Child maltreatment is one of the most difficult and challenging aspects of nursing and midwifery practice.
- The overarching aim of safeguarding work is to make sure that children and young people are able to reach their potential and enter adulthood successfully.
- Safeguarding children and young people is primarily accomplished through good parenting. Nurses and midwives can provide advice and support to encourage this.
- Universal services, such as health and education, have a key role to play in early intervention and support to families experiencing difficulties.
- The importance of the Victoria Climbié inquiry and its findings and recommendations are of particular significance to the nursing profession.

- Nurses and midwives who are practising in what might be considered to be 'adult services' (e.g. gynaecology, occupational health) will also have a contribution to make to safeguarding and promoting the welfare of young people.
- Attributes of modern nursing and midwifery have much in common with the core attributes of safeguarding, i.e. assessing need, working in partnership with individual children and young people, their families and multidisciplinary teams to promote physical and emotional well-being and ensure safety.
- Children and young people have a right to be heard and to be protected from maltreatment, to be healthy, to be safe, to be well cared for and to have the opportunities to achieve their potential.

Recommended reading

Archard, D.W. (2003) *Children, Family and the State.* Aldershot: Ashgate.

DH (Department of Health), DfES (Department for Education and Skills) (2004) *The Chief Nursing Officer's Review into the Nursing, Midwifery and Health Visiting Contribution to Vulnerable Children.* London: Department of Health.

DH (Department of Health), DfES (Department for Education and Skills) (2004) *National Service Framework for Children, Young People and Maternity Services: Core Standards.* London: Department of Health.

HM Government (2004) *Every Child Matters: Change for Children.* London: Department for Education and Skills.

HM Government (2006a) *Working Together to Safeguard Children: A Guide to Inter-agency Working to Safeguard and Promote the Welfare of Children.* London: Department for Education and Skills.

Laming, Lord (2003) *The Victoria Climbié Inquiry: Report of an Inquiry by Lord Laming,* CM 5730. London: The Stationery Office.

NSCAN (National Safeguarding Children Association for Nurses) (2006) *Professional Core Competencies for Nurses Specialising in Safeguarding Children.* Huddersfield, NSCAN.

Welsh Assembly Government (2005) *National Service Framework for Children, Young People and Maternity Services.* Cardiff: Welsh Assembly Government.

chapter **two**

WHY EVERY CHILD MATTERS

Learning outcomes

This chapter will help you to:

- debate and discuss the concept of child- and family-centred care;
- appreciate the trends in the demography of children, young people and families within the population as a whole;
- consider the effects of poverty on child health and welfare;
- analyse the meaning of childhood and the position of children within the UK;
- practise with confidence in relation to issues of consent and parental responsibility;
- support positive parenting approaches.

Introduction

Safeguarding activity is based on a tacit belief that children and young people are a distinct group of vulnerable individuals who have not yet reached a certain chronological age. This chapter explores the nature of childhood and aims to help nurses and midwives to understand the position of children and young people in the UK today. How childhood is viewed is an important aspect of safeguarding practice, both in terms of understanding why children and young people may be maltreated, and in supporting actions to protect them from harm.

The contents of this chapter, which draw on the book's underpinning philosophy of child-centredness and children's rights, may challenge the preconceptions of some readers, particularly those who may share the somewhat traditional view of children as appendages of their parents, rather than individuals in their own right. However, the objective is to support best practice and help nurses and midwives to provide high quality '*child* and family centred care'[1] as part of their safeguarding role. Maintaining a child-centred focus not only helps in identifying concerns about possible maltreatment, but also reflects the need to consult with children and young people on decisions concerning their health care. Nurses and midwives may thus be required to advocate on behalf of children and young people to promote or to protect their best interests, especially in the case of very young children, or those with disabilities.

The chapter begins by providing an overview of some key facts and figures concerning children and young people in the UK. This is followed by an analysis of contemporary childhood, which in turn leads to a discussion of the rights of children and some of the ways in which these are being upheld in the twenty-first century. As part of this debate, we consider the usefulness of the *child friendly healthcare initiative* standards for health care providers, which are based on the principles of the United Nations Convention on the Rights of the Child (UNCRC). The task of parenting, in particular the components of 'good-enough' parenting, which can provide a useful benchmark when assessing how well the needs of children and young people are met, and the need for any intervention are then considered. Linked to parenting is the question of discipline and the chapter concludes by debating the issues around the use of corporal punishment and advocating the promotion of 'positive parenting' techniques as a means to help to make both childhood and parenthood a rich and rewarding experience.

Children in the United Kingdom

According to the Office for National Statistics (ONS) (2004) there were 14.8 million children and young people aged 0-19 years living in the UK in 2001. This number had remained fairly static in the preceding decade, with children and young people comprising approximately 25% of the population as a whole. What is noticeable, however, is that the proportion of those under 16 years of age (20%) is now smaller than the proportion of those in the 60 years plus age group (21%). This looks set to be a trend that will continue as the population of older people increases. In terms of the four countries of the UK, the ONS report noted that most children (88%) lived in England and Wales, a slight increase in the proportion since 1990. This increase was said to be due to changes in birth rates, although overall it was noted that the proportion of children in the 0–4 year age group had decreased. The highest proportions of children and young people live in Northern Ireland (30% of the population), with similar proportions found clustered in and around major conurbations in England, Wales and Scotland. In some areas, such as the South West peninsula, the proportion of those less than 20 years of age is under 23%. The ratio of males to females is noted to be fairly consistent at 105 males to 100 females.

The ONS report (2004) records an increase in the number of children from ethnic minorities from 9% of the total child population in 1992 to 10% in 2000. Of these, the largest group are those from Indian and Pakistani groups and the smallest group those from China. The Black-African group had the largest proportional increase in average growth from 1998–2000.

Family size and structure

Readers, especially midwives, are likely to be aware that the average age at birth of first child has been steadily increasing. The ONS (2004) data demonstrates that this increased from 27.5 years of age in 1990 to 29.2 years of age in 2001. The report suggests that this was partly related to the age distribution of the female population, but also the increase in the age at which women first became mothers. Between 1990 and 2001 there was also an increase in the numbers of multiple births, especially among mothers in the 40 plus age group. This is reported to relate to the increased use of infertility treatments, as well as the increase in the numbers of first births at these ages. Whilst the average age at birth of first child has gone up, teenage pregnancy remains an important public health and policy issue. Britain has been noted to have the highest teenage pregnancy rate in Europe, and is second only to the

United States in terms of rates in industrialised countries (ONS 2004). The links between social disadvantage, including experience of the care system, poor educational outcomes and teenage pregnancy are well known. There is also growing concern about the sexual health of adolescents with an increase in the numbers of young women with chlamydia (many of whom will be asymptomatic). Chlamydia infection poses a significant risk to future fertility in the female population, and has also been linked with male fertility problems (Paavonen and Eggert-Kruse 1999).

One of the predictions contained in the ONS report (2004) is that the proportion of women who remain childless will increase. In addition the authors of the report note that average family size is continuing to reduce, with the numbers of families with four or more children on the decline and the numbers with only one or two children rising. The report links these statistics to evidence that suggests that children and young people living in lone parenthood and/or larger families do less well educationally and have a higher level of behavioural problems. The number of children born outside of marriage has also increased, although it is notable that the majority of births are registered by both parents. This has implications in relation to the concept of 'parental responsibility' discussed later in this chapter. The report notes that in 2001 four out of 10 live births in the UK occurred outside of marriage, the highest proportion of which relating to children born in Wales, where a figure of just under half (48%) was documented (ONS 2004). While not exclusive to single parenthood, the implications in relation to poverty and disadvantage and the links to poorer outcomes for children and young people are important.

Although the majority of births are registered to two parents, it is becoming much more likely that family structure will change during individuals' childhoods. There are thus a range of family types including lone mother, lone father, co-habiting couples with children, married couples with children, same-gender couples with children and stepfamilies. In 1991 just over one million children lived in stepfamilies, although only 3% of stepfamilies include children from both partners' previous marriages or cohabitations, reflecting the fact that children are more likely to remain with their mother after separation or divorce (ONS 2004). Adoptions of children have been decreasing due to the fact that fewer babies are 'put up' for adoption, with the result that there has been an increase in overseas adoptions. The numbers of children and young people who are 'looked after'[2] has remained constant. Children from different ethnic backgrounds had diverse experiences of family structure. Families headed by two parents are most common amongst Asian families, followed by White families. In contrast just under half of Black-headed households are lone parent families.

In summary, this brief statistical review of children in the UK has demonstrated that the population of children over the 10-year period until 2001 remained fairly static; that the proportion of children in the population is now less that that of older adults; that mothers' average age at the birth of their first child is increasing; and that there are more multiple births and more births outside of marriage. A higher proportion of children live in urban areas. An understanding of the demography of childhood is helpful in contextualising contemporary patterns and determinants of family life. The following section considers children and young people's well-being in the twenty-first century, with an emphasis on the effects of childhood poverty and 'modern life'.

Children and young people's wellbeing in the twenty-first century

A UK wide commission set up in April 2004 to examine the relationship between the state and the family in the upbringing of children reported on its findings in 2005 (Commission on Families and the Well-being of Children 2005). While they noted that the outcomes for most children in the UK are favourable, they also documented their concerns about the high numbers of children living in relative poverty and the numbers of parents who are experiencing undue stress. The Commission linked parental stress with behavioural issues and safety concerns within communities and families. They also noted a rise in the number of young people with mental health problems.

The UK is widely recognised to have one of the highest rates of child poverty in the industrialised world, although there are some indications that the numbers of children and young people living in poverty is decreasing (HM Government 2006e). The Commission on Families and the Well-being of Children (2005: 10) outline the current accepted definition of poverty as 'income that is below 60% of the median level of the population at the time'. They argue that an assumption of normal population statistical distribution rates of income generating human potential (allowing for factors such as intelligence and health) should result in 2% of the population falling below the poverty line. However, they add that the reality is that in 2002 the proportion of children in poverty in the UK was approximately 30%, or more than 10 times the number expected. Poverty can have a significant effect on the health and well-being of children; for example, it is linked with low birth weight, infant mortality, low rates of breastfeeding, high teenage conception rates and poor educational attainment. Writing in the journal *Paediatric Nursing*, Jose (2005) provides a useful debate on the definitions of poverty and its links with child abuse and neglect. She argues that with 1:4 children living in poverty, health professionals have a duty both to recognise poverty and its effects on children, and to provide help and support to disadvantaged families. These themes will be revisited in the concluding chapter of the book.

Points for reflection

As universal service providers, nurses and midwives may be in a position to support and advise disadvantaged pregnant women and families as to welfare benefits and sources of local help.

Consider what advice you may be able to give in the following practice examples:

A 15-year-old girl who is pregnant with twins asks you how to find out about her entitlement to benefits.

A couple with a new baby say that they are not able to afford a car safety seat.

Parents of a child who has to attend the outpatients department at frequent intervals say that they are finding it difficult to afford the bus fares.

Following a house fire in which a young child has died, neighbours are keen to fit smoke detectors and wonder if there are any local sources of financial or practical help.

A couple who are struggling to make ends meet would like some help with buying a stairgate for their nine-month-old.

Although poverty is clearly an important determinant of children and young people's well-being, there is concern about the ways in which children and young people are spending their childhoods. As this book is being prepared to go to press, there have been calls from a large group of professionals and academics for an urgent debate on the effects of 'modern life' on children (Abbs et al. 2006). In a letter to a daily broadsheet newspaper Professor Abbs and his 110 co-signatories suggest that the ways in which people live now leads to neglect of the developmental, emotional and social needs of children and young people resulting in poor outcomes such as substance abuse, violence and self-harm. They link their concerns to the rising numbers of children and young people with depression, behavioural problems and developmental conditions. A range of factors are suggested including rapid technological and cultural change, processed food, screen-based entertainment and lack of interaction with 'real-life significant adults'. The authors are also critical of early schooling (and it is notable that other developed countries commence formal education at the age of 6 or 7 years) and what they refer to as 'an overly academic test-driven primary curriculum'. Clearly it is difficult not to have some sympathy with the views expressed in the letter and to be concerned about the potential implications for child health.

Chapter 1 highlighted the 'new morbidity' of child health in terms of the growing prevalence of psychosocial and behavioural problems. As part of this spectrum there will be health problems that are related to 'couch potato' lifestyles that include a lack of outdoor exercise and eating 'junk' food. Childhood obesity is an obvious candidate here, but perhaps less well publicised is a growing incidence of rickets (Bishop 2006). One enduring feature of modern society appears to be a high level of parental anxiety about letting children 'out to play', matched by a big decrease in the numbers of children who walk to school. Yet there is actually very little evidence to suggest that today's society is more dangerous for children and young people than that of the previous generations. Midgley (2006) points out that the (very small) numbers of children who are murdered shows no sign of increasing (see Chapter 8). Given that far more of these murders are perpetrated by parents or other members of the family or others known to the victims, and that most of these deaths occur in the first year of life (Dale et al. 2002), 'stranger danger' is a mantra that is perhaps somewhat overstated. As Wilczynski (1997) has cogently concluded 'It is much more comforting for us as a society to fear the lurking shadowy stranger rather than those ostensibly responsible for the protection of children – the very people with whom they have been locked indoors' (p. 176).

Thus, broadly speaking, whilst most key indicators relating to the well-being of children and young people, including those of disadvantage, are improving, it will be increasingly important to develop measures to address today's challenges of childhood obesity, sexual health and mental health problems. The expansion of child and adolescent mental health services is one example, but it is notable that local health needs assessment and targeting of services to those suffering the effects of poverty and deprivation will be a crucial aspect of any future strategy. Whilst SCPHNs must have clearly defined proficiencies in searching for health needs and influencing policies that affect health (NMC 2004b), the increasing focus on delivering an ever wider range of health services in community settings (as opposed to institutions) means that all nurses and midwives will need to develop broader competence in health needs assessment, political awareness and community advocacy skills.

Although this section has detailed some key facts and figures about *children* in the UK, it has not considered the nature of *childhood* per se. An understanding of contemporary childhood is fundamental in enabling nurses and midwives to achieve their potential in safeguarding children practice. The following section draws on the sociology of childhood literature and aims to highlight the ways in which children and young people have been perceived in recent times. This, in turn, provides an understanding of the development and importance of the children's rights movement.

Contemporary childhood

Childhood (and therefore child abuse and neglect) is largely socially constructed and influenced by historical, social and cultural change. An important aspect of the debate, which many in the safeguarding field believe to be a key contributory factor in the problem of child maltreatment, is the position of children in society. Corby (2006) provides a useful historical review that illustrates the tensions between those who believe that the notion of a period called 'childhood' is a recent construction, and those who suggest that the concept of childhood, as separate to adulthood, has always existed. Undoubtedly, the nature of childhood has changed as countries have developed, largely in response to workforce demands brought about by industrialisation. As Corby notes, richer societies can allow for longer childhoods, albeit to enable a better educated workforce for increasingly complex markets and technology. Poorer countries, in contrast, are perhaps notable for their presence of street children and child labour. Although most people now understand childhood as relating to those who have not yet reached a certain chronological age, Qvortrup's assertion that childhood is '[T]he life-space which our culture limits it to be' (1994: 3) reflects the differing experiences of children as viewed within a historical as well as a global context.

In the UK (and elsewhere) the legal definitions of childhood rest on age. However, my experience in the education and training of health professionals suggests a lack of awareness in some quarters as to when childhood legally ends and adulthood begins. Some of the confusion appears to arise from issues about consent and the age at which 'children's services' hand over patients to those serving adults. The question of consent is discussed later in the chapter. The legal definitions of 'children' in the UK reflect the UNCRC which regards children to comprise all those who are under 18 years of age. Whilst unborn children are not included, it should be noted that their need for protection is encompassed in safeguarding policy and practice, and that professional intervention to ensure future well-being may be required.

Points for reflection
Think about the area in which you live or work and the diversity of the health care services that are on offer for children and young people. Which of these services do you think teenagers access? In what ways do you think these services safeguard and promote their welfare? What difficulties might they encounter?

Although childhood is usually recognised in terms of attainment of a chronological age, there is clearly a developmental aspect too. Childhood is a time of rapid, and somewhat uneven, development of physical, psychological, intellectual, emotional and social attributes. It is therefore important that children and young people receive optimal health and social care during what is a potentially vulnerable time. Safeguarding work recognises the potential vulnerability of children, and there is a growing body of evidence to suggest that those whose development is delayed or hindered through learning or physical disability are especially vulnerable and face a greater risk of child maltreatment. This important issue is discussed in greater depth in Chapter 5.

The oppression of children

While chronological and developmental cut-off points are clearly understood, one of the most important aspects of contemporary definitions of childhood is the suggestion that childhood is in fact circumscribed in negative terms. This negativity is sometimes reflected in the perception of children, the language used to describe them and the way in which they are treated. It is nearly 40 years since the feminist writer Shulamith Firestone proposed that the concept of childhood dictates that children are a *species* different not just in age, but in other attributes from adults (Firestone 1970). She further claimed that this perceived difference has led to the creation of an ideology of childhood in which children are viewed as asexual, pure and innocent. Firestone added that the result of such an ideology is that children are oppressed, segregated from mainstream society, vulnerable to abuse, lacking in civil rights and physically and economically dependent on their parents or carers. In a similar vein, Holt's (1975) revolutionary text on the state of childhood still provides, I believe, a superb opening for any contemporary debate on the position of children:

> 'I have come to feel that the fact of being a "child", of being wholly subservient and dependant, of being seen by older people as a mixture of expensive nuisance, slave and super-pet, does young people more harm than good'
>
> (p. 15).

Points for reflection

Debate and discuss Holt's assertion with a small group of fellow students or colleagues.

Do you think that the UK is a child-friendly society?

You may want to include issues such as availability of good quality childcare, the suitability of public transport and building designs (especially for pushchairs), tolerance of young children in restaurants and public houses, levels of maternity, paternity and child benefits, provision of safe play areas, etc.

Importantly, the voices and views of children may not be heard because they are considered to be *only children*. Miller (1987) suggests that discrimination against children and young people is persistently transmitted from one generation to another. The notion that children should be seen but not heard has apparently become enshrined in Western culture and beliefs. Franklin's work (1986) adds a further dimension to this argument by suggesting that the language used to describe children is often used in a derogatory way. He illustrates this by giving the example of the title 'boy' being used in the past to address adult male slaves. A more contemporary example could be the use of the epithet boy or girl to address a pet dog throughout their lifespan. Archard (1993, 2002) has argued that the predominant notion of childhood is that it represents a stage of incompetence in relation to adulthood, childhood is seen as an *absence of adultness*. Similarly, Lee (2001) proposes that the notion of children being 'human becomings' rather than 'human beings' has allowed unjust attributions to be made. More recently, Webb (2004), a senior lecturer in child health in Wales, has suggested that children are viewed by many as being incapable and immature or 'unfinished adults' rather than people in their own right and that this leads to persistent discrimination against them.

Language can be very powerful; the term 'childish', for example, is widely used in a disparaging manner across the age-range (and full marks go to any child who answers back that they are indeed a child!). As I have argued elsewhere, labelling a child as 'it' is another offensive term, yet one that is frequently heard within health care settings, particularly in relation to babies and younger children (Powell 2006). To describe children as 'it' devalues childhood and may contribute to continuing discriminatory and abusive practices. A 1980s report concerning the treatment of children who presented to paediatricians with suspected sexual abuse, was critical of these children and young people being portrayed as 'objects of concern' rather than individuals in their own right (Butler-Sloss 1988). We would not refer to adults in our care as 'it' and children, at whatever age, are equally worthy of respect.

The issue of equality is an important aspect of the way in which children are perceived and treated. Holt (1975) challenges the minority status of children and cogently puts the case for children to have the same rights as adults in the exercise of freedom of choice in matters such as politics, sex, justice, school, work and where and with whom to live. The issue of whether or not, and at what age, children and young people should be given the vote, has recently been aired in the UK. The burden of disenfranchisement was also discussed by Franklin (1986) who noted that children share many characteristics of other historically oppressed groups (for example, ethnic minority groups, women and lower social classes). As Webb (2004) comments, discrimination on the basis of gender, ethnicity, disability or *older* age groups is unlawful. Furthermore, Lee (2001) notes that while contemporary sociologies of childhood have put the case for children being treated as equals, he adds that the presumption of stability and independence of adults is often misguided. In an article in *The Times* Morgan (2006) quotes the Archbishop of Canterbury's recent reference to 'infant adults' in relation to those who are shirking their parental responsibilities because their own neglectful childhoods have not engendered the emotional maturity to parent. The degree to which nurses and midwives have the ability to provide intensive and specialist support to dysfunctional and socially excluded families is a core element of the debate on future family policy.

An assumption of the incompetence of children is often put forward as a reason for not allowing children and young people to make choices. However, this is hotly disputed by Lansdown (1995) who illustrates children's competence through the example of those experiencing chronic illness or facing major surgery who are often well able to make informed choices about treatment options (and presumably therefore in other areas of their lives; see also Alderson 1993). The ability of children to engage in meaningful discussions about their health care is a scenario that will be familiar to those health care professionals whose practice is predominantly with children and young people. What is often less clear is whether child-centredness and capability to engage with children and young people at their level is reflected at all points at which health care is delivered. Although 'busyness' is often given as a reason for obtaining histories of illnesses or accidents from parents rather than the child themselves (and, yes, this may well be quicker) competence in communicating with children and young people and valuing their worth may also be a factor. This will be especially important in seeking explanations for presenting injuries in cases of possible child maltreatment. As Lee (2001: 9) has argued 'Chronological age can serve as a cloak of invisibility that conceals adults' shortcomings'.

Case example

Molly, aged 11 years, has been sexually abused by her uncle. She has been taken to see the family GP because of unexplained abdominal pain. Molly longs to tell someone about what has been happening to her, but her mother has just told the GP that there are no problems at home.

The issue here is that Molly has been unable to disclose what has happened, first because she does not feel able to speak of the abuse with her mother and second because, as in many health professional encounters, mother has accompanied Molly to the appointment and furthermore the GP has directed questions to her rather than to the child.

The commonly held misconception of children's incompetence is particularly important in addressing the response to disclosure in child abuse and neglect. Alderson (1993) has argued that denying children's rationality can trap them into a lethal silence. She gives the example of an 8-year-old boy, Lester Chapman, who repeatedly ran away from home to escape daily beatings. Despite his protests, and the fact that his injuries were recognised by a police surgeon to compare with grievous bodily harm on an *adult,* Lester was always returned home. The final time he ran away, he was not found until his body was discovered in sewage sludge.

Franklin (1995) suggests that because children are politically disenfranchised they are frequently subjected to the sort of treatment that, if meted out to any other group in society, would be considered a moral outrage. Indeed there are many who believe that we treat our animals better than we treat our children. It is notable that the first case of child maltreatment that was successfully prosecuted in the United States (in 1871) had to resort to laws relating to cruelty to animals (as no laws in relation to children existed at that time). A letter to the journal *Children Now* reported on a conversation with a nursery nurse who said that the reason that she chose to work in childcare was that she did not manage to pass the examinations required to work with animals (McEvoy 2006). Negativity about children, and more particularly about older children, is born out by the treatment that is meted out through the use of 'anti-social behaviour orders' and vilification in the popular press. Perhaps an overarching view of contemporary childhood is that it is often misunderstood (Brooks 2006).

Children's rights

More optimistically, the notion of children's rights is gaining prominence and social policy and legislation are beginning to emphasise the importance of listening to, and respecting, the child. It is, perhaps, this shift to a focus on the centrality of the child that will eventually see an end to the oppression of children as well as the needless misery that child abuse and neglect entails. As Daniel (2005: 12) notes 'We are developing a sophisticated language of children's rights that locates children not only as members of families, but also as members of society who are entitled to protection and services in their own right.' One of the ways in which children's rights are being recognised is in their increasing participation in policy, service design and delivery. For example, the *Every Child Matters* programme in England (HM Government 2004) lays claim to being built upon the five outcomes 'that children and young people told us they wanted', which are:

- To be healthy
- To stay safe
- To enjoy and achieve
- To make a positive contribution and
- To achieve economic well-being.

A useful model for describing the movement from what may previously have been seen as a tokenistic approach, to full engagement of children and young people in projects, has been conceptualised by Hart (1992). His 'Ladder of Participation' identifies eight levels of participation (see Figure 2.1). For me the involvement of children and young people in designing services was epitomised by posters advertising the opening of a new London children's hospital in 2005. The Evelina Children's Hospital, boasted that 'Morgan, aged five, designed the chairs' and 'Tyei, aged five, chose the menu'. I am sure that I am not alone in reflecting that such publicity would simply have been inconceivable in the not too distant past.

Points for reflection
Think about recent developments in your service. How did children and young people participate? Grade their involvement according to Hart's 'Ladder of Participation' (see Fig. 2.1).

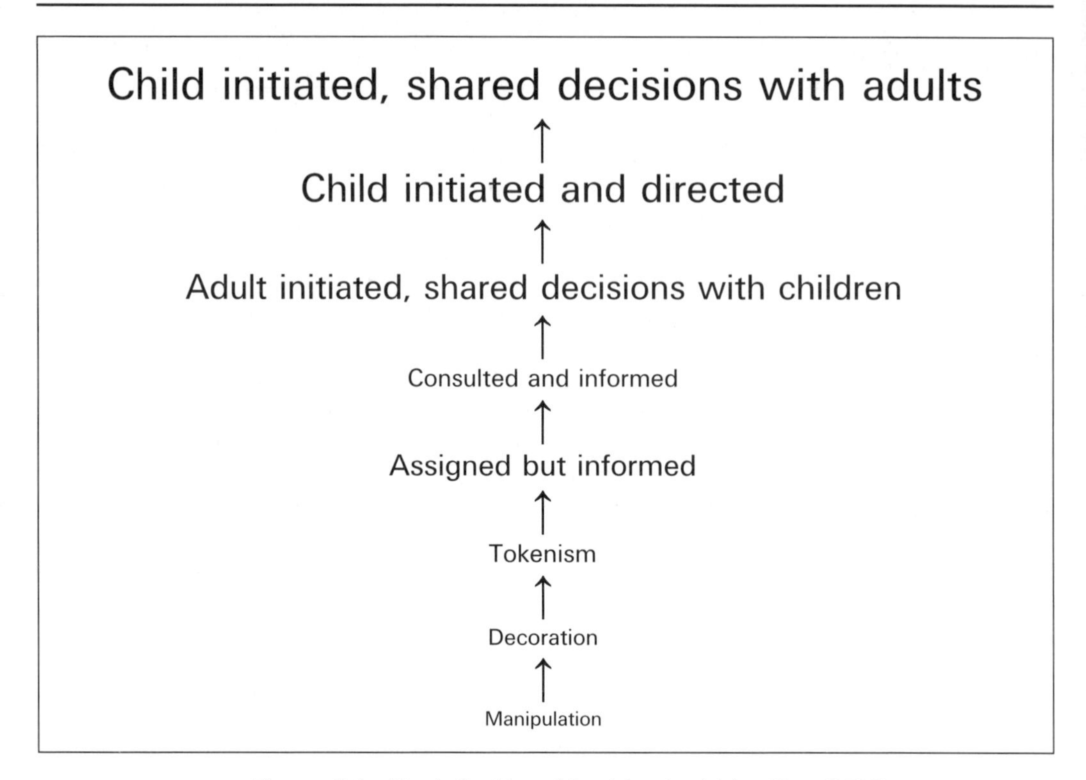

Figure 2.1 Hart's 'Ladder of Participation' After Hart (1992)

Children and young people may now be invited to partake in interview panels for those whose jobs will affect them. This has been increasingly the case in schools when new teachers are being appointed, although as with health services, it is important that such initiatives go beyond a tokenistic approach. Children and young people were also said to have been involved in the appointment of the Children's Commissioners. The role of the Children's Commissioner, a relatively recent initiative in the UK, is outlined below.

Children's Commissioners

The UK now has four Children's Commissioners (one for each country) variously representing or promoting the provision, protection and participation rights of children and young people as laid down in the UNCRC. These posts, which are independent from government, were created to ensure that the views and interests of children are well represented across the piece. As well as raising awareness of the rights of children, the commissioners have the power to initiate inquiries and deal with individual complaints in relation to public services provided for those under the age of 18 (and in certain cases, for example for those with a disability or leaving care, for older young people). Wales was the first of the UK countries to appoint a Children's Commissioner and England the last, following the provision in the Children Act 2004. According to the Children's Rights Alliance (2005) the English commissioner has the weakest general function both in the UK and across Europe. Particular regret was expressed by the Alliance at the failure to link the post explicitly with the UNCRC at the time of the appointment of the incumbent.

Priorities for Children's Commissioners include children's health and well-being, tackling discrimination and physical punishment, ensuring participation, dealing with anti-social behaviour and the needs of children who are vulnerable, seeking asylum or disabled. A report by the English commissioner details how the post holder has attempted to challenge stereotypical negative images, especially of teenagers (Office of the Children's Commissioner 2006). The Welsh commissioner has been involved in engagement with children and young people, the respect agenda, issues around bullying, advocating for looked after children and promoting the UNCRC. Future projects include further work to promote school nursing and child and adolescent health services, improving the safeguarding of children at activity centres and safe use of the internet (Children's Commissioner for Wales 2006). In Scotland key issues for the Children's Commissioner include, amongst other issues, the moving and handling of children with disabilities, gypsy families and communication aids for children who cannot speak (Scotland's Commissioner for Children and Young People 2006). Current priorities for the Northern Ireland commissioner include mental health issues, bullying, road safety, child protection and 'children and the troubles' (Northern Ireland Commissioner for Children and Young People 2006). The commissioners each have their own interactive websites, which give more country-specific information and are easily accessible to children and young people, parents and professionals alike (see appendix).

The 'child friendly healthcare initiative'

A further positive development that neatly brings services that provide health care to children and young people under the umbrella of the UNCRC is the 'child friendly healthcare initiative' (CFHI). This global initiative aims to improve the health care of children wherever it is delivered and provides some practical guidance that will help to ensure confluence with many of the concepts debated in this chapter thus far.

The CFHI is concerned with the physical, psychological and emotional needs of children and their families and sets standards to ensure that visits to health care settings are 'child friendly'. The standards may be of particular interest to those who meet children and young people in the course of their work, but may not have had an opportunity to have the benefit of a child-centred education for their professional practice (see Chapter 1). Importantly, these standards embed many of the key principles of safeguarding practice and will help to ensure that children and young people will be protected from maltreatment from within the health care system (Kendrick and Taylor 2000) as well as from others who may harm them. The following section is taken verbatim from the 2006 standards, although it should be noted that this is still work in progress. The website link is provided below.

Standards for health care providers

'Health care providers, organisations and individual health workers, share a responsibility to advocate for children and to reduce their fear, anxiety and suffering by ensuring that:

1 They are admitted to and kept in an in-patient health facility only when this is in their best interests.
2 The highest attainable (best possible) level of care, evidence based where possible, is provided for them and for pregnant women.
3 The environment in a health facility is secure, safe and clean.
4 The resources and expertise are available to provide separate, age-appropriate care in partnership with parents in child friendly surroundings.
5 They and their parents/carers are kept consistently and fully informed and involved in all decisions affecting their care.
6 They have equal access to health services and are approached without discrimination as individuals, with their own age and developmentally appropriate rights to privacy, dignity, respect and confidentiality.
7 Their physical and psychological pain and discomfort is assessed and controlled.
8 When they are severely ill, undergoing surgery, or have been given systemic analgesia and/or sedation, trained health workers and the necessary resources are available to provide appropriate critical and emergency care.
9 They are able to play and learn when attending a health facility.
10 They are protected from child abuse by appropriate and clearly defined systems, and are supported by health workers familiar with its signs and symptoms.
11 Their health and the health of pregnant women is monitored and promoted.

12 Breastfeeding is supported and optimal nourishment is provided by the promotion and practice of globally acceptable feeding programmes.'

(from www.childfriendlyhealthcare.org, accessed 07/09/06)

In introducing the CFHI standards to the nursing profession, Clarke and Nicholson (2001) note the importance of the participation of children, young people and their families in contributing their experiences, both positive and negative, of health services delivery. Such experiences form the bedrock of the development and review of standards locally and, as the authors cogently argue, focus on the care that has been received rather than the care that is said to have been given.

Points for reflection
How well are the CFHI standards embedded where you practise?

Consent

Linked to the development of children's rights and the implementation of CFHI is the issue of consent to health care and treatment. Although it is difficult at the time of writing to report with confidence that there is as yet full sign-up to the principles across the piece, there is increasing recognition that children and young people can and should participate in determining their care. The capability of children and young people to make decisions about their health care, including giving consent for procedures, is referred to as 'competence' (Larcher 2005). Competence is based on children and young people's ability to understand what is proposed and is based not only on intelligence but also on personal experience of their illness or disability. In the UK competence is presumed for those over 18 years of age. In England, Wales and Northern Ireland, those aged 16 and 17 years may freely consent to treatment, but, where those with 'parental responsibility' dictate otherwise, cannot necessarily refuse and there have been cases where young people's wishes have been overruled; examples reported by Larcher (2005) include the administration of psychiatric medication, blood transfusion in leukaemia and heart-lung transplantation. In Scotland, aspects of parental responsibility are lost once the young person reaches the age of 16 years, although parents may continue to give 'guidance' (BMA 2006a).

Children under the age of 16 years may be able to consent if they are considered to be competent. The law in Scotland is more straightforward on this issue than in other UK countries; here children of any age may consent to treatment unless they lack the capacity to do so. The legal definitions of competence are given in the box below.

Legal definitions of competence

'As a matter of law, the parental right to determine whether or not the minor child below the age of 16 will have medical treatment terminates if and when the child achieves sufficient understanding and intelligence to understand fully what is proposed.' (Gillick v West Norfolk and Wisbech Area Health Authority [1985] 3 All ER 402HL).'

'The validity of a child's consent turns on personal capacity as judged by the opinion of a qualified medical practitioner attending him (Age of Legal Capacity (Scotland) Act 1991:S2 (4).'

(Larcher 2005: 353)

Determining competence is the responsibility of medical practitioners, although evidently nurses and midwives may be asked to contribute to the assessment. Criteria for testing competence may include understanding (in simple terms) the nature, purpose and necessity of proposed treatment; the benefits, risks and alternatives; the effect of non-intervention; and being able to retain the information in order to make a choice. The child or young person must believe that the information relates to them – and make their choice without being under pressure.

It is also important to note that 'Some competent adolescents may wish to share decision-making with trusted adults or let others decide for them. Assessment of competence must be done in situations that maximise competence – after giving adequate information in an appropriate environment' (Larcher 2005: 354). Where children and young people are unable to consent, those with 'parental responsibility' (see below) are able to give consent for medical treatment on their behalf. In most cases parents will wish to make the best decision possible for their children. This should be done in consultation with them and based on appropriate information giving and choice. Support from professionals, particularly in cases of chronic or serious illnesses, is clearly vital (BMA 2006a). The British Medical Association (BMA) recognises that occasionally there may be a conflict between the views and decisions of those with parental responsibilities and the best interests of the child. Their advice to doctors in such cases is to provide only emergency treatment that is essential to preserve life or prevent serious deterioration and to seek a view from the courts as to any other treatment. The various UK Children Acts[3] recognise that the welfare of the child is the paramount consideration. This legislation also recognises that children and young people can contribute to decisions affecting their welfare and this is a positive step in the children's rights movement.

The primacy of the child has necessarily been the focus of the chapter thus far. However, it is also important to consider the child within the family and the roles of the parents, in recognition of the expressed notion of child- and *family*-centred care. The following section considers some key aspects of modern parenting.

Parenting

Within the safeguarding field much has been written about the need for children and young people to receive 'good enough' or 'adequate' parenting. This inevitably leads to discussion and debate about what this may be. In a seminal review of the challenges in ensuring proactive child protection, the National Commission of Inquiry into the Prevention of Child Abuse (NCIPCA) (1996) suggests that the fundamental nature of good enough parenting is to satisfy successfully the health, safety and developmental needs of children. More detail on what good enough parenting may entail is provided by Reder et al. (1993) in their succinct evaluation of the concepts of parental care and control. Care, they suggest, involves anticipating children's age-appropriate needs and providing for them through antenatal care, adequate feeding, warmth and protection from harm. Control, they add, encompasses action to meet the child's safety requirements, as well as the setting of consistent limits to behaviour. Although the notion of 'control' may appear antithetical to children's rights theories, Reder et al. are reassuring in their suggestion that the child must both be wanted and treated as a person in their own right and the parents able to put the child's needs above their own. Achieving this, they add, is particularly difficult for parents who themselves have suffered punitive controls and unmet caring needs during their own childhood. Miller (1987) reflects the cyclical nature of parenting and family life in arguing that children need to be fully accepted, loved, supported and understood in order to parent successfully in turn. Linked to this is the importance and quality of 'attachment' to a parent or primary caregiver (Bowlby 1969). Maltreated children tend to be less securely attached, which can result in difficulties in forming relationships with siblings, peers, intimate partners and in parenting their own children in turn (Browne and Hamilton 2003).

Practitioners may find themselves dealing with uncertainty and anxiety about whether or not they are applying ethnocentric 'middle-class' values to their assessment of parenting ability, especially where parents are struggling with poverty and hardship. As Taylor et al.

(2000) comment, parenting is culturally and contextually determined and good enough parenting difficult to define and measure. Nevertheless, they provide a list of characteristics of good and poor parenting which is drawn from the parenting literature; their examples of good parenting include child centredness, provision of a secure environment and teaching by example, whereas the characteristics of poor parenting (depressingly a much longer list) include hostility, lack of empathy for the child, aggression, high criticism and poor mothering (sic), this last characteristic seemingly reflecting the bias towards mothers in the study of parenting (Ramchandani and McConachie 2005).

Whilst there is likely to be agreement amongst practitioners on what is very good parenting and what is so bad it constitutes maltreatment, difficulties lie in the middle range of parenting behaviours, where parenting may be not quite good enough to ensure optimum health and well-being of children and young people, yet the nature of any intervention is unclear. In such cases, the daily lived experience of the child provides an important benchmark and this should be the primary focus for assessment. Assessment tools, such as the 'graded care profile' (Srivastava and Polnay 1997) which is discussed in more detail in Chapter 7, aim to provide objective measurements of the balance of risk and protective factors in the parent and child dyad. Similar approaches are advocated in government guidance, and this is a welcome reflection of the need to build upon family strengths wherever possible. However, the tension between giving failing parents 'long enough' to improve their parenting in the face of the damaging effects of neglectful care during crucial periods of children's development is a very real practice dilemma (Walker and Glasgow 2005).

In the UK and elsewhere, failure to have a good parental role model in the formative years is compounded by a lack of opportunity to learn about and prepare for the challenges of parenting. As Wilczynski (1997) has argued, it is often assumed that the ability to care for a child is inborn, yet it is in reality a complex and learned skill. Parentcraft does not appear to have a high priority in the packed British school curriculum and the problem may be compounded by other factors. Demographic influences such as the trend for women to have their first babies later in life, and to have fewer children, together with the effects of geographical mobility may well contribute to an unprecedented lack of exposure of the experience of caring for children by parents to be. This lack of preparation combined with poor personal and socio-economic resources must make good enough parenting difficult to achieve. Wilczynski (1997: 103) succinctly sums up the trials of parenting in noting that 'Parenting can be a very exhausting and stressful task even for the most ideal of candidates.'

Points for reflection
What do you think the components of good enough parenting are?

When parents have their first child, what previous knowledge and experience of the demands of caring for an infant are they likely to have had?

In what ways do you think nurses and midwives can offer help and support to new parents?

Expectations of parental duties are enshrined within UK legislation. An understanding of the concept of 'parental responsibility' is important for nurses and midwives, who need to be clear as to who is able to give consent on behalf of non-competent minors or seek access to the health records of their child. The following section may also provide an essential update to changes in the law in relation to parental responsibility.

Parental responsibility

Parental responsibility is defined as the 'rights, duties, powers, responsibilities and authority' that most parents have in respect of their children (BMA 2006a). Importantly, there are some notable differences in respect of who has parental responsibility, depending on when and where in the UK children have been born. For children born after 1 December 2003 (England and Wales), 15 April 2002 (Northern Ireland) or 4 May 2006 (Scotland), both of a child's biological parents have parental responsibility if they are registered on a child's birth certificate. For children born before the above dates, the mother automatically has parental responsibility with both biological parents having parental responsibility if they were married at the time of the child's conception or sometime afterwards. Even if the parents subsequently divorce, the father does not lose parental responsibility. Unmarried fathers can acquire parental responsibility through entering into a parental responsibility agreement with the mother, or through a court order. A person other than the child's biological parents can acquire parental responsibility by being appointed as a guardian (e.g. on the death of the parents) or by having a residence order in their favour (BMA 2006a). If a child is subject to care or supervision proceedings parental responsibility is shared with the local authority.

Those with parental responsibility can exercise their rights independently, for example in consenting to their child's treatment. The BMA website http://www.bma.org.uk/ap.nsf/Content/Parental provides useful advice as to steps that can be taken in cases of parental disagreement (e.g. male circumcision for religious purposes) and the way in which the Children (Scotland) Act 1995 has some differences in this respect. In England, Wales and Northern Ireland, parental responsibility is lost when the young person reaches 18 years of age (or is adopted, given up for adoption or dies). In Scotland all but the 'guidance' aspects of parental responsibility are lost when the young person reached the age of 16 years, although they remain minors until they are 18 years old.

We have considered some key aspects of modern parenting, such as the notion of good enough parenting and the challenges that arise from demographic changes. This knowledge builds on the earlier sections on contemporary childhood and the position of children in the UK today. An understanding of parental responsibility complements that of consent, and has been included to help ensure that health professionals give due regard to the relevant legislation and guidance in the course of their practice. The final section of this chapter considers the sometimes contentious subject of discipline and corporal punishment.

Discipline and corporal punishment

Peter Newell, who has been a tireless campaigner for an end to physical punishment in childhood (Newell 1989, 2006; Children are Unbeatable! Alliance 2006), sees the issue of hitting children as both a simple issue, in that hitting people is wrong and children are people too, and also a very difficult issue to address. He recognises that the difficulty in addressing this problem is its personal dimension. As Newell notes, most people in almost every country of the world were hit as children by their parents and most parents have hit their children (2006). He adds that because none of us likes to think badly of our parents, or indeed our own parenting skills, this makes it very difficult to consider the issue with 'humanity and logic' (p.14).

Case example

Sally, a sister in the emergency department, witnessed the father of one of her child casualties hit the sibling, aged 2 years, with the back of his hand. It had been an extremely stressful day for the family.

How would you decide if this was reasonable chastisement? Is it acceptable to use 'hitting' as a way of relieving tension? Would this be viewed differently if this father had hit his wife?

The UK has been criticised by the United Nations Committee on the Rights of the Child for its record on allowing the continuing practice of hitting children. Lawrence (2004: 9) finds the fact that this has been raised only recently 'remarkable'. While cultural attitudes favouring physical punishment remain strong (Baldwin and Spencer 2005) there is a growing recognition that the use of violence against children is not only an ineffective way to discipline children but also a fundamental issue of human rights (Commission on Families and the Well-being of Children 2005). The Commission share Newell's concern below about the links with child maltreatment:

> The idea that breaching a child's human dignity and physical integrity is acceptable, normal, or even as some still suggest in their best interests, perpetuates children's status as objects or property. *It makes every other sort of extreme abuse and exploitation more likely and easier.* 'But children are different' is the usual response. True, and in this particular respect: the babies and small children who research suggests are the victims of most corporal punishment in the home are different in that they are very small and very fragile. Children's vulnerability, their developmental status, their dependence on adults and the huge difficulties they face in seeking protection for themselves – all these differences suggest that they should have more, not less protection from being hit and deliberately hurt.
>
> (Newell 2006: 14)

A particularly powerful supporting argument is the experience of Sweden, who introduced a ban on corporal punishment, supported by parent education more than 20 years ago. They have since seen a marked decline in child mortality rates from maltreatment (Hammarburg 2006). It is notable that in recent years many health professional bodies have joined with over 400 organisations and individuals, including the UK's four Children's Commissioners, to sign up to the campaign to end the use of corporal punishment in childhood (see http://www.childrenareunbeatable.org.uk/). This would appear to be entirely congruent with nurses' and midwives' responsibilities to 'protect and support health' as per the Code of Professional Conduct (NMC 2004a). However, at the time of writing the UK's largest professional organisation for nurses, the Royal College of Nursing, remains divided on the issue, presumably reflecting the cultural milieu. As I have argued elsewhere (Powell 2002, 2004) it is timely for nurses to acknowledge the dangers of this outmoded practice and to help a move towards supporting parents in non-punitive forms of discipline. An understanding of the principles of positive parenting is extremely helpful in this case.

Positive parenting

Positive parenting techniques are essentially those which encourage positive interactions with children and reduce coercive and inconsistent parenting practices (Sanders 1999). In a National Society for the Prevention of Cruelty to Children (NSPCC) publication aimed at parents, Hayes (2002) provides an extremely practical approach to dealing with the challenges of demanding behaviour at various ages through childhood. Her 'top ten tips' include praising good behaviour (it will increase if you do) and ignoring bad behaviour as much as possible. She also stresses the importance of criticising bad behaviour rather than the child, and trying to use a degree of choice as opposed to saying 'no'. The need for love and warmth from the outset is seen as vital. Nurses and midwives who are unfamiliar with the principles of positive parenting will find this guide very accessible and a useful tool to help support good parenting practice.

Conclusion

This chapter opened with the suggestion that safeguarding practice recognises that children and young people are a separate and somewhat vulnerable group. It has explored the nature of childhood and considered how the children's rights movement has sought to challenge discrimination and address fundamental inequality. The text has been provocative at times, but has been written to challenge those who may unwittingly hold somewhat negative entrenched cultural views of children and young people. An understanding of contemporary childhood, and the risks and challenges that children and young people face, is an important prerequisite to an understanding of the nature of child maltreatment, which we explore next in Chapter 3.

Messages for practice

- Safeguarding activity is based on a tacit belief that children and young people are a distinct group of vulnerable individuals who have not yet reached a certain chronological age.
- Nurses' and midwives' training and education should include knowledge and understanding of the United Nations Convention on the Rights of the Child.
- The legal definition of children and young people is all those under 18 years of age. This definition does not include unborn

babies, although their needs should be considered as part of safeguarding practice.

- An understanding of contemporary childhood is fundamental in enabling nurses and midwives to achieve their potential in safeguarding children practice.
- Maintaining a child-centred focus not only helps in identifying concerns about possible maltreatment, but also reflects the need to consult with children and young people on decisions concerning their health care.
- Nurses and midwives are ideally placed to help to support and advise parents. An understanding of the principles of positive parenting will help to underpin practice.

Recommended reading

Commission on Families and the Well-being of Children (2005) *Families and the State*. http://www.nfpi.org.uk/data/research/docs/family-commission-exec-summary-31.doc (accessed 4/07/06).

Corby, B. (2006) *Child Abuse: Towards a Knowledge Base, 3rd edn.* Maidenhead: Open University Press.

HM Government (2004) *Every Child Matters: Change for Children.* London: Department for Education and Skills.

Newell, P. (1989) *Children are People Too: The Case Against Physical Punishment.* London: Bedford Square Press.

ONS (2004) *The Health of Children and Young People*. London: ONS.

Powell, C. (2004) Why nurses should support the 'Children are unbeatable!' Alliance, *Paediatric Nursing*, 16(8): 29.

Sanders, M. (1999) Triple P-Positive Parenting Program: towards an empirically validated multi-level parenting and family support strategy for the prevention of behaviour and emotional problems in children, *Clinical Child and Family Psychology Review*, 2(2): 71–90.

chapter **three**

CHILD MALTREATMENT

Learning outcomes

This chapter will help you to:

- understand the differing ways in which 'child maltreatment' has been defined, debated and constructed;
- consider the issue of risk and the benefits and pitfalls of risk analysis in individual cases;
- appreciate the scale of the problem and the difficulties in measurement;

- recognise the importance of context and the 'lived experience' of the child;
- discuss the theoretical perspectives that have been applied to the analyses of the causes of child maltreatment.

Introduction

In the opening chapter we noted that safeguarding and promoting the welfare of children and young people encompasses a number of separate, but interrelated activities that include protecting children from maltreatment, preventing impairment of their health and development and ensuring that they are safe and well cared for (HM Government 2006a). The overarching aim of safeguarding work is to make sure that children and young people are able to reach their potential and enter adulthood successfully. The role of good parenting is seen to be vital to achieving this aim, but the supporting roles of nurses and midwives and others who work with children, young people and their families may be highly significant, especially where families are experiencing the stress of multiple disadvantage.

In Chapter 2, an exploration of contemporary childhood included a review of some of the current threats to children and young people's health and development. The concept of 'good enough' parenting was explored together with the recognition of the challenges of carrying out the parenting role in the context of lack of preparation and poor personal and socio-economic resources. An understanding of parenting, childhood and children's rights is thus an important precursor to an understanding of child maltreatment. As Corby (2006) has suggested, views on the status and rights of children and the ways in which they are treated by adults, will help to determine what is and what is not considered to be abusive.

This chapter considers child maltreatment, both in terms of defining and measuring the problem. Child maltreatment is often viewed as an 'incident' or 'event', but the importance of context and the cumulative effect of ongoing sub-optimal parenting are increasingly being recognised, particularly in relation to neglect and emotional abuse. Children and young people in this instance are often referred to as living in situations of 'high criticism – low warmth'. Whilst maltreatment is generally viewed as an issue of intra-familial dysfunction, the problem cannot be understood adequately without due consideration of the structures that (dis)enable successful child-rearing. Therefore this chapter begins by outlining a number of different perspectives, including a consideration of structural child maltreatment. Following on from this we discuss the problems of quantifying the scale of child maltreatment in the UK and provide, with caution, some evidence on the possible incidence and prevalence. The chapter concludes with a brief outline of theories that have considered the causes of child abuse and neglect, with the intention that a deeper understanding will help nurses and midwives to offer sensitive and thoughtful care both to children and young people who are at risk of, or suffering from maltreatment, and also to parents and carers who may be suffering from irrevocable circumstances that have, in turn, led to them harming their children.

Points for reflection

How would you define child maltreatment?

Discuss with fellow students or colleagues the factors that you would take into account in making a judgement as to whether or not a situation is abusive or neglectful to a child or young person.

Defining the problem

Defining child maltreatment is challenging. Lawrence (2004) argues that there is no substantive definition of the term. Child maltreatment is a complex construct that has been (and will probably always be) interpreted in many different ways. The ideology of inter-agency working that underpins good safeguarding practice is paradoxically unhelpful in defining the problem as professional attributes, gender, cultures and beliefs can play an important part in deciding what is, and is not, maltreatment. However, it is important to note at the outset that while there is no cultural or ethnic group that sanctions child maltreatment (Debelle 2003), it is also important to remember that interpretation by others may view some child-rearing practices and childhood experiences outside their cultural experiences as abusive or neglectful. Despite attempts to categorise maltreatment in the past, there is a growing awareness that definitions should reflect the context of harm and longer-term impact on the individual and family, rather than being event specific. A move to consider context rather than incident is borne out in child protection literature. Such texts support the notion that child abuse and neglect are highly complex issues that are not easily defined or measured as they represent socially circumscribed constructs that vary across time and culture (Lawrence 2004; Corby 2006).

Points for reflection

Is this child maltreatment?

An expectant mother is smoking small quantities of cannabis.

On the advice of her mother-in-law a new mother frequently leaves her new baby to cry herself to sleep.

Timothy's father often tells him that he was not wanted.

A mother lashes out at her 4-year-old who has wet the bed for the third time in three nights. She leaves a small bruise on his back.

Rosie and John who are 10 and 8 years old are often home before their mother in the evenings.

Jim, aged 12 years, is missing school because he has to help to care for his disabled father.

Tyler, aged 2, has sustained a fractured femur. There appears to be no history of how it happened.

Joshua, aged 5 years, never seems to be appropriately dressed in cold weather.

Usha, aged 14 years, is sleeping with her 19-year-old boyfriend.

The parents of Sam, who has cystic fibrosis, have rejected conventional medicine and are treating her with homeopathy.

Abdul, aged 14 months, travels unrestrained in his parents' car.

Parents with learning disabilities are feeding their 6-month-old baby infrequently.

A father insists on tucking up his 7-year-old stepdaughter; he says it is their 'special time'.

What else would you need to know? In all these cases further information needs to be gathered. The focus of decision-making, however, must always be on the impact on, and perspective of, the child.

Child maltreatment is now usually understood to embrace a more extensive range of behaviours and features than those initially identified (i.e. deliberate and severe physical maltreatment), with typical reference to four key (but not exclusive) categories of physical abuse, sexual abuse, emotional abuse and neglect. This so-called *diagnostic inflation* (Parton et al. 1997) clearly contributes to difficulty in defining, quantifying and researching the problem. This in turn presents a challenge for practitioners who are on a quest for the evidence base for safeguarding practice. Furthermore, although there is perhaps a predominant understanding of maltreatment as an occurrence between a parent, carer, or (less frequently) a stranger and a child, *structural* forms of child abuse, such as those related to the provisions for children in society are also important. The opening section of this chapter attempts to provide a range of views and perspectives that have contributed to the present-day understanding of the problem.

Paediatrics and child maltreatment: the medical model

Not surprisingly, the definition of child abuse and neglect may reflect the academic concerns and professional background of the interpreter. For example, as celebrated paediatricians in the field of child maltreatment, C. Henry Kempe and colleagues may have used the term in the *Battered Child Syndrome* in an attempt to gain widespread public attention to the issue of severe physical abuse by parents and carers (Kempe et al. 1962). Although a number of paediatric radiologists have been reported as describing fractures that were indicative of abuse prior to Kempe's work (as noted by Radbill 1968), it is the seminal and influential work of Kempe and his colleagues in the early 1960s that serves as a typical starting point for many health professionals. Crucially, in addition to describing clinical indicators of physical abuse, this work also provided health care practitioners with a mandate for the identification and referral of children and young people who exhibit signs of maltreatment. Perhaps of greater significance however, is the widespread belief that Kempe's work heralded the re-emergence of child maltreatment, conceived as an essentially medical problem with accompanying aetiological, diagnostic and epidemiological features. Indeed, it is notable that the World Health Organisation (WHO) has applied specific diagnostic coding for physical and sexual abuse (Z61.4; Z61.5 and Z61.6) and outlined diagnostic features and treatment (WHO 2003–4a). However, a paediatric (and *de facto* medical) model of abuse and neglect may be simply too narrow a focus, especially in terms of prevention. In their analysis, Newman et al. (1998) expressly question the concept of physical abuse as a *disorder*, arguing that it is a description of *behaviour*. Thus in contrast to an earlier notion of a disease or syndrome (where parents are the carriers) many wider contributory factors and alternative constructs are now recognised.

The legal and forensic perspective

For some, current responses to child maltreatment represent a move away from a notion of curing and preventing the *syndrome* or *disease* to an increasing emphasis on investigation, assessment and the weighing up of forensic evidence (Parton et al. 1997). Thus, whereas Kempe's work in the 1960s may be considered in hindsight to reflect the medicalisation of child abuse, Parton and colleagues describe a paradigmatic shift from a socio-medical perspective (with paediatrician as expert) to a socio-legal reality where legal expertise takes precedence. Archard (1993) and Speight and Wynne (2000) urge caution with such developments, arguing that the legal slant will inevitably lead to raised thresholds for intervention in cases of child abuse and neglect.

It is thus remarkable (and perhaps reassuring) to find that the current legal definitions of child maltreatment in the UK are rather vague. In the Children Act 1989 (England and Wales), for example, the concept of *significant harm* is used to denote the threshold that justifies compulsory intervention in family life. Such a definition appears to lack the concrete evidential basis suggested above: 'Where the question of whether harm suffered by the child is significant turns on the child's health and development, his health or development shall be compared with that which could be reasonably expected of a similar child' (The Children Act 1989, Section 31 (10)). As Poblete (2003) notes, this is a very broad definition of child maltreatment that fails to identify clear thresholds of concern and leaves professionals to judge what is meant by both 'reasonable' and by 'significant' harm. Government guidance (HM Government 2006a) lists a number of factors to take into consideration in order to understand and identify significant harm. These include: the nature of the harm and its impact on the child's health and development; the child's development within the context of their family and wider environment; any special needs including medical conditions or disability, and; parental capacity to meet the needs and the wider family and environmental factors.

Archard (1993) suggests that it is the crucial context of harm, and the right and means to the best possible upbringing, that have led to divisions of opinion as to the nature of child maltreatment. These arguments are founded on the lived experiences children have within the social context of their world and thus reflect communities, cultures, organisations, legislation and policies as well as care within the family. Yet the dyadic representation of child maltreatment that fits both the medical and legal models continues to dominate. As Archard suggests, the very agencies that seek to define maltreatment may have a stake in its ongoing representation as something that affects individual children and their families, rather than resulting from social inequities. There is some evidence to support this suggestion in the literature. Hobbs et al. (1999a: 2), for example, appear to reject broader definitions, such as that given in the report *Childhood Matters* by the NCIPCA (see below) as being too 'all-inclusive' and concentrate instead on clinical observations of harmful interactions between family members. It appears that to consider a structural basis to child maltreatment is to be critical of society itself, yet the following section explains why structural interpretations are important.

Structural definitions of child abuse and neglect

Importantly (and controversially), the *Childhood Matters* team adopted a comprehensive sociological definition of child maltreatment to underpin their review. At the time of writing their defining attributes continue to influence the broader concept of safeguarding: 'Child abuse consists of anything which individuals, institutions, or processes do or fail to do which directly or indirectly harms children or damages their prospects of safe and healthy development into adulthood' (NCIPCA 1996: 2). The NCIPCA report concluded that poverty allied to factors such as unemployment and bad housing leads to a build up of stress within the home and a stronger likelihood of child maltreatment by parents. It is, however, the Commission's use of a definition that acknowledges child maltreatment by institutions and processes as well as by individuals, that is equally important in any consideration of the means by which children are harmed, and the actions that may be taken to prevent this. I believe that the notion of structural forms of child maltreatment is highly significant. The importance of this perspective lies in the context in which child maltreatment is most likely to take place, as well as the precursors to it. Certainly, the significance of extra-familial factors is reflected in the work of those who have theorised about the aetiology of child maltreatment. Belsky (1993: 418), for example, notes that 'Child maltreatment is multiply determined and arises as the result of transactional processes involving the parent, the child, the family, and the community, the cultural context, and even evolutionary context in which they are embedded.'

It is widely acknowledged that even in the most caring of homes, children and young people who live in poverty are more likely to suffer a higher level of illness and accidents, and have a higher rate of mortality, when compared with those born into affluent families. Thus, it could be suggested that a society that allows social inequalities that lead to increased likelihood of childhood illness and accidents has failed to act to ensure safe and healthy development into adulthood. As Archard (1993) suggests, many more children are likely to be harmed through living in conditions caused by poverty and deprivation than by any act of commission or omission on the part of their parents. However, he also notes a significant correlation between poverty and what he refers to as standard definitions of child maltreatment. At an individual level the link between poverty and maltreatment is not straightforward. For example, there is clearly a need to distinguish between material impoverishment and emotional impoverishment when assessing child neglect (Hobbs et al. 1999b). Despite these concerns, I have found reluctance, albeit anecdotally, among certain practitioners to acknowledge the links between multiple disadvantage and a greater risk of child maltreatment. The reasons that are given for this appear to centre on a fear of being seen as 'politically incorrect' or causing further damage through labelling or stigmatisation of families. However, while it is important for nurses and midwives to acknowledge that child maltreatment may indeed occur across the social spectrum, and that all children and young people are potentially 'at risk', not to recognise the greater risk for some is unrealistic and detrimental to the development and resourcing of targeted programmes for prevention.

The NCIPCA (1996) definition also makes reference to *institutional* abuse. Current concerns in relation to institutional abuse perhaps most readily summon up high profile scandals of systematic physical and sexual abuse that have been a feature for many children in institutional care (e.g. Utting 1997; Hobbs et al. 1999b). As Walker (1992) comments, children's lack of power and autonomy are intensified within institutional settings and opportunity for exploitation (by whatever means) is common. Nevertheless, institutional child maltreatment is not just confined to children's homes. Kendrick and Taylor (2000) consider a number of high profile cases where children have been harmed in hospital settings. Perhaps the most notorious of the perpetrators was the state enrolled nurse, Beverly Allitt, who was found guilty of four murders, three attempted murders and six instances of grievous bodily harm. These appalling crimes were committed over a three-month period in 1991 and the subsequent inquiry report has led to important changes in recruitment processes and occupational health screening (Clothier 1994). However, cases such as this are seemingly rare. Most harm that occurs to children and young people in health care settings is less sensational than the Allitt case, but nevertheless important. For instance, it is concerning that children and young people may still be harmed unnecessarily by outmoded practice, such as failure to allow parental presence and support for certain elements of health care provision (for example painful or intrusive procedures) in accordance with the wishes of the child (Glasper and Powell 2000). Other examples include the inappropriate application of restraint and lack of adequate analgesia (Kendrick and Taylor 2000; Pearch 2005). Whether or not these examples of institutional abuse constitute child maltreatment will depend on the context in which the definition is used, as well as the beliefs and purposes of the interpreter.

Points for reflection
How have children's nurses addressed the evidence (Carter 1994) that suggests that infants and young children are not always given adequate pain relief?

The classifications considered thus far (i.e. the medical model, the legal and forensic perspective and structural definitions) rest on professional interpretation, policy and academic debate. Arguably however, important definitions of child maltreatment are those that have been provided by victims of abuse themselves. The following section gives some insight into the views and experiences of *survivors* of child abuse and neglect.

Survivors' construction of child abuse and neglect

A number of survivors of child maltreatment gave evidence to the NCIPCA (1996). Survivors addressed a wider range of abusive behaviour than those portrayed thus far. Examples include bullying, the deliberate subjection of a child to danger, the witnessing of domestic violence and a lack of concern for children's rights. The survivors also contextualised abuse in terms of the sense that they, as a child, have made of their situation and the longer-term impact on them as individuals and also on their family. The dynamic and reflexive approach to the construction of child maltreatment portrayed by survivors appears to have the support of experts within the field. Parton et al. (1997), for example, have reasoned against the use of standardised definitions of child maltreatment noting that human beings actively construct their own world and make sense of it. Thus, they suggest that an abusing mother or victim of child sexual abuse may not define themself as such. As Cawson et al. (2000: 5) comment, considerable differences exist between perceptions of child maltreatment by professionals and those of recipients:

> Professionals judge by what was actually done to the victim, by whether the victim suffered harm or by a mixture of these factors. Victims take other things into account, such as their relationship with the person harming them, an understanding of the health problems or pressures on that person . . . or by comparison of their treatment to that of other children in the family and neighbourhood.

The issue of bullying is likely to be of interest to those working with school-aged children and young people. Essentially this can be seen as 'peer child maltreatment'. The WHO (2003–4b) recognises that bullying can have a major impact on the physical and mental health of the victims, as well as disruption to their education. Children who are being bullied are likely to present with a variety of psychosomatic disorders including sleeping difficulties, anxiety, bed-wetting, depression, suicidal ideation and deliberate self-harm. Wolke et al. (2001) undertook a large-scale study of bullying within primary schools and their findings suggest that those who are victims or bully/victims (i.e. both bullies and victims of bullying) may have higher rates of reported sore throats, coughs and colds that may have been 'made up' to allow them to stay off school when compared with those who were 'pure bullies'. However, they also found higher levels of behavioural and mental health problems.

The 'lay' definition

The lay definition is important because this may well represent the starting point for nurses and midwives both at the beginning of their careers or with little experience, education or training in working with children, young people and families, and in safeguarding work in particular. In contrast to the definitions of those with personal experience or academic and professional concerns, the lay definition of child maltreatment may well reflect the occasional horrific case of repeated cruelty or severe neglect. Efforts by organisations such as the NSPCC to raise public awareness of different types of abuse through campaigns such as *Full Stop* may also (one hopes) change public perception of the problem, although the danger of reification has been noted (Lawrence 2004).

Child maltreatment as a continuum

Despite any perceived advantages of agreement on what is and what is not child abuse and neglect (or good enough parenting), there are those who would dispute the helpfulness of a precise definition. Greenland (1987), for example, suggests that child maltreatment exists as a continuum from parental incompetence at one end to homicide at the other. In a similar vein Thyen et al. (1995) suggest that there is a continuum of behaviour that is socially accepted at one end and abusive and neglectful at the other. Labelling, they add, fails to recognise this by dichotomising parents' behaviour as normal or deviant and prevents a helpful response by agencies. Hay and Jones (1994: 380) propose a more complex social and developmental continuum model that may better represent the complexities of child maltreatment whereby 'Child maltreatment is an extreme on a continuum, a severe manifestation of dysfunction in the inter-play between a child's development and the conditions and relationships that affect that development'.

Whilst there are undoubtedly advantages to consideration of a continuum, the identification of acceptable cut-off points from acceptable to unacceptable to abusive is difficult (Cawson et al. 2000). Perhaps what is important here is that for professionals at least, the 'threshold' for intervention in cases of child maltreatment has been lowered and the spectrum of what is considered abusive broadened since Kempe and his colleagues first raised the problem of grievously injured children in the 1960s. Nevertheless, as Archard (1993) notes, it would not do to define child maltreatment in such a way that the majority of parents cannot but help being abusers of their own children. This would be particularly important if the root cause of the abuse or neglect lay in factors over which the parents had little perceived control.

A more practical definition, and one that is broadly applied throughout UK, may be that provided by government guidance on safeguarding policy (HM Government 2006a). An appreciation of current safeguarding policy is extremely important for nurses and midwives as it links directly with their roles in line with the statutory duties of health authorities. In England, the Children Act 2004 (Section 11) placed a new duty on agencies working with children and young people to safeguard and promote their welfare. The policy definitions are given below; Chapter 4 will provide more details as to what this means for practice.

Policy definitions

In England the policy definitions are set out in the *Working Together* guidance, first published in 1988 and now in its fourth incarnation. The latest guidance has built upon previous definitions of the four categories of child maltreatment highlighted above (i.e. physical abuse; emotional abuse; sexual abuse; neglect). Midwives should note that this edition alludes to maternal substance misuse in pregnancy and neglect. Another addition is 'overprotection' as a form of emotional abuse which seems pertinent given our reference in the previous chapter to 'cotton-wool' children and the exaggerated concerns about 'stranger danger' (Midgley 2006). Reference is also made to neglect incorporating 'exclusion from home' reinforcing perhaps the enduring nature of parental responsibility until adulthood.

The document sets out the four categories of maltreatment as follows:

Physical abuse

Physical abuse may involve hitting, shaking, throwing, poisoning, burning or scalding, drowning, suffocating, or otherwise causing physical harm to a child. Physical harm may also be caused when a parent or carer fabricates the symptoms of, or deliberately induces illness in a child.

Emotional abuse

Emotional abuse is the persistent emotional maltreatment of a child such as to cause severe and persistent adverse effects on the child's emotional development. It may involve conveying to children that they are worthless or unloved, inadequate, or valued only insofar as they meet the needs of another person. It may feature age or developmentally inappropriate expectations being imposed on children. These may include interactions that are beyond the child's developmental capability, as well as overprotection and limitation of exploration and learning, or preventing the child participating in normal social interaction. It may involve seeing or hearing the ill-treatment of another. It may involve serious bullying causing children frequently to feel frightened or in danger, or the exploitation or corruption of children. Some level of emotional abuse is involved in all types of maltreatment of a child, though it may occur alone.

Sexual abuse

Sexual abuse involves forcing or enticing a child or young person to take part in sexual activities, including prostitution, whether or not the child is aware of what is happening. The activities may involve physical contact, including penetrative (e.g. rape, buggery or oral sex) or non-penetrative acts. They may include non-contact activities, such as involving children in looking at, or in the production of, pornographic material or watching sexual activities, or encouraging children to behave in sexually inappropriate ways.

Neglect

Neglect is the persistent failure to meet a child's basic physical and/or psychological needs, likely to result in the serious impairment of the child's health or development. Neglect may occur during pregnancy as a result of maternal substance abuse. Once a child is born, neglect may involve a parent or carer failing to provide adequate food and clothing, shelter including exclusion from home or abandonment, failing to protect a child from physical and emotional harm or danger, failure to ensure adequate supervision including the use of inadequate care-takers, or the failure to ensure access to appropriate medical care or

> treatment. It may also include neglect of, or unresponsiveness to, a child's basic emotional needs.
>
> (HM Government 2006a: 8–9)

Although these 'categories' of child maltreatment are well established in policy and practice, their helpfulness has been brought into question. The concern here is that categorisation may promote the over-reliance on identifiable incidents of abuse. There is also a significant co-morbidity of different types of abuse and this may become hidden in reporting mechanisms. As the following section demonstrates, the policy definitions play a prominent role in determining the possible extent of the problem of child maltreatment across populations.

Measurement and reporting

In the opening chapter we noted the suggestion from one expert that at the time of writing, child maltreatment was *the* major cause of morbidity in children. However, substantiation of this claim is difficult to prove. It is widely agreed that efforts to monitor and report the scale of child maltreatment are fraught with difficulties. There is general consensus in the field that many instances of abuse or neglect go unreported. This is not surprising as it is a largely hidden problem. As Jenny and Isaac (2006: 265) claim 'at its essence, child maltreatment is a deceptive and easily disguised entity'. Recognition is generally dependent on those outside of the family, such as neighbours or professionals, identifying possible concerns. Recognition also rests on the perception of the identifier as to what they understand as child maltreatment. In a few cases children and young people themselves will disclose that they are being abused, but this is by no means a common feature. For example, on the evidence of literally hundreds of letters the NCIPCA (1996) received from those who were abused as children, it was concluded that at least half of child maltreatment that occurs was undisclosed and unrecognised at the time. Although this evidence may be somewhat dated it does indicate that there may be both a reluctance to disclose on the part of the child and a failure to recognise concerns by those around them. The fact that child maltreatment is more common in very young children and those with a disability is highly relevant here.

Disclosure

Walker's (1992) research highlights the real difficulties that children may face in disclosing abuse. One victim, who was subjected to multiple beatings, recalled how her mother used to sit opposite her at health checks ensuring that the right impression was given and remembers feeling powerless to report the beatings, not only because of a lack of privacy, but also because of what she feared would happen when they returned home. Walker suggests that abusers are systematic in planning to manipulate victims and those around them so that the abuse does not come to light. She reports the words of another survivor (1992: 10–11):

> She [mother] emotionally and physically abused all of us ... I couldn't have told anyone, but somebody did because the NSPCC came. They went away again. They talked to my mother. They didn't talk to me. My mother was a powerful figure; a power in the house, and what she said went. But she never protected me.

Points for reflection
Consider the vignette above in light of your knowledge and experience.
Why do you think that the abuse was not recognised?
What are the key lessons for practice?

Perhaps one of the most distressing accounts in Walker's book relates to a girl who was sexually abused by her father. After unsuccessfully trying to tell a teacher and her doctor what was going on she finally told her mother, only to realise that her mother appeared to be already aware of the abuse. In relating this and other similar accounts, Walker (p. 92) notes the 'climate of blind faith' in the family as reflected to children by storybooks, schools and the wider media. The work with adult survivors, and the evidence that much abuse goes unreported or unrecognised, illustrates the need for this section on measurement and reporting to be read with some caution.

Prevalence and incidence

There are two key aspects to measurement of any health issue within a population. One is to consider 'prevalence' and the other 'incidence'. Prevalence refers to the proportion of a defined population who have experienced a particular problem (e.g. child maltreatment) within a specified time (such as during childhood). Incidence, on the other hand, is a term that is used to describe the number of 'new cases' occurring within a population over the period of one year. Both are now considered.

The prevalence of child maltreatment

The conservative estimate that at least one in ten children in the UK is likely to encounter physical, emotional or sexual abuse or neglect during the course of their childhood as suggested by the *Childhood Matters* (NCIPCA 1996) team was open to some debate on publication (House of Commons Hansard Debate 1996). However, in 2000 the NSPCC undertook a widely acclaimed retrospective self-report survey of the experiences of a representative group of 18–24-year-olds in the UK (Cawson et al. 2000). Their findings broadly support the NCIPCA work. In other words, they found that 90% of respondents reported that they had been well cared for as children and had enjoyed a warm and loving family background, thus leaving the remaining 10% to indicate that they had not. More worryingly, subsequent analysis by the researchers suggested that as many as one in six children experienced serious maltreatment within the family, with one in three experiencing maltreatment of a lesser extent (Cawson 2002). Thus it appears that within the broader professional interpretations of child maltreatment at least, the prevalence of child maltreatment is really quite striking.

I have found their following analogy helpful in conceptualising the prevalence of child maltreatment:

> Every full double-decker [70 seater] school bus at the end of a day is likely to be taking home around seven seriously unhappy children. Most of the lower deck would at some time during their childhood have been going home to serious worries. Approximately 10 children may be going home to a 'double-shift' of cleaning, laundry, shopping and preparing meals, and two or three will be in fear of violence between their parents while they were out, or what might happen that evening.
>
> (Cawson et al. 2000: 93)

The incidence of child maltreatment

The incidence of child maltreatment, i.e. new occurrences in a one year period, is commonly illustrated by the statistics relating to numbers of children and young people whose names have been placed on traditional child protection registers. Registration reflects the need for continuing protection for children who have suffered, or are at risk of suffering, significant harm. Clearly, because of this, the register cannot provide an accurate measure of child maltreatment, but nevertheless may be a useful guide to trends. The registers reflect the policy definitions and categories of child maltreatment given above. Important changes in this process in England are discussed in the next chapter.

Figures for child protection registration are readily available for all four countries of the UK. The child protection register is dynamic, with names being added and removed during the course of the year – the figures given are therefore those on a certain date, sometimes referred to as a 'point prevalence'. Readers are advised to view the relevant websites to check for updates.

England

The numbers of children and young people on child protection registers in England are collated by the Department for Education and Skills (DfES). The main finding for the year ending 31st March 2006 (DfES 2006) was that there was a small increase in the number of children on the register. In total there were 26,400 children on the register reflecting 31,500 additions and 31,000 de-registrations during the year. Risk of neglect, which has become more prominent since, represented 43% of registrations; emotional abuse 21%; physical abuse 16% and sexual abuse 9%. The remaining 11% were 'mixed' categories (see Tables 3.1, 3.2 and 3.3).

Table 3.1 Children and young people on child protection registers at 31 March 2006, broken down by age

Under 1	3000
1–4	7600
5–9	7600
10–15	7300
16 and over	490
Total:	25,990

Table 3.2 Numbers, rates and percentages of children and young people on child protection registers (England) during the year ending 31 March 2006, by gender

	Numbers[1]
Boys	13,200
Girls	12,800
Total children[2]	26,400
	Rates per 10,000
Boys	23
Girls	24
Total children	24

Table 3.2 (contd)

	Percentage[3]
Boys	51
Girls	49

Notes: 1 Figures may not add due to rounding.
2 The 'all children' figures include unborn children.
3 Percentage calculations exclude unborn children.

Table 3.3 Comparison of percentages of registrations between countries of the UK, year ending 31 March 2006

	England	*Wales*	*Scotland*	*Northern Ireland*
Neglect[1]	43	49	45	35
Physical abuse[2]	16	16	27	20
Emotional abuse	21	19	16	15
Sexual abuse	9	7	12	15
Mixed category	11	9	–	15

Notes: 1 Physical neglect in Scotland
2 Physical injury in Scotland

Wales

In Wales the numbers of children and young people on child protection registers are collected by the Local Government Data Unit on behalf of the Welsh National Assembly. Figures for the year ending 31 March 2006 showed that there were 2163 children and young people on the register, reflecting 2870 additions and 2971 de-registrations. There were fairly similar patterns to England in respect of the categories with neglect representing 49% of registrations; emotional abuse 19%; physical abuse 16% and sexual abuse 7%. The remaining 9% were 'mixed' categories (National Assembly for Wales 2006).

Scotland

In Scotland the numbers of children and young people on child protection registers are collected by the Scottish Executive. Figures for the year ending 31 March 2006 showed that there were 2228 children and young people on the register reflecting 2791 additions and 2774 de-registrations. In comparison with England and Wales there appears to be an upward trend since 2000. The categories of child maltreatment in Scotland are slightly different, with 45% of children registered for physical neglect; 27% for physical injury; 16% for emotional abuse and 12% for sexual abuse. The statistics report notes that Glasgow is seeing a rise in the numbers of children registered for neglect due to parental addiction (Scottish Executive 2006).

Northern Ireland

In Northern Ireland the numbers of children and young people on child protection registers are collected by the Department of Health, Social Services and Public Safety (DHSSPS). Figures for the year ending 31 March 2005 showed that there were 1593 children and young people on the register. This is an increase of 12% on the previous year, although the figures for 2003 were higher. Neglect represented 35% of registrations; emotional abuse 15%; physical abuse 20% and sexual abuse 15%. Mixed categories accounted for the remaining 15% (DHSSPS 2006a).

Overall these figures represent a rate of child protection registration of approximately 21:10,000 children and young people under the age of 18 years. Broadly speaking the rates for boys and girls are similar. Younger children, especially those under the age of 1, feature more prominently. Further details as to a breakdown of registration by age, gender and also by local authority are readily available from the website.

Why child maltreatment happens

Nurses and midwives who come across child maltreatment in the course of their practice will, understandably, find the actions of parents or carers who have harmed their children very challenging to comprehend. This is particularly the case when a child has died or been irreversibly damaged by child abuse or neglect. Nurses may find themselves in the position of having to provide information and support to parents at the bedside of a grievously injured infant or child in the light of growing suspicion and concern that one or both of them may well be responsible for the injury. Midwives may provide intra-partum care for women whose past history or current circumstances may be judged as being too risky, warranting the infant's removal at the time of birth. In such cases sensitive support and debrief is extremely important. An understanding of why child maltreatment happens can also be helpful in managing these very difficult situations.

Corby (2006) provides a useful overview of theories that have been applied to an understanding of the causation of child maltreatment. He groups these into three broad perspectives:

- psychological theories;
- social psychological theories;
- sociological perspectives.

Generally speaking, the above perspectives, and the different theories that they embrace, reflect a development over time that has moved from a focus on the individual towards an integrative approach that recognises the interplay between the individual, their environment and the way in which they adapt to stressors and change. Nurses may find some resonance here with the work of Parse who based her theory of nursing on adaptation (Parse 1992).

Corby promotes the work of Jay Belsky (1980) who described an ecological framework that reflects a four-level approach; ontogenic development (the parents' developmental background and experiences); the microsystem (the interaction of individuals within the family); the exosystem (the immediate social environment within which the family functions); and the macrosystem (the broader structural factors, such as cultural attitudes to violence). The way in which these systems interact with each other is important in determining the likelihood of child maltreatment occurring or indeed of parents being able to parent adequately. Ecological approaches have been utilised in the development of assessment tools, such as the 'Common Assessment Framework' (HM Government 2004), which help practitioners to work with children, young people and their families to identify both strengths and needs. As Corby notes, a broad range of integrated knowledge provides a strong basis for practice. This is particularly important in helping nurses and midwives to provide care in very difficult situations, because it can help them to understand that the precursors for abuse are, to a certain extent, outside the perpetrators' control.

The NCIPCA Report (1996) also recognises that there has been a shift away from a notion of the abusing parent as manifesting a major psychopathy to a psychosocial context of the causes and consequences of maltreatment. The authors describe as misconceived any belief that abuse and neglect occur when the parents are abnormal or intractably evil, or that the abused have provoked their ill treatment. Rather, they argue that abused children and their families require identification, acknowledgement of their concerns, help and support. This is borne out by Roberts (1988: 44) who notes, 'Having interviewed numerous child abuse parents I am convinced that the last thing these people wanted to do was harm their children – somehow neither they, their families, nor the professional helpers could prevent them from doing so.' Nurses and midwives will almost certainly be among the 'professional helpers' that Roberts alludes to. The rights of children and young people to be heard and to be protected from maltreatment, to be healthy, to be safe, to be well cared for and to have the opportunities to achieve their potential, should be at the heart of a proactive and evidence-informed approach to safeguarding practice. The following chapter aims to inform and support practitioners in their role in preventing, recognising and referring children, young people and their families who are at risk of, or suffering from maltreatment. The potential to make a difference is huge.

Conclusion

This chapter has sought to help nurses and midwives understand the issue of child maltreatment by outlining a number of different perspectives. It has also sought to quantify the scale of child maltreatment in the UK, while acknowledging that there are challenges in identification and reporting. At a time when advances in maternal and child health care have led to improvements in children's and young people's health and well-being, maltreatment features starkly as a major and potentially preventable cause of morbidity and mortality. An understanding of the causes of maltreatment is helpful in providing sensitive child- and family-centred care. Nurses and midwives have a crucial role to play in prevention, identification and reporting of child maltreatment. Chapter 4 will help to achieve this.

Messages for practice

- Child maltreatment is a complex construct that has been (and will probably always be) interpreted in many different ways.
- All children and young people are potentially 'at risk' of child maltreatment; however, there is a significant correlation between poverty and a greater risk.
- Policy definitions in the UK typically categorise four types of child maltreatment: physical abuse, emotional abuse, sexual abuse and neglect.
- Considerable differences may exist between professionals' perceptions of child maltreatment and those of victims and perpetrators.
- There are important distinctions between the measurement of the prevalence and the incidence of child maltreatment.
- Research with young adults has found that approximately 1:10 people suffered from some form of abuse and neglect in the course of their childhood.
- An understanding of the causes of child maltreatment has developed over time.

Recommended reading

Cawson, P., Wattam, C., Brooker, S. and Kelly, G. (2000) *Child Maltreatment in the United Kingdom: A Study of the Prevalence of Child Abuse and Neglect.* London: NSPCC.

Corby, B. (2006) *Child Abuse: Towards a Knowledge Base,* 3rd edn. Maidenhead: Open University Press.

NCIPCA (National Commission of Inquiry into the Prevention of Child Abuse) (1996) *Childhood Matters*, vols I and II. London: The Stationery Office.

Southall, D.P., Samuels, M.P. and Golden, M.H. (2003) Classification of child abuse by motive and degree rather than type of injury, *Archives of Disease in Childhood,* **88**: 101–4.

chapter **four**

SAFEGUARDING CHILDREN: PROFESSIONAL ROLES AND RESPONSIBILITIES

Learning outcomes

This chapter will help you to:

- successfully enact your role in the prevention, recognition and referral of cases of possible child maltreatment;
- understand the importance of the early identification of concerns and provision of support to families;
- appreciate the need for the judicious application of risk factors;
- be aware of the importance of contextual factors, behavioural factors and background;
- understand the procedural aspects of safeguarding children and young people and the contribution that nurses and midwives can make;
- recognise the importance of a multi-agency response and the roles of other agencies;
- consider the importance of access to clinical supervision and support;
- discuss the leadership role of named and designated safeguarding professionals.

Introduction

Chapter 3 defined child maltreatment and introduced some of the theoretical perspectives that have been applied in order to explain and understand the nature of the problem. The reader may thus be somewhat relieved to learn that the current chapter focuses much more on *practice*. In doing so the aim is to inform and support nurses and midwives in successfully enacting their crucial roles in the prevention, recognition and referral of cases of possible child abuse and neglect. Working with children, young people and families where child maltreatment is suspected, or confirmed, is difficult and demanding work and should not be tackled alone. However, the experience of being part of a team that has worked together to ensure a child or young person's safety and well-being can be extremely rewarding.

The chapter begins by considering some of the indicators of risk and early signs that may alert the practitioner to the possibility of child maltreatment. Early intervention in these instances may rest on the provision of extra support to parents and judicious monitoring of children's safety and well-being. In these cases the 'threshold' for formal child protection referral may not be reached. Both the risk factor approach and the identification of early indicators of possible abuse or neglect can be viewed as secondary preventative approaches to child maltreatment. The next part of the chapter considers the history and presentation of children who can be more readily recognised as likely to be suffering from 'significant harm' and for whom a child protection referral may well be needed. For ease the 'signs of child maltreatment' are discussed within the categories of physical abuse, emotional abuse, sexual abuse and neglect. However, it should be noted that neglect is also discussed in some depth in a later chapter, and that fabricated and induced illness (an aspect of physical abuse) is outlined in Chapter 6. Despite the use of the four categories to exemplify different types of child maltreatment, it is also important to remember that children and young people may well be suffering from more than one form of abuse simultaneously.

Following on from the sections on recognising maltreatment, we consider the response. The aim here is to explain the way in which government guidance and legislation informs local child protection procedures and consequently professional practice. The response to child maltreatment also reflects the requirements of the Code of Professional Conduct (NMC 2004a). One of the key features of success in safeguarding children work is that it is reliant on a coordinated response from a multi-professional and inter-agency team. Thus the chapter also provides insight into the roles of others who are key players in ensuring that children are healthy and safe. The chapter concludes with a discussion on the roles of named and designated professionals.

Recognising risk

Although this section highlights a range of factors that have been found to be linked to a greater risk of child maltreatment, two important points should be understood from the outset. First, just because a family appears to 'score' very highly in terms of risk, it does not mean that child maltreatment is occurring; it is more than likely to be the case that it is not. The injudicious application of risk factors has been widely criticised for its stigmatisation of families. Corby (2006) adds that past efforts to 'predict' the likelihood of child maltreatment may even have been 'ethically suspect', with families not necessarily engaged in the risk assessment process. Crucially, he adds that working with parents on the basis of shared concerns is an effective strategy in ensuring the safety of a child. This is of vital importance to nurses and midwives who need to be able to challenge parents on issues of concern about the health and safety of their children, and work with them towards a resolution. However, it is recognised that in a minority of cases, sharing concerns may place the child, young person or worker in danger. In these cases a discussion with children's social care and the police on how parents will be informed will be needed. Second, as was stated in the previous chapter, it is important to acknowledge that any child or young person can be vulnerable to maltreatment, even within 'a normal looking family' (Poblete 2003). Nevertheless, the issue of risk is important because it is helpful in informing practice priorities and the provision of services that optimise opportunities for prevention at a variety of levels.

Risk factors have been identified for both children and for parents, although clearly there are some risk factors that affect the well-being of the whole family. These include issues such as poverty and social exclusion. Table 4.1 summarises the risk factors that have been drawn from the literature.

Table 4.1 Summary of risk factors

Child	*Parent*
Previously abused or neglected	Mental health problems
Younger age	Substance misuse
Pre-term or low birth weight	Domestic violence
Male	Abused or neglected as a child
Congenital abnormality or chronic illness	Aged 20 years or less at birth of first child
Development delay, disability	Single parent/separated; partner not biological parent of child
Prolonged separation from mother	History of maltreatment or deprivation in childhood
Parental criticism, indifference, intolerance, over-investment or over-anxiousness	Unemployed/unskilled worker
Cries frequently/difficult to settle	Low level of education/learning disability
Difficulty in feeding/elimination	Poor self-esteem
Adopted, foster or stepchild	Chronic illness
	Acute and chronic stress
Family	
Social exclusion	
Frequent moves	
Poor housing	
Poverty and social deprivation	
Family violence (animals, elder abuse)	

Source: Adapted from Greenland (1987); Browne et al. (1988) and Browne and Hamilton (2003)

Points for reflection

Discuss with fellow students or colleagues how you could utilise a risk factor approach to help to prioritise and target services.

How may children, young people and families be engaged in this process?

The notion of a 'cycle of abuse', whereby abused children may become abusing parents reflects the intra-generational transmission of child maltreatment (and indeed other disadvantage) that is often noted in the literature on risk factors. Thus, any attempt to 'break the cycle' may include a consideration of the risk factors for child maltreatment as part of routine clinical practice, especially when caring for vulnerable adults. However, in relation to adults who were maltreated in their childhood, it is equally essential to recognise that there is no inevitability that an abused child will become an abuser (Royal College of Psychiatrists 2003) and to do so discriminates against those adult survivors who work hard to overcome the experiences of their childhood (Wattam and Woodward 1996).

In short, it is important that caution is applied in utilising a risk factor approach. Lawrence (2004: 79) helpfully suggests that 'Although possible risk factors associated with child abuse have been identified, research has not yet proved a direct causal relationship between specific circumstances and confirmed abuse.' Therefore, whilst the use of risk tools and assessments is common in safeguarding children work, they do not, and cannot, predict that child maltreatment will actually happen or that it will not. It is important to recognise that there are no assessment tools that can determine with certainty which situations are dangerous (Beckett 2003). My own reflection on practice is that there are many vulnerable individuals who competently manage the challenging task of parenting, despite multiple disadvantages, and that we have much to learn from the resilience of these families. A focus on the day to day 'lived experience' of the individual child or young person, together with a child-centred holistic assessment, which includes an evaluation of the ability of parents to meet their child's needs, may ultimately be more meaningful than professional discourse on the existence or not of multiple risk factors in families. The following sections thus outline the clinical indicators and signs of possible child maltreatment that may be identified by nurses and midwives in the course of their practice. We start by reviewing the evidence base for 'early indicators' of child maltreatment.

Identification of child maltreatment

One of the driving forces of the current government policy for children and young people is that there should be 'early intervention' and help when problems arise (HM Government 2004). The recognition of risk factors (as outlined above) and the identification of *early indicators* of possible maltreatment are viewed as a secondary prevention strategy for child maltreatment (Thyen et al. 1995; Sidebotham 2003). There is an important role for health professionals. An 'early diagnostic' approach to secondary prevention differs from the risk factor approaches in that it focuses on early signs of possible maltreatment. In his classic text on levels of prevention Caplan (1964: 91) notes that an early preventative approach can be undertaken when 'diagnostic tools are sharpened so disorders can be identified from fewer and milder signs and symptoms . . . sufferers and their social networks can be alerted to weaker indications of the disorder and can be motivated to enlist intervention earlier . . . facilities can be provided to investigate without delay . . .'. This begs the question 'what milder signs and symptoms' might suggest possible child maltreatment?

Early indicators

My own research focused on the importance of early indicators (Powell 2003a). This area of study was chosen partly in response to the *Childhood Matters* review which called for priority research into the determination of indicators that may help in diagnosing abuse and neglect at 'an earlier stage' (NCIPCA 1996), and also in recognition that retrospective serious case reviews (see Chapter 8) frequently highlight individual cases where there is evidence of a progression from 'mild' to severe abuse. Such reviews have found evidence to suggest that universal service providers, such as health professionals, may miss these early signs and that as a result, opportunities for early intervention may be missed (Reder et al. 1993; Reder and Duncan 1999). The notion of a linear progression from mild to severe abuse thus denotes potential opportunities for earlier and more timely intervention to safeguard a child or young person's welfare. The study utilised the Delphi technique (Powell 2003b) to harness expert opinion from a multi-professional panel of child protection experts as to what features they may consider as 'early indicators' of possible child maltreatment. The findings suggest a wide range of physical, behavioural and contextual signs that might prompt early concerns as to the possibility of maltreatment. There was very strong agreement that early indicators included a number of features that could be identified in pregnancy such as: failure to book for antenatal care, domestic violence in pregnancy and substance misuse in pregnancy. Participants also agreed that unexplained patterns of minor injury, failure to attend for routine appointments, use of excessive punishment, a miserable child, lack of provision for safety, unrealistic expectations of the child, alienation of support network and high levels of conflict with agencies and people in 'authority' were important early signs of possible maltreatment.

The study concluded that the early indicators of child maltreatment identified by the expert panel may help in detecting abuse and neglect at an earlier stage, although they are not by any means *diagnostic*. There was a significant overlap with the existing work on risk factors, which was perhaps not surprising. The early indicators may also signify that a child is suffering from other adverse experiences in childhood, i.e. not necessarily abuse (for example, 'a miserable child'). However, in these cases a professional response, such as increased parental support and guidance, may still be needed. What was seen to be important, on the other hand, was the potential for the above indicators to alert service providers to enquire more deeply into the welfare of the (unborn) child or young person, to focus on their everyday lived experience and to consider how best to support the family.

Where early concerns are identified, it may be possible to work within the framework of service provision for 'additional needs' rather than make a child protection referral. This may include a referral to children's social care as a child 'in need' under the auspices of section 17 of the Children Act 1989 (England and Wales). However, where assessment suggests that the child or young person is more clearly at risk of, or suffering from, child maltreatment, then a child protection referral needs to be made (see below). Signs or indicators that may be suggestive of child maltreatment are now discussed.

Signs of child maltreatment

Nurses and midwives will come across child maltreatment in the course of their practice in different ways and in diverse settings. In some instances they may be made aware that concerns about child maltreatment have already been identified or are strongly suspected. In other cases, concerns of possible maltreatment may be raised during a routine visit or an episode of care for an unrelated problem. In some cases (that may typically involve more junior staff such as nursing students, health care assistants or ancillary staff) a child may choose to disclose their maltreatment because they have established a trusting relationship with that person. Any of these presentations will be emotionally challenging for the practitioner and their team. It is not surprising that when alternative explanations can be offered, they may readily be accepted. As Pace (2003: 15) has argued 'It is important to acknowledge the range of emotions, values, attitudes, beliefs, knowledge and skills that may impact on our ability to "hear" when presented with a child who may have been abused. It is natural to respond to child abuse with feelings that can range from anger to distrust, pity, horror etc. The response may lead to blocking and denial . . .'. Recognising that a child or young person is at risk of, or suffering from, child maltreatment can be difficult. It is widely recognised that there are no signs or symptoms that are 100% pathognomic of child maltreatment. The difficulties inherent in the field are reflected by Lord Laming in his report into the death from maltreatment of Victoria Climbié: 'The diagnosis of deliberate harm is far from an exact science and failure to recognise it can be fatal' (Laming 2003: 248). Poblete (2003) suggests that an allegation of maltreatment made by the child themselves is now considered to be the 'most important diagnostic sign' (p. 5).

Case example

Tonia, aged 14 years, had been on the children's ward for a number of weeks suffering from chronic fatigue syndrome. On one occasion when she returned from 'weekend leave' she seemed more withdrawn than usual. While she was being settled for the night she disclosed to a student nurse that she had become close to that her father had been sexually abusing her for some time and that she was worried about her younger sister. She asked the student to promise to keep the information 'a secret'.

Nevertheless, many children will not tell, even if they are of an age to do so. Therefore it falls to those who routinely see children, young people and families in the course of their daily practice, as well as the wider community, to be alert to the possibility of child maltreatment and to know how to respond when suspicions are raised. However, it seems likely that cases of child maltreatment are missed, either because of a failure to detect the signs or because of uncertainty in knowing how to respond. This was borne out by a recent review of the evidence on reporting of 'non-accidental injury' by accident and emergency staff, which suggested that the frequency of child maltreatment reporting does not match the expected prevalence in local populations (Sanders and Cobley 2005).

Signs that may alert nurses and midwives to the possibility of child maltreatment are discussed under sub-headings for the four key categories: physical abuse, emotional abuse, sexual abuse and neglect. In all cases the signs will need to be contextualised in light of the history (given by the child if at all possible), presentation and information gathered about the wider circumstances of the child or young person and their family. In some cases it will be the context, rather than any specific sign, that alerts professionals to the possibility of maltreatment. In all cases where concerns have been raised the definitive clinical assessment of the child or young person normally rests with a consultant paediatrician, although forensic nursing may well expand to embrace this role in the future (Regan et al. 2004).

Physical abuse

Bruising is usually considered to be the most common sign of physical abuse and one that nurses and midwives will be well placed to spot. Hobbs et al. (1999a) remind us that 'considerable force' is involved in producing a bruise. They add that bruising in babies is particularly serious, and even a small bruise in a baby may be a predictor of later serious or fatal maltreatment. Non-accidental bruising is often distinguished by the site of the bruise (e.g. buttocks, lower back, outer and inner thighs, abdomen, genitalia, head, neck, ears, eyes, cheeks and lower jaw) and also the patterning. Children who have been intentionally injured generally have a larger number of bruises than those who have been bruised as a result of accidents. In some cases the marks of implements (e.g. straps, belts, canes or flex), hand prints or finger marks may be seen. At the time of writing, ageing of bruises is not recommended (WCPSRG 2005a). Accidental bruises are more likely to be seen distal to the elbow or knees (e.g. shins) in *mobile* children. The use of a paediatric 'skin map' as part of the documentation of the physical examination is strongly recommended.

Case example

Sandra rarely took her baby to be weighed at the 'Well Baby Clinic' so the health visitor was pleased to see her. Although the baby had gained adequate weight, a small bruise was noticed just above the clavicle. Sandra told the health visitor that she 'did not know how it had happened'.

Bruising in young babies is always of concern and requires follow up and investigation. In some cases the bruise may overlie a fracture. Thus investigations in the above case may include a skeletal survey.

Sometimes a bruise may result from a bite. According to Hobbs et al. (1999a) bites are always non-accidental in origin. Teeth marks may be seen, and in vicious bites the skin may have been broken. Hobbs et al. add that a forensic dentist or odontologist may be able to help to identify a suspect from an assessment of the pattern of the marks. An analysis of saliva may also be undertaken. Sometimes children may be kicked. Bruises on children that result from being kicked are usually seen as large irregular shapes on the lower half of the body and these may reflect the shape of the shoe.

Hobbs (2003) lists some of the differential diagnoses for bruising as; clotting defects such as idiopathic thrombocytopenia, or (rarely) leukaemia; collagen disorders such as Ehlers Danlos; congenital lesions such as a Mongolian blue spot (Horner 2005) and even felt tip or marker pen. Thomas (2004) reminds us, however, that children may suffer from both a haematological disorder *and* child maltreatment. There may be other explanations. One possible 'urban myth' that does the rounds of safeguarding training events is the story of the middle-class schoolboy who presented with bilateral linear, horizontal bruising on the back of his lower legs, highly suggestive of being hit by an implement. However, as the anxious mother explained to the social worker who was called to investigate, the child had worn a new pair of wellington boots to school, in which his name had been hastily written!

Suspicious fractures are clearly a serious indicator of child maltreatment. Fractures that are the result of physical abuse are said to occur most often in infants and pre-school children, especially those under the age of 18 months. In infants the fracture may involve the proximal limb bones. Concerns should always be raised where there is a femoral fracture in a non-mobile child. Rib fractures are also associated with child maltreatment and approximately one third of complex skull fractures may also be associated with physical abuse (WCPSRG 2005b). Specialist advice from orthopaedic surgeons and radiologists is usually sought in the case of suspicious fractures. Where there is suspicion of child maltreatment, a skeletal survey and bone scan may be ordered, and in some cases multiple fractures of different ages and stages of healing may be seen. Birth injuries are sometimes suggested as a cause for fractures of the clavicle or humerus, but these will generally be noted at birth or immediately afterwards, and callus formation will be present at 10 days of age. Differential diagnoses for multiple fractures and fractures in non-mobile children include osteogenesis imperfecta (brittle bones) but this is rare, and certainly 'far less common' than child maltreatment (Hobbs 2003).

Case example

Jodie, aged 14 weeks, was brought to the emergency department because she had stopped moving her arm. On examination the arm was swollen and bruised. Father said that he had been putting her back in the cot when she slipped in his arms and he grabbed her to stop her falling. On this occasion the history was accepted. Three weeks later Jodie was admitted following a 'near miss' cot death. A different paediatrician who was on call asked for a skeletal survey. This showed two healing posterior rib fractures that pre-dated the fractured humerus.

This is a case that should have been rigorously assessed from the outset. Staff later admitted that they were distracted by the fact that father was a confident and successful businessman.

Burns and scalds may also be indicative of serious physical abuse (and neglect) and there is a link to sexual violence (Hobbs 2003; Horner 2005). Hobbs notes that burns and scalds that are abusive can be anywhere on the body, but may be found on the backs of hands, buttocks, soles of feet and the face. Demarcation lines (c.f. glove or sock) suggest that a child has been deliberately held. 'Splash marks' are less common than with accidental scalds (Horner 2005). Hobbs adds that cigarette burns may also feature in deliberate injury – here there will be a circular crater of approximately half to one centimetre in diameter. An accidental cigarette burn is much more of a superficial injury; there may typically be a 'tail' from brushing past the lit end. Bilateral burns (e.g. both hands or both feet), or burns on more than one area of the body, should raise serious concerns. Horner (2005) notes that between 10% and 25% of burns in young children are likely to be the result of child maltreatment and suspicion should be raised for any burn in a child under 3 years of age.

Case example

Ricky, aged 14 months, was taken to a nearby NHS walk-in centre with minor burns to both his hands. Mother's boyfriend was reported to be looking after him when he put his hands in a bowl of spaghetti rings that had been heated in a microwave. A children's nurse who was on duty at the time commented that it would be very unusual for a child to suffer accidental bilateral burns and suggested that Ricky was taken to the local hospital for paediatric follow up. This was not done. Had Ricky been fully examined a number of fading bruises would have been seen on his abdomen and back.

Young children who present with injuries should be subject to a full examination and assessment. Concerns need to be followed up.

Head injuries are the leading cause of deaths from child maltreatment and may involve either or both shaking and impact injuries. Reece and Sege (2000) noted that mortality from non-accidental head injury was higher than for many other conditions, including meningitis, although the latter may feature more prominently in the consideration of differential diagnoses in neurologically compromised infants and young children. In terms of prevalence, Mayer and Burns (2000) estimate that 25% of all head injuries in the under-2s are caused by maltreatment, with a mortality rate of approximately 30%.

As well as the risk imposed by their social situation, young children are particularly vulnerable to head injuries because of anatomical differences in their brain and skull. In a young child the head comprises approximately 10% of body weight (compared to 2% in an adult). In addition, the neck muscles are somewhat weaker and unable to absorb the energy generated during a 'whiplash' injury (Fulton 2000). Non-accidental head injuries in young children include injuries produced by shaking as well as impact to the head caused directly by hitting the head or as a result of the head hitting another object or surface. Other important factors that increase the risk of death or irreversible brain injury following a head injury include a larger subarachnoid (potential) space, a higher water content of the brain, and the fact that the brain of a young child is not fully myelinated. Case et al. (2001) note that the rotational movement of the brain that occurs in a severe inflicted head injury creates shearing forces that cause diffuse axonal injury (DAI) with disruption of axons and tearing of bridging veins. These injuries are particularly significant because they lead to immediate unconsciousness and long-term neurological damage in non-fatal cases (David 1999). Further complications arise as a result of the oxygen deprivation during a shake injury. According to Kemp et al. (2003) there is an ongoing debate as to the mechanisms and forces involved and whether DAI or hypoxic ischaemic injury is of greatest importance. Pathological findings of intentional head injuries include subdural haemorrhage or effusion, subarachnoid haematoma and retinal haemorrhage (Case et al. 2001). Dale et al. (2002) note that the triad of injuries including subdural haematoma, DAI and retinal haemorrhage is highly suspicious of intentional head injury especially when there are associated grip injuries such as fractured ribs, fractured long limb bones and finger tip bruising. However, in some cases there will be no visible external signs of injury.

It is commonly suggested that intentional head injuries in young children arise when there is loss of anger control in parents or carers as a result of inconsolable crying. However, it is also important to note that parents may shake a child perceiving this to be a less violent way than other means to enforce discipline (Fulton 2000). The majority of children who are injured in this way are under 2 years of age, with most aged less than 1 year. Although the provision of statistics is fraught with difficulty, it has been suggested that subdural haemorrhage associated with inflicted head injury occurs in 21–24.6 per 100,000 infants under 1 per year in the United Kingdom (Jayawant et al. 1998). There appears to be a peak incidence at 4 to 6 months of age. Boys seem to be affected more commonly than girls; perhaps because their crying is more 'high pitched' or because of an expectation that 'boys don't cry' or that they should be able to tolerate 'rougher handling' than girls (Jayawant et al. 1998). The statistics may belie the number of young children whose injuries fall into the 'mild or moderate' category, who may not receive medical attention at the time of their injury, but nevertheless suffer neurological or cognitive problems as a result. In these children mild/moderate learning difficulties may not be detected until they start school (Fulton 2000; Blumenthal 2002).

Emotional abuse

Recognising emotional abuse can be very difficult because, unlike physical abuse, there will be no obvious signs or specific 'incidents' to focus on. This may be exacerbated by the fact that the child is even less likely to disclose their maltreatment, as their situation may feel 'normal' to them. It is important to remember that some level of emotional abuse is involved in all types of child maltreatment. Corby (2006) notes that addressing emotional abuse requires a sensitive approach as it is essentially about questioning approaches to the task of parenting. Emotional abuse includes acts of commission, which may be conscious and deliberate in extreme cases (e.g. public humiliation, threats or verbal abuse), but it can also comprise a lack of emotional warmth or stimulation. Other features of emotional abuse include a failure to respond to the child's needs to ensure the development of their social competence and individuality. There may be an unconscious pattern of parenting behaviour transmitted from one generation to another as a result of ongoing dysfunctional parenting styles (A. Hall 2003). As noted previously such parent–child situations are often referred to as being of 'high criticism, low warmth' and are widely believed to affect some 350–400,000 children in the UK (DH 1995; NCIPCA 1996).

Points for reflection

How may the promotion of 'positive parenting' (see Chapter 2) help to address the inter-generational cycle of 'high criticism, low warmth' parenting styles?

Although all nurses and midwives need to be alert to emotional abuse, health visitors have been identified as being particularly well placed to recognise emotional abuse and to contribute to an evaluation of the family circumstances (Hall 2003). Others who have an ongoing relationship with the child or family such as practice nurses, school nurses or mental health nurses are also in a good position to identify possible emotional abuse and contribute to multi-agency discussions on whether or not a threshold for child protection referral has been reached. A decision may also be made to undertake a thorough assessment of the child (including specialist mental health assessment) and a trial of an intervention to improve the quality of parenting before resorting to child protection routes.

Sexual abuse

Mott (2003: 99) defines child sexual abuse as 'the sexual exploitation of a child for the gratification of an adult'. She adds that both boys and girls of any age may be sexually abused, but that boys may be both less likely to report the abuse and less likely to be believed if they do disclose. As highlighted in the policy definition of sexual abuse (see Chapter 3) sexual abuse may take a variety of forms that range from non-contact activities to violent penetrative acts. In most instances of sexual abuse the abuser is a member of the child's family, a friend of the family or in a position of power over the child, not, as one might interpret from the media, a stranger. The issue of 'on-line' grooming and other internet activities are discussed in the following chapter. Children can also be sexually abused by another child or young person; the issue here is the child's lack of consent or ability to make an informed decision. Sexual activity involving a 16- or 17-year-old may also, in some circumstances, be considered harmful or put the young person at risk of harm (HM Government 2006a).

Presentation of child sexual abuse may include physical indicators, such as vaginal or rectal bleeding, bruising or sexually transmitted diseases; psychosomatic indicators such as recurrent abdominal pain; behavioural indicators such as sexualised play; or contextual concerns arising from contact with a sexual offender. However, there are often few observable signs and thus it is usually the child's testimony that is the most important indicator (Corby 2006). Nevertheless, it is not uncommon for disclosure to follow months, or even years after sexual abuse (i.e. in adulthood), particularly if the abuser was a family member (Hobbs et al. 1999a). If a child or young person discloses abuse it is important to acknowledge what has been said, to keep accurate and contemporaneous notes and to let them know that you will have to share the information to help to keep them, and other children, safe. It is not the role of nurses and midwives (or indeed other health professionals) to 'interrogate' the child; specially trained social workers and police officers follow specific guidance in collecting evidence, usually in the form of a video-recording of a joint interview that may later be used in court (Home Office et al. 2002). The child or young person may also need to undergo a specialist forensic examination (aided by the use of a colposcope), especially in the case of an 'acute presentation'. In some cases, an appropriately trained nurse will undertake the forensic examination (Regan et al. 2004) and in all cases the nurse has a vital role in helping to support children, young people and their families throughout the examination and may assist in collecting specimens. The nurse may also be in a position to ensure that a child does not experience unnecessary repeat examinations.

Case example
Gemma, 11 years old, was admitted to the ward with an injury to her vulva and perineum that required suturing under anaesthetic. She had been reported to have slipped off a swing. Her clothing was noted to be intact. On visiting the house, police found evidence of equipment that was being used to make films. Gemma did not disclose abuse at a subsequent joint interview, but three weeks later she contacted the ward saying that she had something important to tell one of the staff nurses.

Nurses and midwives working with young people will be aware that a proportion of those under 16 years of age (i.e. below the age of consent)[1] will engage in sexual activity. Guidance from the DH on best practice for the provision of advice for contraception, sexual and reproductive health notes that health professionals have a duty of care and confidentiality to all patients including those under the age of 16 years, as enshrined in professional codes (DH 2004). Best practice embraces a discussion of the emotional and physical implications of sexual activity, an assessment of the consensual nature of the relationship and, if possible, encouraging the young person to have a discussion with a parent or carer. The duty of confidentiality is not absolute, and where there are concerns about the health, safety or welfare of young people (including a risk to other children) local child protection and information-sharing protocols should be followed.

Points for reflection
Should contraceptive services be provided to a 15-year-old girl who refuses to provide any information about her sexual partner?

The latest edition of *Working Together* (HM Government 2006a) has sought to provide clarification on the question of sexual activity in those under the age of 13 years. It notes that children of this age are not legally capable of consenting to sexual activity and that there would always be reasonable cause to suspect that they are suffering, or likely to suffer, significant harm. The guidance adds that 'cases involving under 13s should always be discussed with a nominated child protection lead in the organisation' (p.105) and that there is a presumption that the case will then be reported as a child protection concern to children's social care and that a strategy discussion will be held (see below). The document also provides a comprehensive checklist that can be used to assess the risk to any sexually active child or young person. This highlights the importance of assessing, amongst other factors, their maturity, family background and any age or power imbalance in the relationship. All decisions taken by professionals need to be documented, including the decision not to share information. Mayor (2006) reports the children's minister's assertion that the guidance 'strikes the right balance between respecting confidentiality and empowering professionals to act where a child is at serious risk of harm' (p.872).

Neglect

The importance of the roles of nurses and midwives in preventing, recognising and responding to neglect led to the decision to cover this form of child maltreatment in more depth in a standalone chapter (see Chapter 7). Neglect may co-exist with the other forms of maltreatment highlighted above. Key indicators of neglect include malnourishment, poor growth and poor weight gain (failure to thrive), a dirty or unkempt child, infestations, inappropriate clothing, hypothermia, cold injury (red, swollen hands and feet) and repeated infections, e.g. gastroenteritis and respiratory infections (Hobbs et al. 1999a).

Points for reflection
Is there a difference between a child who is always dirty and one who is never clean?

Other important indicators of child neglect include a persistent failure to supervise a child or to provide a safe environment for them. This may result in mortality and morbidity from road traffic accidents, falls, scalds, ingestions, drowning and house fires. Clearly there are some children and young people who present to emergency departments or walk-in centres on a regular basis, and this should provide opportunities for conveying preventative messages and making an assessment of the need for family support or, in some cases, child protection referral. In contrast to these 'regulars', nurses and midwives may also suspect neglect because of a *failure* to attend for health care; including antenatal care, routine outpatient appointments and well child provision such as immunisations.

Case example
Harry had been referred to the ophthalmologist because of a squint. His rather chaotic circumstances meant that he missed three appointments and was subsequently dropped from the list. By the time the school nurse caught up with him he had missed the developmental 'window of opportunity' for the operation to be successful.

The above sections provide a brief overview of some of the key indicators of physical abuse, emotional abuse, sexual abuse and neglect. However, none of these offer 'diagnostic certainty' that a child or young person is being maltreated. The signs are rarely straightforward and often comprise a mixture of clinical signs, behavioural characteristics and contextual factors. In practice, it is often the case that concerns about the possibility of child maltreatment hinge more on the contextual factors than any one sign (Beckett 2003). These are now discussed.

Contextual factors for child maltreatment

There are a range of contextual factors that nurses and midwives need to be aware of, as they should alert them to the possibility of maltreatment, and the need for further evaluation and enquiry. These include:

- Minor (i.e. as well as major) injuries in babies (especially those less than nine months of age)
- There is a delay in seeking medical treatment or refusal to comply
- There is 'doctor shopping' i.e. the use of different health care facilities to avoid detection
- The parent seems angry or has a history of interpersonal violence
- The family appear to be under undue stress
- There is a previous history of abuse or neglect (including that of siblings)
- A vague history or no history or explanation is offered
- The injury is not consistent with the history (NB developmental abilities)
- A major injury is discovered following reports of a minor injury or no injury at all
- There are repeated injuries or many injuries of the wrong kind, distribution and different ages
- There is no history of pain, even where there is a scald or fracture
- The child gives a different account of how they got their injury, to that given by the parents
- The child gives a 'rehearsed' account of how they got their injury
- The child appears frightened or uncomfortable in the presence of their parent(s)
- The child appears watchful or withdrawn, or lacks self-esteem
- The child appears over-anxious to please
- The child appears restless or hyperactive
- There is denial and defensiveness

(from Hobbs et al. 1999a; Beckett 2003; Hobbs 2003; Horner 2005)

In my experience there are many nurses and midwives who are well-versed in their ability to describe the key indicators that may lead them to suspect that a child or young person is at risk of, or suffering from, child maltreatment. This is not surprising and reflects the ongoing and intensive relationship that many practitioners have with the children, young people and their families in their care. Coupled with this is the fact that experience of largely well-functioning families drawn from the wider population will help them to spot when things are not as they should be. However, a key driver for writing this book is the recognition that nurses and midwives may not always be clear as to how to take their concerns forward or easily access supportive advice. In some cases nurses and midwives may even find that their concerns are refuted, minimised or blocked (Pace 2003). In these instances it is *essential* to seek the advice and support of the named or designated professional.

Case example
Ronald, aged 15 years, was seen briefly on the ward after an argument with his father over his refusal to wash and shave had led to his father grasping him rather too tightly around the neck. He appeared to be a deeply unhappy teenager who reportedly rarely left his room. Mother was quiet and subdued. Medical staff were of the opinion that this was a difficult young man who had 'asked for trouble' and as he was basically unhurt discharged him. Nursing staff felt more concerned, particularly when the school nurse informed them that Ronald had reported escalating domestic violence between his parents. Old records showed a number of attendances at the emergency department including an attendance after a dinner plate thrown by his father had caused a head wound. Three weeks after the admission Ronald attempted suicide.

What to do if you are concerned about child maltreatment

Nurses and midwives may become suspicious about possible or actual child maltreatment through identifying specific signs of abuse or neglect, by recognising contextual factors that are indicative of concern or by being party to a disclosure. A natural reaction to this suspicion might be to feel upset and anxious or even to question their judgement. It is thus vital that help and advice is sought, both to assist in validation (or not) of suspicions and also to ensure timely action to safeguard the welfare of the child or young person. In the first instance, a discussion with a senior colleague or the named or designated professional can be extremely helpful (see below for an explanation of these roles). At this point, it may not be necessary to divulge the name of the child. In some instances more specialist advice may be sought, for example from children's social care. Again this discussion can take place in the context of maintaining confidentiality until the point at which a decision is reached that a child protection referral is obligatory. It is important to recognise that 'blocks' to the recognition of child maltreatment happen and to be clear on the objective evidence that has contributed to *your* professional opinion that a child or young person is at risk of, or suffering from, significant harm as defined in policy and legislation (HM Government 2006a). The facts and opinions should be carefully documented, even if the decision is that no further action be taken.

It is important to recognise that concerns may relate to the actions of the parent or carer, rather than the presentation of the child. Bajaj et al. (2006) discuss the role of a nurse 'child protection coordinator' who assists in the identification of, and response to, concerns that may be raised about children or other family members within a variety of hospital settings. Documentation is without a doubt a key part of the process and records should be clear and contemporaneous or written as soon as possible after a consultation or visit. Clift (2003) notes that health visitors' records kept by parents should match any records kept in the base unless there are exceptional circumstances. Systems need to be in place in hospital settings to ensure that concerns are recorded and acted on. The use of chronologies and summaries can be helpful, especially where there have been multiple contacts and a range of contextual concerns. A genogram (see box, p. 86–7) is a useful tool for readily capturing the family structure and members of a child's 'household' (Walker et al. 2003).

Any disclosure of maltreatment should be recorded verbatim – the words used by the child to describe parts of their body may form an essential part of the evidence in any criminal investigation and subsequent court proceedings. As noted above, the child must be allowed to speak freely about their experiences.

Referral

If after initial discussion it is apparent that further action is needed, then a referral to children's social care (or in an emergency, to the police) will be required. The process of referral described below is that for England, although there are parallels with the other countries of the UK. Nurses and midwives will be guided by their local procedures as to how this is facilitated and who takes the lead responsibility for making the referral (e.g. in hospital this will usually be a paediatrician). Telephone referrals to children's social care should be followed up in

Genograms

The following symbols are used to represent the gender of family members

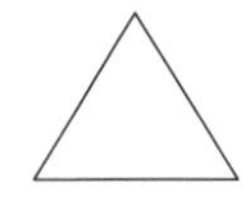

Female

Gender unknown

If a family member is deceased, this is indicated by placing a cross inside their symbol:

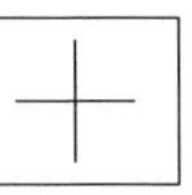

Enduring relationships, such as marriage and cohabitation, are illustrated by a single unbroken line:

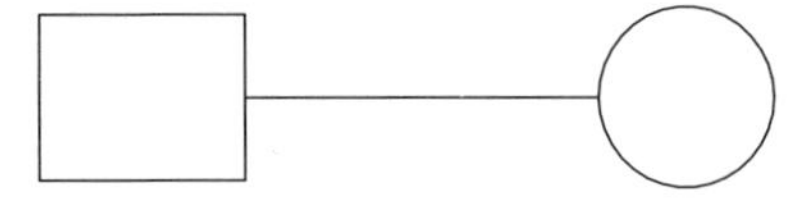

Transitory relationships are illustrated by a single broken line:

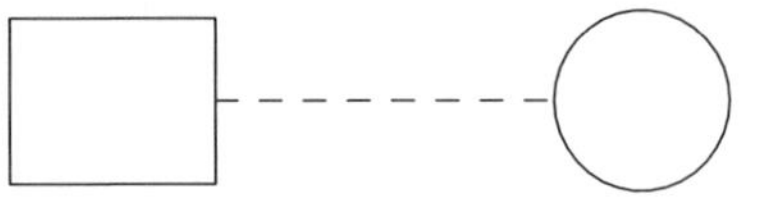

Separation is shown by a single short diagonal line across the relationship line:

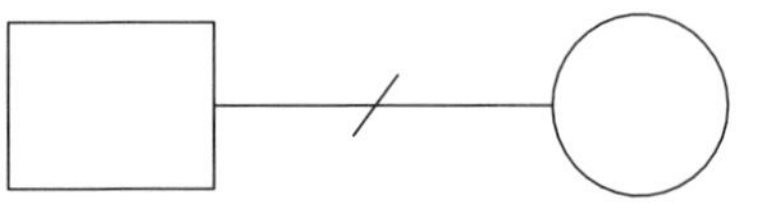

Divorce is shown by two short diagonal lines across the relationship line:

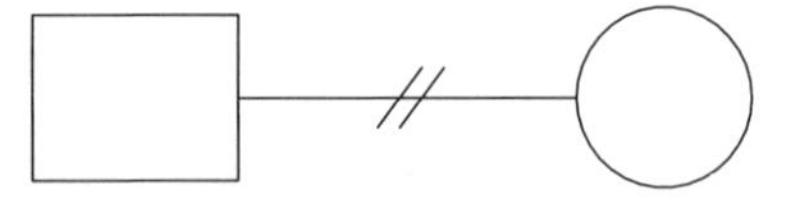

When there are a number of children from a relationship the eldest child is placed on the furthest left, followed by the second eldest and so on, with the youngest child appearing on the right.

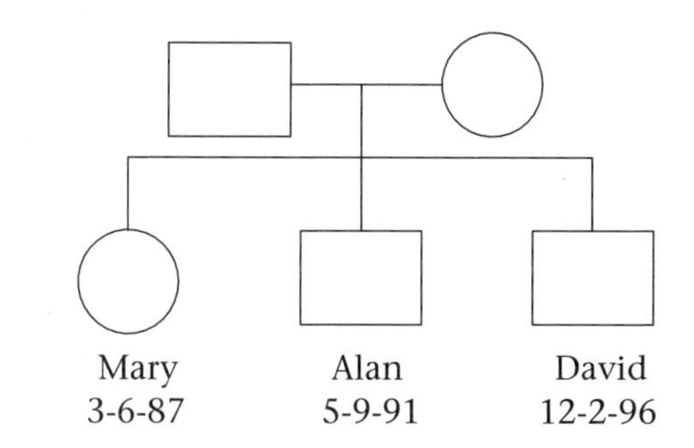

Twins are indicated by two symbols coming from a single 'stalk'.

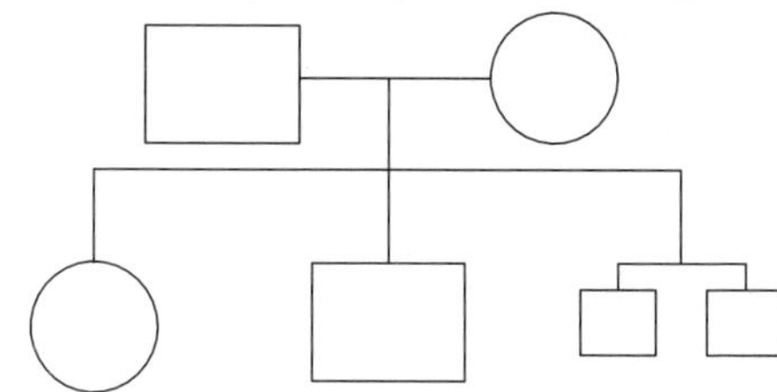

A miscarriage or abortion is indicated by a diagonal cross. In the genogram the miscarriage or abortions should be placed in the diagram in the same order as other children. So, for example, if a couple had a daughter, Mary, followed by a miscarriage, followed by a son David, their genogram would look like this:

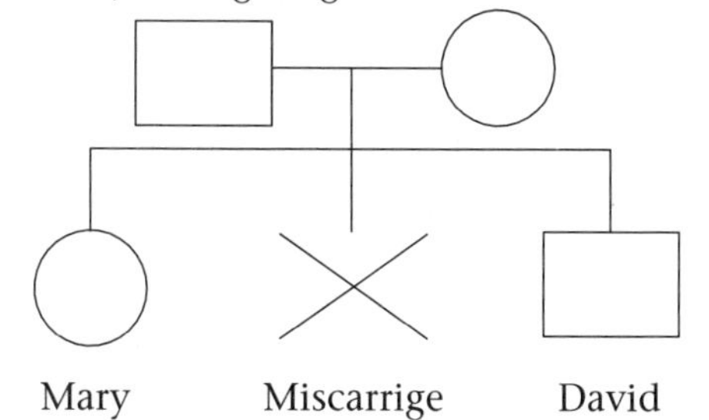

The family members who are part of the same household are indicated by a dotted line which is placed around the household members.

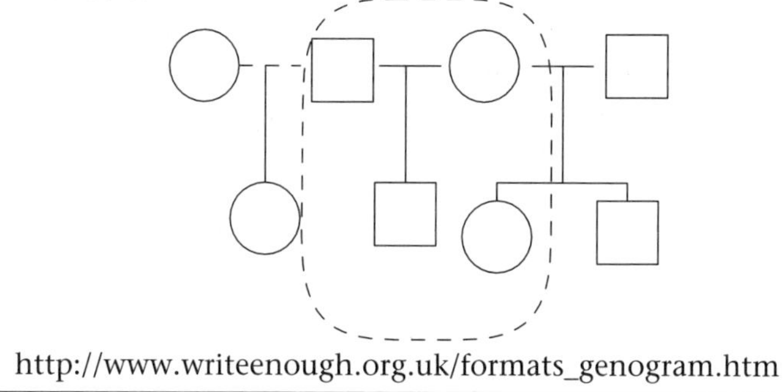

http://www.writeenough.org.uk/formats_genogram.htm

writing within 48 hours. Local (i.e. individual Trust or other health care provider) policies and procedures will reflect the Local Safeguarding Children Board's policies and procedures which will, in turn, reflect national *Working Together* guidance. Copies of all of the above documents should be easily accessible to practitioners.

The decision to make a referral to children's social care should normally be shared with the child or young person in a way that is appropriate for their age and understanding. Children have a right to understand what is happening and why and, if possible, to give their permission for the referral. It is also usual practice for parents to be informed of the decision to refer, unless to do so would place the child (or another child or young person) at additional risk or undermine the prevention, detection or prosecution of a serious crime. As Poblete (2003: 9) notes 'talking to parents is an essential aspect of the management of child abuse, as it is important that parents understand the facts which raise professional concern and that they receive information on the process of referral and involvement of social services'.

In the majority of cases one or both parents will be responsible for the future safety and welfare of the child. It is thus essential that they are engaged in safeguarding processes at the earliest opportunity and included in any discussion about the identification of the risk of significant harm. Where a child or young person is suspected to be suffering, or likely to suffer, significant harm the local authority (i.e. children's social care) is required (under s.47 of the Children Act 1989) to make enquiries to decide whether action should be taken to safeguard and promote their welfare. An initial assessment, structured on *The Framework for the Assessment of Children in Need and Their Families* (DH 2000b), is undertaken to consider the child's developmental needs, the capacity of parents to meet these needs and the family and environmental factors that influence these. A decision is then made by children's social care on whether or not to proceed to a *strategy discussion* and undertake further enquiries.

Strategy discussion

A strategy discussion may take the form of a face to face meeting or via the telephone. It should involve the police, the referring agency and others thought to be appropriate such as the health visitor or school nurse. *Working Together* (HM Government 2006a: 116) specifically states that 'If the child is a hospital patient (inpatient or outpatient) or receiving services from a child development team, the medical consultant responsible for the child's healthcare should be involved, as should the senior ward nurse if the child is an inpatient'.

The purpose of the strategy discussion is to share information, agree the conduct and timing of further assessment and enquiries and any criminal investigation, and to determine how the outcomes of the strategy discussion will be shared with the family. Those present may also need to agree actions to immediately safeguard the child and any other children who are thought to be at risk. The processes that follow may be referred to as 'Section 47 enquiries' after the part of the Children Act 1989 that provides the statutory basis for action.

Core assessment and s.47 enquiries

A 'core assessment' and s.47 enquiries will be undertaken by an experienced social worker and consider the safety and welfare of the child in relation to the three domains outlined above (i.e. child's developmental needs, parenting capacity, and family and environmental factors). Health professionals should be engaged in this process and have a statutory duty to contribute and cooperate as necessary. The input from nurses, midwives and specialist community public health nurses is likely to be of key importance. Practitioners should focus their contribution on the strengths of the families as well as on any concerns. The child, and in most cases the parents, will be fully engaged in the process. Children's social care will make a decision as to how to proceed following their enquiries and should discuss this decision with all those who have been involved. If the enquiries conclude that the child continues to be at risk of, or suffering from, significant harm then a *child protection conference* will be convened. This will normally take place within 15 days of the strategy discussion. If a decision is made that the child is *not* at risk of harm, it is important to consider whether the family would benefit from any additional service provision to meet their needs. This may involve a higher level of contact with universal services, such as health visiting or school nursing.

Child protection conference

The purpose of the child protection conference is to determine whether or not the child is at risk of continuing harm, and if so to establish a core group to develop and implement a formal *child protection plan*. The category of maltreatment (i.e. physical, emotional, sexual abuse or neglect) will also be determined. The decision of the conference should be circulated to all those invited to the conference within one working day. In England at the time of writing the use of a 'child protection register' (sometimes referred to as an 'at risk' register) is due to be discontinued; however, if a child or young person has a 'child protection plan' this should be identifiable from the children's social care electronic records system.

Those invited to attend a child protection conference should have a significant contribution to make arising from their professional expertise and/or knowledge of the child and their family. Health contributors may include those working with the child or young person (e.g. GP, midwife, health visitor, school nurse, paediatrician or NHS Direct) and those who are providing services to parents (e.g. mental health professionals). While child protection conferences can have numerous members, the possibility of large numbers intimidating the family or inhibiting discussion should be considered. There should be a 'quorum' of children's social care and at least two other professional groups or agencies that have had direct contact with the child. Parents, and children of appropriate age and understanding, are important members of the conference, although there may be rare occasions when one or both parents are excluded for all or part of the meeting (HM Government 2006a). Examples may include where one parent is the alleged abuser or if there is a high level of conflict between family members.

If the child or young person is thought to be at continuing risk of harm a 'core group' will be formed. The core group will include a social worker, who is allocated as key worker to the family, family members, the child where appropriate, and professionals who will have direct contact with the family. The group should meet within 10 days of the initial child protection conference and at regular intervals afterwards. The focus should be on the welfare and best interests of the child or young person. Health visitors and school nurses have an important role to play as members of core groups working with others to help to ensure the future safety and well-being of children and young people at risk of, or suffering from, harm.

The child protection plan

The overall aim of the child protection plan is to ensure that the child is safe and to prevent them from suffering further harm, to promote their welfare and, provided it is in the best interests of the child, to work with the family in achieving this. The plan should set out clearly what the roles and responsibilities of those who have direct contact with the child and family are. Planned outcomes and timescales will be agreed. Where a child or young person is subject to a 'child protection plan' their ongoing safety, health and development will be formally reviewed.

The child protection review conference

The first 'child protection review conference' takes place three months after the initial conference and thereafter at intervals of not more than six months. Those who have been working with the child and family will be invited to attend and to submit a written report that evaluates the progress of the outcomes and any ongoing health and safety needs of the child. Once it is judged that the child is no longer at risk of significant harm the child protection plan will be discontinued, although the need for further support and services should also be discussed with the family.

Legal proceedings

In addition to child protection proceedings, cases involving the maltreatment of children and young people may be subject to legal proceedings. In some cases, nurses and midwives may be asked to attend court to give supporting evidence. Civil proceedings, which are generally dealt with in family courts include those for adoption and also for 'contact' or 'residence' orders in relation to parental visiting rights and where a child will live. Family courts may also issue a variety of care and supervision orders in relation to the ongoing safety of a child or young person, including the emergency protection order outlined below. A worker from the Children and Family Court Advisory and Support Service (CAFCASS) will be appointed to ensure that decisions made in the family courts are in the best interests of the child. In some cases, the police investigation of child maltreatment may lead to criminal proceedings in a Crown Court. Where nurses and midwives are called to give evidence in court they should be prepared and supported by a senior colleague, such as the named or designated nurse. In many cases a 'pre-hearing' visit to the court can be arranged. Employers (i.e. Trusts) will also be able to ensure access to a solicitor who can be engaged to support staff in the legal proceedings. In addition, nurses and midwives may seek assistance from their professional organisations.

Immediate protection of children and young people

In some child maltreatment cases there may be a need to ensure urgent and immediate protection of children, and nurses and midwives should know how to secure this. Where it is becoming apparent that parents or carers are unlikely or unable to comply with assessment or enquiries there can be recourse to legal proceedings. Any person, but more usually the local authority (i.e. children's social care), the police or the NSPCC may apply to a magistrate for an Emergency Protection Order (EPO) under s.44 of the Children Act 1989, if they believe that a child is likely to suffer significant harm if they are either not removed from where they are being accommodated, or in the case of, for example a hospital, removed from a safe place. The magistrate can give specific directions; for example, to enter premises to search for a child and/or other children thought to be at risk of harm. Medical examinations can also be ordered (subject to consent by the child, as appropriate). Those applying for an EPO gain parental responsibility, though this will be shared with those who already hold this (see Chapter 3). An EPO lasts for up to eight days in the first instance, but it can be challenged after 72 hours. In some cases the order may be extended by a further seven days.

In exceptional circumstances, the police have the powers to take a child into Police Protection (s.46) of the Children Act 1989. This allows them to ensure that a child stays in a safe place such as a hospital, or to remove a child to suitable accommodation in the case of an emergency. The longest time that a child can remain in police protection is 72 hours as it is expected that this would allow time to seek an EPO from the courts, if necessary. In practice I have found that where there may be a need for police protection, for example where a parent who is a suspected perpetrator is threatening to remove an ill or injured child from a hospital, early discussion with children's social care and the police enables a specific telephone contact and 'incident number' to be recorded on the ward in case it may be needed (we had a case where an aggrieved parent started to remove 'Gallow's' traction and were rapidly able to secure police protection).

This section has outlined the statutory processes for safeguarding children and the reader is encouraged to access their own national guidance and local policies and procedures to aid their learning.

Points for reflection

Do you know how to access your local safeguarding policy and procedure?

How do you contact your named and designated professionals?

What is clear is that the process is dependent on close collaboration with colleagues both within and outside of the practitioner's usual team. An important aspect of successful safeguarding practice is sharing information. This is now discussed in the context of the NMC code of professional conduct and the law.

Confidentiality and information-sharing

Nurses and midwives may naturally be anxious about sharing information with those from other agencies. The protection of confidential information is an important component of the NMC code of professional conduct (NMC 2004a). However, you should be reassured that the code (sections 5.3 and 5.4) recognises that:

- information can be shared with the patient's or client's consent;
- information can be shared without their consent if it can be justified in the public interest (i.e. if it is essential to protect the patient, client or someone else from the risk of significant harm);
- where there is a child protection issue, action should be taken in accordance with national and local polices.

Further clarity has been provided for all of those working with children and young people in England through the publication of information-sharing guidance (HM Government 2006b). This recognises that the safety and welfare of children and young people should take priority in any decision to share information. The guidance also supports the notion of being honest and open with children and their families as to why information needs to be shared and to seek to obtain their agreement and informed consent to do so. It recognises that as well as sharing information in the context of safeguarding practice, information may also be shared with other agencies to secure additional services such as help with learning, parenting support and to prevent anti-social behaviour.

Additional guidance on legal issues has been published alongside the information sharing guidance (HM Government 2006c). This provides a useful overview of the Human Rights Act 1998, the Common Law Duty of Confidentiality and the Data Protection Act 1998. Whilst the Human Rights Act states the need to respect private and family life, it also has regard to the protection of children and young people as per the United Nations Convention on the Rights of the Child (see Chapter 1). Information-sharing has to be 'justified and proportionate'.

The Common Law Duty of Confidentiality recognises that information can be shared if the person to whom the duty is owed has given explicit consent, where there is overriding public interest in a disclosure, or when sharing is required by a court order or other legal obligation. The Data Protection Act 1998 was enacted to protect 'sensitive personal data'. However, similarly this Act allows information to be shared with consent, to protect the person, or others interests, to comply with a court order, to fulfil a legal duty or statutory function and in the public interest. As the Information Commissioner notes in the foreword to the *Practitioner's Guide* (HM Government 2006b) 'The Data Protection Act is not a barrier to sharing information but is in place to ensure that personal information is shared appropriately'. The statutory basis to safeguarding and promoting the welfare of children and young people is also important here. The Children Act 1989 contains express powers for children's social care to respond to children 'in need' of additional services (s.17) and to make enquiries about any child who may be suffering significant harm (s.47). The Children Act 2004 promotes the cooperation of agencies (including Strategic Health Authorities and Primary Care Trusts) with the local authority in relation to children's well-being as defined by the *Every Child Matters* outcomes (s.10) and to place a duty on key people and bodies (including NHS bodies) to ensure that their functions are discharged with regard to the need to safeguard and promote the welfare of children (s.11). Good practice in information-sharing is seen to be key to collaborative working in both the planning and the delivery of services. Understanding each other's roles is also crucial.

Roles and responsibilities of other agencies

Working Together (HM Government 2006a) provides a comprehensive outline of the various agencies with responsibilities in safeguarding and promoting the welfare of children. In addition to health services, these include: the local authority, criminal justice organisations (including youth offending teams), the Connexions partnerships,[2] schools and further education institutions, childcare services, CAFCASS, the armed services, the voluntary and private sectors and faith communities. In essence, like health services, all of the above share a responsibility (and in most cases a statutory duty) to safeguard and promote the welfare of children. Here we briefly consider the role of children's social care, the police, probation and education.

Children's social care

In England children's social care is the term for what was previously known as 'children's social services'. Children's social care is part of the wider local authority provision for children and families. Details of local provision should be clearly signposted for families. Local authorities now host websites, 'children's service directories', that provide a range of information on local provision for children, young people and their families including details of children's centres, extended schools, childminders, playgroups, nurseries, leisure facilities as well as links to other local statutory and voluntary agencies and organisations.

Points for reflection
Visit your local children's service directory. How easy is it to find information on what to do if you are concerned about a child?

Children's social care staff (i.e. social workers and their teams) act as the 'principal point of contact' where there are concerns about the welfare of children and young people. Referrals to children's social care may come from children and families themselves or from neighbours, friends or other professionals, including those from health services. Local authorities, together with other agencies and organisations, have a duty to make enquiries if they suspect that a child in their area is suffering or likely to suffer significant harm; this duty is enshrined within the Children Act 1989. Encompassed within this role is the responsibility to coordinate an assessment of the child's needs, the parents' capacity to keep the child safe and the wider family circumstances (as discussed above). Nurses and midwives may be asked to assist in, or contribute to the assessment, especially when they are actively involved with the child, young person or family or have initially raised a possible child protection concern.

The police

The main roles of the police are to uphold the law and prevent crime and disorder. As the *Working Together* guidance explicitly notes, children and young people have the right to the full protection offered by the criminal law (c.f. the case of Lester Chapman outlined in Chapter 2). All police forces have a 'child abuse investigation unit' which will take the lead in investigating allegations of child maltreatment. However, as the guidance notes, every police officer has a role to play in safeguarding children and a given example is their role in ensuring the safety and welfare of any children when called to a domestic violence incident. Where there are concerns that a criminal act has been committed, or is suspected to have been committed, against a child, children's social care are expected to notify the police as soon as possible and a decision will be made as to the need to undertake a full criminal investigation. In some cases, specially trained officers will undertake a 'joint interview' of the child. As we have discussed, the police also have emergency powers to ensure the immediate protection of children believed to be suffering from, or at risk of suffering, significant harm; nurses and midwives may seek to use so called 'police protection' in urgent situations.

Probation services

The main role of the probation service is to supervise offenders in the community. As such they aim to reduce re-offending and protect the public. The role of probation officers may include supervising and supporting young offenders (16 or 17 years of age), offenders who are parents or carers and those who may present a risk to children. In some cases they may offer a service to children who have been victims of a serious sexual offence (HM Government 2006a).

Education

As well as creating a safe learning environment for children and young people, schools and further education institutions have a crucial role to play in early identification of concerns about possible maltreatment and in making appropriate referrals to children's social care. In a role that has some parallels to that of a designated health professional, a senior member of staff in each institution will be designated to take the lead in dealing with child protection issues, providing support and advice to staff and engaging in inter-agency processes (HM Government 2006a). In addition to the recognition of and response to suspected child maltreatment, schools can also contribute to safeguarding children through the curriculum by developing children's understanding, awareness and resilience. This is an important function of the framework for personal, social and health education.

Integrated services

Although the above sections have by no means introduced the roles of all the services that are involved in safeguarding children, one of the notable changes of the *Every Child Matters* programme (HM Government 2004) is that it promotes the benefits of integrated service provision across the range of children's services as part of its 'change for children' programme. Thus, increasingly, those who provide front-line services to children, young people and their families will find themselves working in multi-agency teams, either co-located in settings such as children's centres or in 'virtual teams' bringing together processes and staff development to ensure a more joined-up delivery of services to families. It will be important to understand the roles as well as the culture and language of a range of professionals.

However, a key aspect of new ways of working will also be for nurses and midwives to be able to 'market' their services and promote the benefits of high quality universal health service provision to children, young people and their families.

Named and designated professionals

All primary care trusts (PCTs) should have a designated doctor and nurse to take a strategic and professional lead on all aspects of the local health services contribution to safeguarding children and young people. This includes taking responsibility for providers of health services in the PCT area. Designated professionals provide advice and support to the named nurse and midwife and provide safeguarding advice to the PCT, local authority children's services and the Local Safeguarding Children's Board (HM Government 2006a). They also play an important role in ensuring the development of relevant training – both on a single and inter-agency basis. This includes ensuring that lessons learned from serious case reviews (see Chapter 8) are incorporated into practice.

Named professionals, including nurses and midwives, are appointed within all NHS Trusts, primary care trusts and foundation trusts. The focus for their work is promoting and supporting safeguarding within their organisation. They will have specific expertise in child health, child maltreatment and local arrangements for safeguarding and promoting the welfare of children (HM Government 2006a). Helpful guidance on roles and competencies for health professionals' roles in safeguarding children, including that of named and designated nurses was published in 2006 (NSCAN 2006; Royal College of Midwives et al. 2006). Named and designated professionals will also have an important role to play in ensuring that systems of clinical supervision are in place for nursing and midwifery staff. Clinical supervision allows for the development of expertise for practice through critical analysis and reflection. While it is vital in providing a focus for discussion on child protection cases, there is clearly a wider potential, including that of developing early intervention strategies. Lister and Crisp (2005) describe the process of clinical supervision for community nursing staff, which they see as a 'right and duty' for all nurses and managers.

Conclusion

This chapter has outlined the professional roles and responsibilities of nurses and midwives in the prevention, recognition and referral of child maltreatment. The role embraces the recognition of the centrality of the child or young person, knowledge and understanding of normal child development, and skills in communicating with children and young people. Where possible, nurses and midwives should seek to prevent child maltreatment. Preventative actions include being alert to risk factors and early indicators of maltreatment and in ensuring the provision of timely advice and support for families struggling to cope with the demands of parenting and daily life. The role of holistic child-centred assessment is vital in decision-making, as is the opportunity to discuss concerns with colleagues from both within and outside the immediate team. Nurses and midwives also need to understand when and how to make a referral to children's social care and to provide input to assessments and child protection proceedings in partnership with the lead statutory agencies. An understanding of national guidance and local policies and procedures, as well as the roles of others engaged in safeguarding processes, is an important aspect of this role.

Messages for practice

- Those who routinely see children, young people and families in the course of their daily practice should be alert to the possibility of child maltreatment and know how to respond when suspicions are raised.
- Working with children, young people and families where child maltreatment is suspected, or confirmed, is difficult and demanding work and should not be tackled alone.
- The use of risk tools and assessments is common in safeguarding children work; however, it cannot predict that child maltreatment will happen or that it will not.
- Where early concerns are identified, it may be possible to work within the framework of service provision for 'additional needs' rather than child protection.
- Signs of child maltreatment are rarely straightforward and often comprise a mixture of clinical signs, behavioural characteristics and contextual factors. Contextual factors are particularly important in helping to identify possible abuse or neglect.
- Once a child protection referral has been made to children's social care they will lead any enquiry, undertake specialist assessments and engage health professionals and others to work

together to ensure the future safety and protection of the child or young person.

- The named and designated professionals provide local leadership, training and support to frontline staff and their managers.

Recommended reading

Bannon, M., Carter, Y. (eds) (2003) *Protecting Children from Abuse and Neglect in Primary Care*. Oxford: Oxford University Press.

Beckett, C. (2003) *Child Protection: An Introduction*. London: Sage.

HM Government (2006a) *Working Together to Safeguard Children: A Guide to Inter-agency Working to Safeguard and Promote the Welfare of Children*. London: Department for Education and Skills (Chapters 2 and 5).

HM Government (2006b) *Information Sharing: Practitioners' Guide*. London: Department for Education and Skills.

HM Government (2006c) *Information Sharing: Further Guidance on Legal Issues*. London: Department for Education and Skills.

HM Government (2006d) *Information Sharing: Case Examples*. London: Department for Education and Skills.

NSCAN (National Safeguarding Children Association for Nurses) (2006) *Professional Core Competencies for Nurses Specialising in Safeguarding Children*. Huddersfield: NSCAN.

Royal College of Midwives, Royal College of Paediatricians and Child Health, Royal College of General Practitioners, Royal College of Nursing, Community Practitioner and Health Visitor Association (2006) *Safeguarding Children and Young People: Roles and Competences for Health Care Staff – Intercollegiate Document*. London: Royal College of Paediatrics and Child Health.

chapter five

SAFEGUARDING VULNERABLE CHILDREN

Learning outcomes

This chapter will help you to:

- safeguard and promote the welfare of vulnerable groups who face a greater risk of child maltreatment;
- recognise the links between domestic abuse and child maltreatment;
- appreciate the extra vulnerability of women living in situations of domestic abuse who are also pregnant;
- understand the risk factors for those children and young people who are disabled;

- support an understanding of childhood prostitution as child sexual exploitation and consider the additional health needs of this vulnerable group;
- provide advice to children and young people on safe use of the internet;
- consider the health and safety needs of those children who are refugees or seeking asylum.

Introduction

This chapter focuses on the safeguarding needs of children and young people who may be particularly vulnerable to child maltreatment. Notably these special groups represent children and families who are likely to have high levels of contact with a variety of health services. The chapter begins by considering the links between domestic abuse and child maltreatment and the roles of nurses and midwives in the provision of information and support. We then explore the increased risk of maltreatment for children and young people with disabilities and discuss the implications of this for practice. Children and young people who are at risk of sexual exploitation form the next vulnerable group to be discussed and links are made to the risk of 'online exploitation'. Suggestions are given for safe practice for those using the internet. The chapter closes with a consideration of the risks to those children and young people who are asylum seekers. Whilst the chapter highlights the key groups who are more vulnerable to child maltreatment, this is not a fully comprehensive review. Other important groups not discussed here include children living away from home, children of drug-misusing parents, children and families who go missing, children whose behaviour indicates a lack of parental control, children whose abuse is linked to spiritual or religious beliefs and those who abuse their peers.

Domestic abuse and child maltreatment

Children and young people (including unborn children) who are at risk of exposure to domestic abuse need to be identified, protected and supported. The health of children and young people is closely related to their safety and security and this will always be at risk in cases of domestic abuse. Children living with domestic abuse are at risk of significant harm through direct physical or sexual violence, the emotionally damaging effects of hearing or witnessing the abuse and from the consequences on the ability of the non-abusing parent (usually, but not exclusively, the mother) to parent effectively. The Local Government Association (LGA) have emphasised the importance of mainstreaming services for domestic abuse and ensuring their integration with the children's agenda (LGA 2006). There is an important role for the local safeguarding children boards. Nurses and midwives need to understand the critical links between domestic abuse and child abuse and know how to enquire and respond to disclosures whilst ensuring their own safety and that of the victim and their children.

Domestic abuse, a term that is increasingly replacing 'domestic violence', is defined by the Home Office as 'Any incident of threatening behaviour, violence or abuse (psychological, physical, sexual, financial or emotional) between adults who are, or have been intimate partners or family members, regardless of gender or sexuality' (DH 2005: 10). There are strong links between domestic abuse and other risk factors for child maltreatment including parental substance misuse and mental health needs. It has been suggested recently that violence against women should be seen in the context of current strategies to tackle social exclusion, drugs and alcohol, anti-social behaviour, child poverty and teenage pregnancy (Amnesty International 2006). Nurses and midwives need to relate to this context in practice and contribute to local strategies that ensure the provision of integrated and accessible services for those with the greatest needs. However, as with child maltreatment, it is also important to recognise that domestic abuse may affect any family regardless of class, culture or ethnicity. Notably, the definition given above is seen to include forced marriage and what are referred to as 'honour crimes' within some groups. An important aspect of the prevention (and response) to domestic violence is to ensure that it is seen for what it is, rather than as 'marital conflict' or 'arguments' (Humphreys and Mullender 1999) and to recognise that the perpetrator is always to blame. Nevertheless, there can be a tendency for victims to underplay or hide the fact that they are suffering from domestic abuse for a variety of reasons that may include fear of bringing shame on their family or of losing their children.

The Domestic Violence, Crime and Victims Act 2004 gives powers to the police to prosecute offenders and offer better protection to victims and their children. PCTs have a legal duty to work in partnership with the police and other groups to tackle domestic abuse and violence and it is important that individual practitioners address this issue in the course of their practice. Baird and Salmon (2006) recognise the importance of health professionals being educated to recognise when a woman is living in an abusive relationship. This includes introducing proactive and sensitive routine enquiry about domestic abuse as part of the assessment process. They add that the social isolation that can be a feature of domestic abuse, means that women may be unable to gain the support that they need from family, friends and voluntary or statutory agencies.

Case example

Penny, who was 22 weeks pregnant, presented to the emergency gynaecological clinic with vaginal bleeding and abdominal pain. Penny reported that she had left her 2-year-old son with a 'friend' saying that her partner could not manage to look after him. On examination fresh bruises were seen on her abdomen and upper arms. She was extremely distressed and refused admission.

Nurses and midwives should be alert to the signs of possible domestic abuse. These may include: frequent appointments for vague symptoms; missed appointments (e.g. antenatal); injuries that are inconsistent with explanations offered; multiple injuries of different ages; hidden injuries; suicide attempts (domestic abuse is given as a reason for half of all attempted suicides in Asian women); anxiety and depression; and the enduring presence of an aggressive or dominant partner (Chantler et al. 2001; DH 2005). Domestic abuse is common. Although it is an issue that is likely to be under-reported, it is widely recognised that domestic abuse is suffered by up to 30% of women at some point in their lives, that it is usually ongoing, and that in England and Wales it results in the deaths of two women every week. It is essential to recognise that an abused woman's risk of being murdered is at its greatest at the point of separating or having just left a violent partner. This is likewise a dangerous time for any children. For this reason practitioners are advised not to encourage a woman to leave her partner but to advise them to seek the specialist help of community-based domestic abuse support and advisory services. The risks that violent offenders (including sex offenders) represent are managed through statutory frameworks or 'multi-agency public protection arrangements' (MAPPA). Multi-agency working is crucial in this context and is likely to involve the police, the probation service, the prison service, housing departments and health and social care services.

At all times it is important to focus on the safety of the woman and her children, to be open and non-judgemental and to provide support and reassurance. In short, as universal providers of health care, nurses and midwives offer a non-stigmatising, but potentially life-saving service. Domestic violence is an important cause of maternal death and the risk is very real. As Humphreys and Mullender (1999: 8) argue:

> The message for practitioners is that when a woman says her abuser has threatened to kill her, or a child has heard this said and discloses it, they must be believed. The only safe way to work with any case of domestic violence is to offer levels of confidentiality and support that assume that this could be, or could become, a 'life or death' situation.

Whilst confidentiality can be largely assured, it is also vital that the risk of significant harm to children and young people is recognised and that referrals to children's social care for 'a child in need' or 'a child in need of protection' (see Chapter 4) are made where appropriate. Where children are already subject to child protection proceedings, professional knowledge of any domestic violence should be shared in order that appropriate safeguarding plans are made. Research suggests that as many as 75% of children subject to child protection proceedings have a background of domestic violence (DH 2005).

What are the risks to children and young people?

Domestic abuse can seriously affect the chances of children and young people living a healthy and rewarding life (DH 2005; LGA 2006). The most obvious risks to children and young people are that of suffering physical or sexual abuse themselves. Research findings suggest that approximately half of all children living with domestic abuse will be directly harmed in this way (Humphreys and Mullender 1999). In some cases the physical abuse will be perpetrated by the adult victim rather than the person responsible for the domestic abuse (Davidson and Lynch 2003). However, this scenario has also been described as 'greater levels of physical punishment' from an over-stressed mother (Humphreys and Mullender 1999).

Points for reflection
From the child's perspective does the end result of severe physical punishment feel any different to the end result of physical abuse?

Children and young people may also be harmed accidentally through being caught up in the violence or by trying to protect their mothers. Children may also be harmed prior to birth with resultant physical or learning disabilities (in some cases the child will be miscarried, see below). In this respect Humphreys and Mullender report on a study that found that a quarter of refuges in a national survey had a disabled child; although arguably these figures need to be seen in the context of the number of children and the nature of the disability.

Children and young people will also suffer from witnessing or hearing the abuse or through being neglected by a parent who has to prioritise their own safety and well-being. Other adverse effects include educational failure and exclusion, the effects of house moves and loss of friends and possessions. The child may also display negative behaviour such as hyperactivity, perpetrating violence or bullying other children (Davidson and Lynch 2003). It is important to recognise that children may blame themselves for the domestic abuse. This clearly affects their self-esteem and can make it difficult for them to form positive relationships in the future (LGA 2006). Like their abused parent, children and young people need to be listened to, believed and supported.

Maternity care

The risks of domestic abuse beginning or escalating in pregnancy are well recognised. There are links with repeated miscarriages, terminations, pre-term labour, stillbirths and maternal deaths (DH 2005). All pregnant women should be given an opportunity to disclose domestic abuse in a safe and private environment and those who have been abused have welcomed the move for midwives to routinely enquire into this aspect of women's well-being in pregnancy (NICE 2003; DH 2005). This means that women need to be seen alone at least once during their antenatal care. Where there are language barriers, women should be supported by professional interpreters and not by family members. Any disclosure should be documented, as should any decision on the part of the practitioner not to enquire as to the possibility of abuse. Documentation should be in the practitioner-held notes, rather than those held by the woman, as this may inflame an already dangerous situation.

Nurses and midwives working in sexual health services also need to be aware of the possibility of domestic abuse. Kipps (2005) notes that the ability of a woman to negotiate the use of condoms may be hampered in a relationship that is based on coercive control and adds that this may lead to women presenting repeatedly with unwanted pregnancies or sexually-transmitted infections. Maternity, gynaecological and sexual health clinics and emergency departments should provide telephone numbers of local and national sources of help for those experiencing domestic abuse. This needs to be done discreetly, for example on the back of lavatory doors, or via credit-card sized leaflets that can be hidden by the woman if necessary.

Female genital mutilation

The cultural and gendered issue of female genital mutilation (FGM) has been seen to be part of the spectrum of domestic abuse, but is also now recognised as an important child protection issue in its own right. The ancient practice of FGM occurs across sub-Saharan Africa and parts of the Arabian and Malay peninsulas, but also features in multicultural communities in the UK. There are variations in the degree of mutilation, the most severe being 'infibulation' which involves cutting off the external genitalia and sewing up the wound to leave a pinhole meatus (Debelle, 2003). The procedure, which may also be referred to as 'female circumcision', is recognised to be medically unnecessary, extremely painful and has serious consequences for the child or young woman's health. Taylor (2003) summarises the international efforts to eradicate this 'traditional practice', whilst recognising the traditional and religious elements that are said to be part of initiation into adulthood and preparation for marriage. FGM is thus a criminal act in the UK, although many girls and young women remain at risk. All nurses and midwives need to be aware of this issue and to advocate against this practice and ensure the protection of vulnerable girls and young women. A recent guide by the RCN is helpful in expanding knowledge in this respect (RCN 2006).

One of the challenges in addressing the issue of FGM is that parents genuinely believe that they are acting in their child's best interests (Taylor 2003). Yet this is clearly seen as a child protection issue within the UK. *Working Together* (HM Government 2006a) provides specific guidance as to safeguarding children and young people at risk of FGM, including recourse to statutory procedures. An FGM protocol developed by Cardiff Area Child Protection Committee that has been adopted throughout Wales (All Wales Child Protection Review Group 2005b) reinforces the child protection aspects of this practice.

Prevention of domestic abuse

An awareness of the issues and an ability to enquire and respond to domestic abuse is an important aspect of the preventative role of nurses and midwives. The LGA (2006) recognise that early education is vital in helping to ensure that embedded cultural issues such as gender stereotyping that sees women and girls as inferior to men and boys are tackled and that a message of zero tolerance to domestic abuse is promoted. As with child maltreatment there is a need to tackle the causes and risk factors for domestic abuse and to seek ways of preventing the risk of inter-generational transmission. On this latter point it is important to note that a child who witnesses domestic abuse will not necessarily grow up to become an abuser. However, good parenting role models are key. As Humphreys and Mullender (1999: 17) comment:

> Many young people (and their parents) are frightened that living with violence marks them out as inevitably bound for a violent future themselves. It is important to dispel such myths, while also providing positive opportunities for parents to learn to discipline in non-physical ways and for young people to learn ... that violence is wrong and is not appropriate as a means of conflict resolution.

In summary, domestic abuse is widely prevalent and has strong links to all categories of child maltreatment. Rather than being viewed as a 'private affair' between spouses (as in the past), it is now seen to be a matter of public interest, not least because of the huge cost to victims and to society in the effect that it has on children and young people. It is also important to recognise that in the female dominated professions of nursing and midwifery, there will be a substantial number of practitioners who are, or have been, victims of domestic abuse themselves. Davidson and Lynch (2003) suggest that this can either inhibit or enhance the ability to respond to domestic abuse issues in practice. The DH guidance on domestic abuse recognises the needs of victims in the workplace and notes that NHS organisations should have workplace guidance and opportunities for confidential counselling in place (DH 2005). There will be a need to consider the safeguarding and welfare needs of any children. Details of national helplines and websites of key organisations that provide advice and support to those suffering from domestic abuse are given in the appendix.

Children and young people with disabilities

The greater risk of child maltreatment to children and young people with a disability is a crucial issue that has become more prominent since the 1990s, although there is still much to be done. The maltreatment of disabled children can be physical, sexual, emotional or neglectful. The risk of serious sexual abuse appears to be particularly high, especially amongst deaf children (Hobbs et al. 1999a). As with any statistical evidence on the incidence and prevalence of child abuse and neglect, difficulties are raised by the defining and reporting of the problem. This situation is compounded by the paucity of studies that have specifically considered the prevalence of maltreatment of disabled children in the UK (National Working Group on Child

Protection and Disability, NWGCPD 2003). As Beckett (2003) notes a lack of literature on this topic may reflect a lack of attention in actual practice. However, it is widely reported that the risk of child maltreatment is some three times greater than for able bodied children and young people, and furthermore, that the more disabled the child, the more severe the abuse may be. In addition, it is also important to recognise that many disabled children will be part of what Sobley (2006) has referred to as a 'vicious circle'. These are the children and young people who are disabled in the first place because of their maltreatment and who will, in turn, be subject to further victimisation and more injury.

Points for reflection

In what ways may child maltreatment cause disability? Discuss with fellow students or colleagues the messages for prevention in these cases.

The maltreatment of disabled children and young people is an important issue for nurses and midwives both in terms of the high levels of contact that these children have with health care services and also because of the opportunities that practitioners have to prevent and detect child maltreatment through ensuring good practice and the provision of high quality care. Prevention may include supporting the child in learning about what is meant by 'safe touch' and what is inappropriate. *Working Together* (HM Government 2006a) notes that disabled children need to receive appropriate personal, social and health education, including sex and relationships education. Guidelines and training for good practice in intimate care; working with children of the opposite sex; handling difficult behaviour; consent; anti-bullying strategies; and sex and sexuality should be in place. School nurses can help to develop policies and protocols for practice.

Case example

Melanie, who has cerebral palsy and communication difficulties, has been refusing to get into the school mini-bus that arrives early each morning to take her to her special school. Her mother has contacted the school who say that she appears to settle quickly once she arrives and they cannot identify any specific problems. A new driver has recently been engaged.

The underpinning philosophy of this book is particularly important here, in that the *rights* of children and young people to be heard and to be protected from maltreatment, to be healthy, to be safe, to be well cared for and to have the opportunities to achieve their potential, apply to *all* children and young people and that those with disabilities are children first. This section considers the reasons why disabled children and young people are more vulnerable to child maltreatment and what nurses and midwives can do to lessen the risk. We start by considering the evidence for a tradition of under-recognition of this important issue.

Discrimination, stigmatisation and disbelief

Hobbs et al. (1999a) recognise that the abuse of children and young people with disabilities has been ignored in the past. They draw on the findings of Marchant (1991) who suggested the common myths that abounded included disbelief that disabled children could be abused as they were not attractive; or that their disability should arouse sympathy rather than exploitation; that maltreatment was not harmful because disabled children would not understand it and that the widespread problems of adults finding it difficult to accept that *any* maltreatment occurs are compounded when they are faced with the possibility of harm to a disabled child.

The NWGCPD (2003) note that society devalues and disempowers those with disabilities and that these negative attitudes both make children with disabilities more vulnerable to abuse and less likely to be listened to. *Working Together* (HM Government 2006a) recognises that children and young people with disabilities face a greater risk of maltreatment. The guidance notes that:

- disabled children have fewer outside contacts than other children;
- they have an impaired capacity to avoid abuse;
- communication difficulties may also be impaired;
- they are more vulnerable to bullying and intimidation; and
- crucially, they receive intimate personal care (such as washing, dressing and toileting) from a number of carers that '... may both increase the risk of exposure to abusive behaviour and make it more difficult to set and maintain physical boundaries' (p.198).

The importance of accepting that disabled children and young people are more vulnerable to child maltreatment and an understanding of why this might be, are important factors in developing strategies to ensure their protection.

Prevention and protection

In their analysis of the factors that lead to disabled children's increased risk of maltreatment, Hobbs et al. (1999a) note the early effects of poor attachment. They suggest that this relates to the fact that the disabled child is not the 'hoped for child'. Importantly, they add that research findings point to a relationship between lack of support at the point at which parents learn that their child is disabled and an increased likelihood of physical abuse later on. This has ramifications for nurses and midwives who need to ensure the provision of expert advice and support at this difficult time.

The NWGCPD (2003) suggest that barriers to safeguarding disabled children must be tackled at a number of different levels. Their proposals embrace:

- recognising disabled people as equal citizens with equal rights and ensuring their full participation in society;
- providing safe and accessible community and leisure services;
- ensuring flexible support that places a value on the views, wishes and feelings of the disabled child or young person;
- developing policies and practices that safeguard, respect and empower disabled children (including sex and relationships education);
- undertaking early multi-agency assessments of need in relation to any causes for concern.

Good employment practices in relation to the recruitment and screening of staff are an important aspect of ensuring safety, especially in institutional or residential settings. Where intimate care is provided there should be guidelines and training on good practice to ensure the safety and protection of the young person. The Royal College of Nursing (2001) guidance on protecting children and *staff* recognises the challenges of providing intimate care and gives the examples of the administration of rectal medication, catheter care and bathing. The guidance highlights best practice principles including respect for privacy and dignity, information-giving and consent, clinical supervision and support, although it lacks specific recognition of the particular vulnerability of children and young people with disabilities. Communication skills, particularly in ascertaining the wishes of the child in relation to their care and treatment are clearly key. *Working Together* (HM Government 2006a) recognises the importance of meeting communication needs for those with communication impairments or learning disabilities and urges agencies not to make assumptions that children and young people who are disabled will not be able to be credible witnesses in court proceedings. The next vulnerable group to be discussed are those children and young people who are at risk of sexual exploitation. It is notable that disabled children have been found to be amongst this special group.

Children and young people at risk of sexual exploitation

There is a growing recognition that children involved in prostitution and other forms of commercial sexual exploitation should be treated primarily as victims of maltreatment who are likely to have a number of health and welfare needs (see, for example, the very powerful report *Whose Daughter Next?*, McNeish, 1998). The UK government recognises that the primary law enforcement activity should be against those who coerce and abuse children and young people, rather than engaging the child in criminal proceedings (DH et al. 2000). A child protection route is seen to be an appropriate way in which to ensure the future safety of children and young people who have become involved in prostitution, although this has been questioned by some (Pearce 2006). At the time of writing, guidance instructs Local Safeguarding Children Boards (LSCBs) to make active enquiries as to the existence (or not) of such activity in their local area (HM Government 2006a). Sexual exploitation incorporates a spectrum of behaviours from child sexual abuse at one end to formal prostitution at the other (Scott and Skidmore 2006). Nurses and midwives are likely to encounter children and young people involved in prostitution through their access to maternity care, mental health services, and sexual health clinics, and also in emergency situations due to violence, self-harm and substance misuse. This section seeks to explore the nature of the problem and to help practitioners understand the reasons that children and young people are drawn into prostitution and how they can help to ensure their safety and well-being. There are also clear messages in relation to prevention. We begin by considering the scale of the problem.

The scale of the problem

In an overview of the issues, Levy (2004) suggests that the number of children and young people involved in prostitution in the UK is increasing. The figures are currently estimated to be around 5000, with a ratio of 4:1 females to males. Levy adds that there is also some evidence to suggest that the age at which children become involved in prostitution in the first place is decreasing, with many children and young people involved before they can legally consent to sex.

Case example
Kristi, who gave her age as 18 years but looked younger, was brought semi-comatose to the emergency department by an older man who said little, but refused to leave her side. Her condition was thought to be related to misuse of amphetamines. She was found to be 12 weeks pregnant.

Why children and young people get involved

Levy (2004) notes that although the dominant view is that children and young people become 'entrapped' into prostitution through the grooming activities of a 'pimp' (usually, but not always, a man), there is evidence to suggest that many will be drawn in through their peers or that they 'drift' into this way of life as a means of survival. Children and young people become engaged in prostitution for a variety of reasons. These may include disengagement from education, poverty, homelessness and family breakdown, leaving care or running away. Although a past history of sexual or physical abuse may feature in the background of these children and young people (McNeish 1998), the links are not as clear as they may seem (Corby 2006). For some a lack of self-worth makes them vulnerable to 'grooming'; for others it may be that their experience of child maltreatment has contributed to them running away from home. The need for money is an important contributory factor. This may include needing money for drugs as well as for shelter, and there is an irrefutable inter-relationship between prostitution and substance misuse. However, it is not clear whether substance misuse leads to prostitution or follows it, as drugs and alcohol may be used to 'block out' past and present circumstances (Levy 2004; Scott and Skidmore 2006). Whatever the contributory factors, it is also important to remember that the demand from clients and the existence of adverse childhood experiences, including child maltreatment, family breakdown and social exclusion, create the conditions for the sexual exploitation of children and young people.

Ensuring safety and well-being

An awareness of the risk factors for children and young people engaging in prostitution means that nurses and midwives can make a contribution to its prevention. This may be through supporting children, young people and their families at times of crisis and ensuring that children who have been abused have access to therapeutic help and support. Nurses and midwives may be able to influence the provision of specialist services to children and young people who are at risk of, or engaging in, substance misuse; these are often seen to be part of 'adult services'. Nurses and midwives can also help to ensure and support education programmes that advise on the dangers posed by those who seek to coerce vulnerable individuals into a lifestyle that places them at risk of sexual exploitation.

A key issue in working with sexually exploited children and young people is to allow space and time for the young person to work through their own, rather than any imposed solution (McNeish 1998). Corby (2006) notes that it may not always be helpful to view these children and young people as victims, and suggests that that it is important to seek to understand the views of the young person as to how they see themselves and the reasons for their engagement in commercial sexual exploitation. This suggestion is supported in a paper by Pearce (2006), who proposes that the problems facing this group are best addressed through interventions that draw on a combination of child protection, domestic violence and youth work policies and procedures, rather than a strictly child protection route. It is likely that the best approach is one that involves both statutory and voluntary organisations, the latter sector having developed expertise in working with this group through a number of key projects. Scott and Skidmore (2006) describe the 'four As' approach used successfully by Barnardo's which focuses on:

- access to services;
- attention to ensure the development of a supportive relationship with a named worker;
- assertive outreach to establish and maintain contact (e.g. regular texting); and
- advocacy to ensure the provision that these young people need.

This is clearly sensitive and specialist work and an important aspect of nurses' and midwives' care is knowledge of local programmes and facilities for children and young people at risk of, or suffering from, commercial sexual exploitation. These are extremely vulnerable young women and men who have often had a lifetime of disadvantage.

Online abuse

The 2006 edition of *Working Together* in England (HM Government 2006a) recognises child abuse in the context of information and communication technology (ICT). The risk posed by 'internet chat rooms', discussion forums and bulletin boards that draw children and young people towards inappropriate and abusive relationships, including the transmission of pornographic images of themselves, are widely reported. This risk also extends to mobile phones (especially those with cameras) and instant messaging services, and it is important to recognise that as well as the risk posed by adults, peer text bullying and the circulation of violence or sexual acts amongst peers also takes place.

Case example
Well aware that a 'love-struck' Year 10 student was infatuated with a girl in the year above, his 'friends' sent a text message allegedly from the girl in question asking him to send her a photograph of his genitalia via the phone. This was rapidly transmitted to the friends' call lists.

The UK has recently established a Child Protection and On-line Protection (CEOP) centre. CEOP maximises international links and combines police powers with the expertise of business, government, specialist charities and other organisation focusing on tackling child sexual abuse (see web resources in the appendix). School nurses and others who provide sex and relationships education to children and young people or who work with parenting groups may like to make reference to CEOP's 'child-friendly' website in their programmes. Here invaluable tips for avoiding sexual exploitation are backed up with links that enable the direct reporting of concerns. The 'Top Ten' tips will be of interest to all those readers who are parents, as well as those working with children, young people and their families in a variety of contexts.

'Think u Know' Top Ten

1 It's best not to give out your personal details to online mates.
2 Personal stuff includes your messenger id, email address, mobile number and any pictures of you, your family or friends.
3 If you publish a picture or video online – anyone can change it or share it.
4 SPAM/Junk email & texts: don't believe it, reply to it or use it.
5 It's not a good idea to open files that are from people you don't know. You won't know what they contain – it could be a virus, or worse – an inappropriate image or film.
6 It's easier to get on with people online and say stuff you wouldn't offline.
7 Some people lie online.
8 It's better to keep online mates online. Don't meet up with any strangers without an adult you trust. Better to be uncool than unsafe!
9 It's never too late to tell someone if something makes you feel uncomfortable.

10 There are people who can help. Report online child abuse, or find more advice and support.

From http://www.thinkuknow.co.uk/topten.aspx (accessed 20/11/06)

In addition to the risks posed in the ways described above it is also important to consider the needs of children and young people who spend a great deal of time engaged in ICT activities. Such children may not only be at risk of obesity, but also of missing out on the development of meaningful social relationships.

There are clear links between the risks posed by 'online' abuse, child well-being and the wider roles of agencies in safeguarding and promoting the welfare of children. Access to programmes and activities to raise the awareness of the safe use of ICT is said to be an issue for all LSCBs to consider (HM Government 2006a).

Points for reflection

Find out about local programmes for the safe use of ICT.

Does your clinical environment offer posters or leaflets about the risks posed by internet grooming activities and sources of help and advice?

Refugees and asylum seekers

In a similar vein to the arguments put forward above in relation to children with disabilities, a report under the auspices of the Mayor of London (2004) suggests that refugee children are not being treated as children first and refugees second. The report outlines the risks of harm caused by a lack of monitoring of children who are accompanied by an adult who is not their parent or usual carer (c.f. Victoria Climbié); the vulnerability of both accompanied and unaccompanied children in relation to the way in which they are accommodated; and the risk, outlined above, of girls being taken out of the country for FGM. There is some mention of unaccompanied children in *Working Together* (HM Government 2006a) which recognises that their health needs are likely to be extensive and may include the need for mental health or counselling services as a result of post-traumatic stress. Definitions of key terms used to describe these children and their families are helpfully provided in the Mayor of London's report (2004: 5–6). These definitions include:

- Refugee: In international law a refugee is someone who, because of a 'well-founded fear' of persecution, has fled their own country; cannot or dare not return to it; and therefore seeks asylum in another country. The persecution that drives them to flee must be related to their race, religion, nationality, membership of a particular social group or political opinion. Recent court judgements have established that this may cover those, usually women, who suffer sexual persecution by state agents.
- Asylum seeker: An asylum seeker is someone who has applied to be recognised as a refugee and is awaiting a decision on their application, whether at initial or appeal stage. Asylum seeker is neither an official immigration status nor an official status under the UN Convention on the Status of Refugees 1951, whereas a person who has refugee status is recognised by the State as fulfilling the terms of the UN Convention on Refugees. Refugee status is an official immigration status.
- Discretionary leave: This is granted to unaccompanied asylum-seeking children who do not have adequate reception arrangements in their home country. Unaccompanied asylum-seeking children are usually granted discretionary leave for three years or until they reach 18. At the end of this time it must be renewed.
- Unaccompanied asylum-seeking children: On the Home Office's strict definition, these are children alone on arrival in the UK who are not known to be joining a close relative. This definition excludes children who are accompanied by an adult who is not their parent or legal/customary carer, and children reaching UK immigration controls with an adult who subsequently abandons them.

Webb (2002), writing in the *British Medical Journal*, recognises that many child care professionals in the UK are concerned about the welfare of refugees and unaccompanied asylum seeking children and young people. She suggests that strategies are needed to ensure that their voices are heard.

As universal providers of health care, nurses and midwives need to make certain that the needs of these children and young people are prioritised. This includes developing awareness and understanding of the physical and mental health issues that arise from the background and trauma that has led to their plight; facilitation of communication through the appropriate use of interpreting services and provision of written material about services in the mother-tongue. Nurses and midwives should also be contributing to strategic developments that ensure the commissioning and provision of services that help to support the integration of those who have been typically marginalised and misunderstood.

Conclusion

While recognising that all children and young people are vulnerable to child maltreatment, this chapter has focused on the safeguarding needs of children and young people who may be particularly vulnerable. Notably these special groups represent children and families who are likely to have high levels of contact with a variety of health services. The chapter began by considering the links between domestic abuse and child maltreatment and outlined the roles of nurses and midwives in identification of domestic abuse and the provision of information and support. The increased risk of maltreatment for children and young people with disabilities, and how this may impact on practice, were then discussed. The issues for children and young people who are at risk of sexual exploitation were explored and links were made to the risk of 'online exploitation'. Suggestions have been given for safe practice for those using the internet. The chapter closed with a consideration of the risks to those children and young people who are asylum seekers. In many cases, specialist advice and help will be essential. Thus readers are advised to make themselves aware of local provision. Links are provided to key websites and other national sources of help in the appendix.

Messages for practice

- Children, young people and families who are at a greater risk of child maltreatment are likely to have high levels of contact with a variety of health services.
- The health of children and young people is closely related to their safety and security and this will always be at risk in cases of domestic abuse.
- An abused woman's risk of being murdered is at its greatest at the point of separating or having just left a violent partner. Referral to specialist services is essential.
- Children and young people with disabilities face a threefold risk of child maltreatment. It is imperative that nurses and midwives see disabled children as children first.
- Children and young people who are being sexually exploited are best safeguarded from harm through interventions that draw on a combination of child protection, domestic violence and youth work policies and procedures.
- School nurses and others who provide sex and relationships education to children and young people or who work with parenting groups may like to make reference to CEOP's 'child-friendly' website in their programmes.

- The high levels of risk to the safety and well-being of asylum-seeking children and young people has been recognised. Like all children and young people, it is important to treat them as children first and foremost.

Recommended reading

DH (Department of Health) (2005) *Responding to Domestic Abuse: A Handbook for Health Professionals*. London: Department of Health.

DH (Department of Health), Home Office, DfEE (Department for Education and Employment), Welsh Office (2000) *Safeguarding Children Involved in Prostitution*. London: Department of Health.

Kipps, S. (2005) Sexual health needs of women in violent relationships, *Primary Health Care*, **15**(8): 27–32.

Levy, A. (2004) *Stigmatised, Marginalised and Criminalised*. London: NSPCC.

Mayor of London (2004) *Offering More than they Borrow: Refugee Children in London*. London: Greater London Authority.

NICE (National Institute for Clinical Excellence) (2003) *Antenatal Care: Routine Care for the Healthy Pregnant Woman*. London: National Institute for Clinical Excellence.

NWGCPD (National Working Group on Child Protection and Disability) (2003) *'It Doesn't Happen to Disabled Children'*. London: NSPCC.

RCN (Royal College of Nursing) (2006) *Female Genital Mutilation: An RCN Educational Resource for Nursing and Midwifery Staff*. London: Royal College of Nursing.

chapter **six**

FABRICATED OR INDUCED ILLNESS

Learning outcomes

This chapter will help you to:

- understand the aetiology of fabricated or induced illness by carers;
- consider opportunities for early identification and support to children and their families;
- discuss the response to suspected fabricated or induced illness;
- reflect on the challenges in the provision of child- and family-centred care in cases of suspected fabricated or induced illness;
- debate the professional and ethical issues surrounding the use of different methods of surveillance.

Introduction

This chapter outlines the difficult and somewhat puzzling form of maltreatment known as 'fabricated or induced illness' (FII) whereby children and young people are presented, usually persistently, by their parents or carers to health professionals for medical assessment and care with false histories of illnesses or with a range of signs and symptoms of illnesses that arise from deliberate harm such as poisoning or suffocation (Royal College of Paediatrics and Child Health, RCPCH 2002). All nurses and midwives need to be aware of the existence of this form of abuse and the important role that they can play in its identification and response. The Department of Health (DH) in conjunction with the Home Office, Department for Education and Skills and the Welsh Assembly Government have issued specific guidance on *Safeguarding Children in Whom Illness is Fabricated or Induced* (2002). This has also been reflected in an All Wales Child Protection Committee Protocol published in 2004. These documents form an important source of information for those who care for families where FII is suspected or confirmed and reinforce the fact that this is essentially a form of child maltreatment.

The chapter begins by considering the definition and key features and explores the development of current terminology to describe the problem. A number of differing presentations are outlined. We also consider the response and emphasise the importance of the involvement of key statutory agencies within the framework for safeguarding and promoting the welfare of children and young people. The implications for nurses and midwives are discussed with the recognition that usual practice in the contemporary care of children, young people and their families is severely compromised when FII is suspected. At all times the focus needs to be firmly on the child, their daily lived experiences and, where age and developmentally appropriate, their own understanding of their signs, symptoms and experience.

Definition of FII

The starting point for most discussions about FII is a reference to a paper by Asher in 1951 that coined the term 'Munchausen Syndrome' to describe patients who repeatedly presented for health care with factitious somatic complaints. There then followed a growing recognition that parents or carers may adopt similar behaviour in repeatedly presenting their child to health care professionals with factitious illnesses or, more worryingly, having deliberately induced illness in their child (RCPCH 2002). The term 'Munchausen Syndrome by Proxy' (MSbP) was subsequently adopted by Meadow (1977) to describe a triad of:

- duped doctor
- harmed child
- fabricating parent.

Cases vary in their presentation. In some cases there will be an urgent need to prevent serious physical harm, or even death. In others the harm to the child will be of a 'chronic disabling nature' which is recognised to be potentially as severe as an acute life threatening event in its nature (RCPCH 2002). The variety of presentations has led to much debate about the key features of this form of maltreatment. In their review of the literature and clinical experience of FII, the RCPCH (2002) broadly accept Meadow's (1995: 8) criteria to describe this phenomenon.

'1 Illness in a child which is fabricated or induced by a parent or someone who is in *loco parentis*;
2 A child is presented for medical assessment and care, usually persistently, often resulting in multiple medical procedures;
3 The perpetrator denies the aetiology of the child's illness;
4 Acute symptoms and signs cease when the child is separated from the perpetrator.'

However, there has long been controversy over the defining attributes of MSbP, including that of the difficult borderline between fabrication and exaggeration. There has also been discussion as to whether pointers to the abuse should be seen as 'diagnostic' (RCPCH 2002). These discussions have been influential in reframing MSbP as 'fabricated or induced illness' to cover the vast array of possible presentations. Linked to this is the debate as to whether MSbP (or FII) is a 'syndrome' and whether it is the child or perpetrator that is the sufferer. A further argument is that FII is more usefully viewed as a label for the form of maltreatment that is being perpetrated. My own preference is for the latter, with the recognition that the focus should be on the presenting features and the health and well-being of the child or young person rather than the 'supposed psychopathy' of the parent (Craft and Hall 2004). The RCPCH suggest that adoption of the term 'fabricated or induced illness' in preference to 'Munchausen Syndrome by Proxy' raises awareness of the wide range of presenting features which may lead to physical injury and psychological harm to the victim. However, it is likely that nurses and midwives will still hear the term 'MSbP' used in practice for some time, although the term FII is now the preferred term and its use should be promoted. Other terms found in the literature include 'factitious illness' and 'Meadow's Syndrome'.

Working Together (HM Government 2006a) notes that there are three main ways of fabricating or inducing illness in a child. These include fabrication of signs and symptoms, including past medical history; falsification of hospital charts, records and specimens of bodily fluids; and/or the induction of illness by a variety of means. FII is incorporated into the policy definition of physical abuse in the guidance: 'Physical abuse may involve hitting, shaking, throwing, poisoning, burning or scalding, drowning, suffocating, or otherwise causing physical harm to a child. *Physical harm may also be caused when a parent or carer fabricates the symptoms of, or deliberately induces illness in a child*' (HM Government 2006a: 8, emphasis added). However, whilst the policy definition refers to 'physical abuse' it is important to recognise that children and young people who are victims of FII are also being 'emotionally abused' and that, in some cases, the presentation is one of alleged behavioural or mental health problems rather than physical signs or symptoms (RCPCH 2002; Hall 2003a). Additionally, allegations of child maltreatment, including sexual abuse, may form a presenting feature in some cases.

Incidence and prevalence

As with other forms of child maltreatment, the provision of statistics in relation to the prevalence of FII is fraught with the difficulties of definition, recognition and reporting. Although Hobbs (2003) claims that FII is a problem that is 'commonly encountered' in primary care and paediatric practice, the RCPCH (2002) draw on a number of different studies that have proposed rates that vary from 0.1 to 45 per 100,000 children per year, which, if accurate, makes it relatively rare. The risk appears to be greatest during the first year of life (Hobbs et al. 1999).

Effect on the child

According to the RCPCH (2002) children who are being abused in this manner may react in a number of ways. Some will be aware of what is happening, but may continue to participate due to being concerned about abandonment by their mother if they stop being sick. Others will believe what they are told and adopt their parents' perception of their illness. Older children may also be at risk of becoming compliant because frequent school absences may have led to a lack of friends and an inability to enjoy school.

Outcomes for children and young people will be dependent on the severity of the abuse and the emotional resilience of the child. Yet the risk of death is very real. Early research on FII tends to show a relatively high death rate (i.e. 10–12%), but this may have been due to the seriousness of cases being studied at specialist centres. Induced harm is linked to a poorer prognosis than fabricated illness, as is FII associated with other forms of abuse and associated risk factors such as domestic violence, substance misuse and social isolation (RCPCH 2002).

Perpetrators

In a review of 313 cases which were highlighted in the RCPCH (2002) report, mothers were found to be by far the most common perpetrators (89%). Although there is a perception that perpetrators of FII have a health care or paramedical background (e.g. health care assistants) this was only found to be the case in 20% of cases where occupation was ascertained and 7% of the sample overall. Hobbs (2003), however, notes that 'many mothers' have a nursing background. Perpetrators are often reported to have existing or previous mental health difficulties such as somatising and somatiform disorder (formerly Munchausen Syndrome), personality disorder, eating disorder, self-harm or substance misuse. Importantly many will have their own history of child maltreatment or other adverse events in childhood, including being in the care of the local authority. Fathers in cases of FII are said to be distant, passive or absent (RCPCH 2002).

Despite the fact that perpetrators are often very personable and engage well with their children's health care providers, they need to be recognised as essentially dangerous and manipulative individuals. The RCPCH (2002: 29) note that:

> Perpetrators may be skilled in concealing their activities and in misleading professionals. They appear on occasion to be strongly motivated to continue or even escalate the abuse. Many deny their activities when challenged, may be very guarded and defensive and may seek alternative healthcare or move to another area with continuing risk of harm to the child.

The RCPCH (2002) also recognise that it is difficult to ascertain the motivation of those who perpetrate this form of abuse. They may be deluded or suffering from excessive anxiety to the point of hysteria. They may even be 'mothering to death'. Meadow (1999) gives a chilling account of three adults from different families who were apparently treated as invalids by their mothers from childhood and subsequently suffered an untimely death. However, perpetrators have also been described as 'doctor addicts' or 'doctor shoppers' who seek personal gain from engagement with health care services. This may include additional financial support. Hobbs (2003) suggests that the motivation is linked to personal gain and the sympathy, attention, status and respect afforded to those with a sick child.

Case example

Robert, aged 8, suffered from cystic fibrosis, and the disease had been relatively well controlled with little need for time off school or hospitalisation for treatment of chest infections. His consultant was somewhat baffled by an unforeseen deterioration which included a demand from the parents for a wheelchair to assist Robert's mobility. Review by the cystic fibrosis team, including home visits by the specialist nurse, suggested that the family sought financial gain from housing and other benefits if Robert could be presented as more of an 'invalid'. Concerns were also expressed that treatment was being deliberately withheld.

Presentation

Working Together (HM Government 2006a: 148) usefully summarises the key aspects of presentations for health care that may raise concerns about the possibility of FII:

- 'reported symptoms and signs found on examination are not explained by any medical condition from which the child may be suffering; or
- physical examination and results of medical investigations do not explain reported symptoms and signs; or
- there is an inexplicably poor response to prescribed medication and other treatment; or
- new symptoms are reported on resolution of previous ones; or
- reported symptoms and found signs are not seen to begin in the absence of the caregiver; or
- over time the child repeatedly presents with a range of symptoms; or
- the child's normal activities are being curtailed beyond that which might be expected for any medical disorder from which the child is known to suffer.'

The RCPCH note that the spectrum of signs and symptoms, the severity of the initial illness, the age at onset, the length of time before action is taken, the likelihood of escalation and whether the child is drawn into collusion, or not, are extremely varied (2002). Fabrications of illnesses are reported to be more common than induced illness. Whilst in many cases the child will be essentially 'well', it is important to be aware that existing chronic illness does not exclude the possibility of fabricated or induced illness and may act as a stimulus for abnormal behaviour, as well as offer the opportunities to induce symptoms.

Case example

Jade, a 9-month-old infant, was transferred to a tertiary hospital for investigations of reflux and failure to thrive. Having been born pre-term, she had spent most of her short life in hospital and was fed via a naso-gastric tube, pending a gastrostomy. The nursing staff bonded quickly with the mother, who seemed very much 'at home' in a hospital setting. One lunchtime mother pressed the emergency bell and Jade was found lifeless and cyanosed. The curtains had been drawn around the cot and an observant ward sister noted that pillows from the adjoining mother's bed had been disturbed. Later covert video surveillance showed attempted suffocation and Jade was removed from the family for later adoption. She thrived in her temporary foster family and began to take a normal diet.

The RCPCH (2002) note that fabrication or illness induction can simulate almost any disorder and a table of possible presentations based on the body systems is included in their review. Examples drawn from this include:

- seizures, collapse, loss of consciousness, ataxia and developmental delay caused by drugs, poisons, suffocation or pressure in the carotid sinus;
- fabricated fits or disabilities, under-stimulation, deprivation or sedation;
- disability through enforced use of wheelchair, nappies etc.;
- apnoea and cyanosis, cardiac arrest, near-miss sudden infant death syndrome caused by suffocation or interference with medical equipment in an inpatient care environment;
- recurrent vomiting and diarrhoea from laxatives, poisons or mechanical induction;
- failure to thrive through restricting intake or diluting feeds, fabricating charts;
- haematuria or bacteriuria from adding parental blood or swapping urine specimens with parent or other patients;
- injecting blood under the skin to cause purpura;
- simulating fever through heating the thermometer;
- causing sepsis through injecting bacteriologically contaminated material;

- applying excessive environmental and dietary measures to avoid 'allergen';
- applying irritants, scratching, scalding the skin to cause rashes;
- inserting caustic solutions in the eyes and mouth;
- dirtying wounds;
- abuse of insulin and adding salt to feeds.

However, the RCPCH urge caution on focusing on 'typical scenarios' which they say can miss cases of FII or lead to a failure to identify genuine disorders. In many instances the presentation is less dramatic than commonly believed.

Points for reflection
Where parents are engaged in caring for their child within a ward setting who monitors and countersigns their contribution to care (e.g. fluid charts)?

The RCPCH (2002) note that the possibility of harm from FII may be recognised by a number of different health professionals working in a range of community and hospital settings. It appears that this is an issue that may be encountered by any practitioner who works with children, young people and their families. Close collaboration between colleagues from primary care and paediatrics, as well as opportunities for joint training in recognition and response to FII, are seen to be important (Horwath 2003).

Although the literature focuses largely on *children*, unborn babies can also be affected. Midwives should note that some mothers may induce harm to their unborn baby, for example through rupturing membranes to cause premature labour (RCPCH 2002). This may result in infants being admitted to neonatal units and neonatal nurses should be aware of the subsequent risk to the child. Midwives who are contributing to assessment for the possibility of FII are encouraged to analyse information obtained at booking. This may include the content of the GP referral letter and information supplied by the mother, particularly a history of strange illnesses, unusual complications of pregnancy, unexpected deaths in the family, family members with untreatable diseases, complicated medical histories in existing children, history of child maltreatment or failure to thrive and any signs and symptoms reported by the mother but not observed by midwife (DH et al. 2002). Mental health professionals caring for mothers or mothers-to-be also need to be aware of the possibility of harm to unborn children.

General practitioners (GPs) and health visitors may be the first to be aware of abnormal illness behaviour, perhaps through numerous primary care consultations and visits to emergency departments and 'walk-in' centres. However, some perpetrators will avoid GPs (who are a repository for notifications and letters from other health practitioners) and may seek consultations whilst on holiday, or via grandparents' GPs, or, in some cases, from alternative private practitioners. In relation to the latter example, the RCPCH note that children and young people who see alternative practitioners may also be at private school which may act to shield them from mainstream NHS services (although developments in school nursing may make this scenario increasingly less likely). School nurses may be aware of children and young people who are spending a great deal of time absent from school and they can provide an important link between health, social care and educational services. Early referral to a paediatrician for a definitive opinion on the child's health in cases of suspected FII is recommended and may even contribute to the prevention of escalation (RCPCH 2002).

In many cases, particularly those that are more severe, the child will be seen in a hospital setting. Whatever the speciality, a paediatrician should have a role in the care of children and young people in hospital (Ministry of Health 1959). The RCPCH (2002) note that all children admitted under general surgeons and other specialists, such as ear, nose and throat consultants, should be in the joint care of a named paediatrician. They suggest that although surgeons are beginning to recognise FII, unnecessary procedures such as the insertion of central lines, gastrostomies and Nissan fundoplication are particularly common features of FII. Those working in CAMHS may encounter fabrication of emotional or behavioural symptoms. It is important to ensure that hospital notes are collated when children and young people are seen in different departments. The use of information technology is helpful here and the future use of electronic care records can only be of advantage to children and young people at risk of FII.

Paediatricians are suggested to be the key group of professionals who are both involved in FII and most likely to be 'duped' (RCPCH 2002). Hobbs et al. (1999a) note that perpetrators may act to feed the self-esteem of medical staff; it is thus important that the interaction between professionals and the carer, as well as that between the carer and the child, forms part of the assessment and that opportunity for clinical supervision and case discussion involving all team members are routine.

Case example

Emily, 10 years old and her brother Adrian, aged 7 years, were regular attendees at the asthma and allergy outpatient clinic. Mother's demands for increased medication and more frequent appointments were met with surprise by the consultant who felt that the children were really quite well. For several Christmas's he had been sent a present of a novelty child-oriented silk tie by the family.

The RCPCH (2002) suggest that the first threshold to be crossed in cases of fabricated or induced illness is that in the mind of the paediatrician. This sentiment needs to be shared with all health professionals caring for children and families. In addition to being aware of the key aspects of FII presentation that are summarised above, the RCPCH add that a history of unexplained illnesses or deaths or multiple surgery in the parents or siblings may also be significant, as is a past history of child maltreatment, self-harm, somatising disorder or false allegations of physical or sexual assault in the parent.

Case example
Shireen Roberts appeared to be an extraordinarily anxious parent. She had consulted her GP, health visitor and NHS Direct on numerous occasions with concerns about her toddler's diarrhoea. Referral was made to a paediatrician when it became clear that there was some tailing off in growth trajectory. It was difficult to assess the child as an inpatient as there was often confusion about who was responsible for completion of the stool chart. In addition 'rota-virus' was present on the ward. At an inter-agency case discussion, the police representative produced a large file containing reports from Shireen of alleged minor assaults and burglary.

Response

The response to concern about the possibility of FII should be broadly the same as concerns about other forms of child maltreatment, although local protocols and policies specific to FII may be used to support national guidance. The key here is that the response should have a multi-agency contribution. Early referral to children's social care may engender an approach that is primarily based on a response to 'children in need' determined through the assessment framework (DH 2000b) rather than one of child protection. However, where there is evidence that the child has suffered or is at risk of suffering significant harm then a Section 47 enquiry will be instigated. The RCPCH (2002) note that there may a tendency for some paediatricians to wait until they are virtually certain that the child is suffering from FII before making a referral to statutory agencies; however, this may mean that the child could be harmed through a prolonged stay in hospital or by invasive, extensive and unnecessary medical investigations. Thus early contact with children's social care and the police is advocated.

The point at which the perpetrator is challenged about the possibility of FII represents an 'immense and imminent' (Hobbs et al.

1999: 302) danger point for the child. Any information-sharing with the parents needs to be firmly centred on the requirement to place the child's best interests first. A key feature of FII is that symptoms cease when the child is separated from the perpetrator (Hobbs 2003). In some cases this means that FII will only be identified if the suspect parent (or other perpetrator) is asked to leave the child in hospital – referred to by some as a 'parentectomy'. If a parent is not able to comply voluntarily, such a request may have to involve the local authority seeking an order for 'no contact' at the family courts.

Implications for practice

The RCPCH (2002) note that in comparison with other forms of child maltreatment, FII is unusual in that health professionals are involved with the child and family from the outset; this should potentially offer important opportunities for early detection and intervention to prevent possible escalation. However, it is recognised that FII can be extremely difficult to identify and that perpetrators may go to great lengths to avoid detection. It is thus important to ensure that concerns are documented and discussed at an early stage with other members of the health care team and then subsequently with children's social care and the police. This may include pooling information from the full range of health care records both for the child and other members of the family in the form of a chronology. The support of a named or designated health professional can be helpful. One local protocol (Avon and Somerset Joint Area Protocol for the Management of Suspected Fabricated or Induced Illness in Children 2005) advocates utilising the expertise of a 'consultative group' comprising designated health professionals, a senior police officer from the Child Abuse Investigation Unit, a children's social care manager with appropriate experience, a specialist consultant e.g. in epilepsy (if indicated), a representative from the Child and Adolescent Mental Health Service and the referring professional. The protocol adds that it may also be useful to invite the health visitor or school nurse and a representative from education, as appropriate.

Teamwork is vital, but it is important to remember that cases of suspected FII have the potential to divide staff and that debrief is an essential part of learning and support. Psychological support and counselling for professionals involved in difficult cases is recommended (DH et al. 2002; Terry 2004).

For nursing staff the real challenge of caring for a child who is thought to be suffering from FII is that the activities of the parent come under suspicion. The situation requires intensive monitoring, extreme sensitivity and a degree of secrecy. Perhaps contra to the progress that has been made since the Platt Report (Ministry of Health 1959) to develop a family-centred approach to care where parents are not just welcome residents on the ward, but supported and encouraged to actively participate as partners in care delivery. Terry (2004) notes that children who are victims of FII need to have an opportunity to build a relationship with a health care professional. This seems to be particularly important in addressing issues of collusion between perpetrator and child but is also essential in cases where parents are excluded.

Points for reflection
How may the notions of partnership with children and families, information-sharing and the traditions of family-centred care and open-access be compromised where there are concerns about possible FII?

Record keeping is key; what was seen, what was reported, what was administered, by whom and when? Nurses and midwives are involved in the collection of specimens, and in the spirit of partnership working may share this task with parents and children. In cases of suspected FII it is vitally important that this aspect of care is carefully managed. Who collected, labelled and delivered the specimen may be part of a so-called 'chain of evidence'. *What* is collected (i.e. urine, blood, vomit, stools or feed) will normally be ordered by the paediatrician, but it is the nurse's responsibility to ensure that this is done. Where there are cases of suspected poisoning laboratories are greatly helped if the possible agents can be suggested on the request form. This means that those caring for the child and family need to be aware of prescribed and over the counter medications that are available in the household. Nevertheless, it is important to remember that not all cases of poisoning are indicative of FII (RCPCH 2002).

The importance of the nursing role

Clearly the role of the nurse in cases of suspected FII goes beyond the collection of specimens and care with charts and records. Seibel and Parnell (1998) suggest that nursing is a very valuable resource in terms of provision of clinical expertise, observation and active participation in the process of diagnosis. They note:

> Of all the professionals in the hospital setting, nursing personnel spend the greatest amount of time with child patients and their parents, and have many opportunities to observe their interaction. Nurses may observe subtle signs [of FII], such as a mother's

> enmeshed interaction with the families of other ill children, a mother's misperceptions of her child, and certain kinds of statements made by a mother during conversations.
>
> (p. 71)

The authors also recognise that nurses may sometimes find it difficult to believe that this form of abuse is being perpetrated within a family that they have got to know well. In such cases it is important that the nurse and/or their manager consider withdrawal from provision of direct care while others seek to establish a confirmation of the diagnosis.

Surveillance

Clearly surveillance is essential not just in confirming suspicions of FII, but also in recognising health problems that have occurred naturally; either outcome will ensure the safety and well-being of the child. Where there is danger of a life-threatening event this needs to be undertaken in an inpatient setting (RCPCH 2002). Physiological monitoring to detect abnormalities in breathing patterns, oxygen saturation or bradycardia can be helpful in identifying or excluding serious natural disturbances of physiology as a cause for apparent life-threatening events. Video-surveillance, both overt and covert may also be used. In some instances parents may be loaned a camera to record unusual episodes in the home setting.

Covert video surveillance (CVS), where hidden cameras record the parental care of the child, has been hugely controversial. Nevertheless, Craft and Hall (2004) suggest that it is now an 'accepted procedure' where there is no other way of confirming a diagnosis of suffocation. However, as Terry (2004) notes, negative findings on CVS recording do not necessarily clear the parents. The welfare and safety of the child is the most important ethical consideration. The RCPCH (2002: 45) suggest that there are now 'fewer cases where this is needed'. However, where a decision is made to undertake CVS then this *must* be led by the police service in agreement with the Trust's Chief Executive and as part of a multi-disciplinary plan. Details of the regulations that now govern this practice may be found in the DH et al. (2002) guidance. The guidance is clear that a decision to use CVS should be shared on a strictly need to know basis and that nursing staff who are involved in the care of the child and family receive special training in this procedure.

Conclusion

This chapter has considered the key features of fabricated and induced illness. FII is recognised as a form of child maltreatment whereby a perpetrator, most usually the mother, repeatedly presents their child to health professionals with false histories of illnesses or more rarely with signs and symptoms of illnesses that are deliberately induced. A range of presentations have been outlined, but it is important to be open-minded about the possibility of organic illness as well as FII. Early referral to a paediatrician is recommended. The multi-agency response to FII involves key statutory agencies and is set within the framework for safeguarding and promoting the welfare of children and young people. Nurses and midwives have an important role to play in the identification and response to FII. Usual practice in the contemporary care of children, young people and their families is severely compromised when FII is suspected. At all times the focus needs to be firmly on the child's well-being and safety.

Messages for practice

- The key features of fabricated or induced illness are duped doctor, harmed child and fabricating parent.
- In comparison with other forms of child maltreatment, health professionals are involved with the child and family from the outset.
- Existing chronic illness does not exclude the possibility of induced illness
- In many instances the presentation is less dramatic than commonly believed. However, there may be an urgent need to prevent serious physical harm, or even death.
- False allegations of child maltreatment may form a presenting feature in some cases.
- An early multi-agency response is advocated.
- The point at which the perpetrator is challenged about the possibility of FII represents a danger point for the child.
- Children's nursing traditions of partnership with parents and family-centred care are severely compromised when FII is suspected. The welfare of the child is paramount.
- In the rare occasions when CVS is used this should be led by the police in accordance with statute and national protocols.

Recommended reading

All Wales Area Child Protection Committees (2004) *Safeguarding Children in Whom Illness is Fabricated or Induced.* Cardiff: All Wales Child Protection Review Group.

DH (Department of Health), Home Office, DfES (Department for Education and Skills), Welsh Assembly Government (2002) *Safeguarding Children in Whom Illness is Fabricated or Induced.* London: Department of Health.

Meadow, R. (1995) What is and what is not Munchausen Syndrome by Proxy? *Archives of Disease in Childhood,* **72**: 534–8.

Royal College of Paediatrics and Child Health (2002) *Fabricated or Induced Illness by Carers.* London: Royal College of Paediatrics and Child Health.

Seibel, M., Parnell, T.F. (1998) The physician's role in confirming the diagnosis, in T.F. Parnell and O. Day (eds) *Munchausen Syndrome by Proxy: Misunderstood Child Abuse.* London: Sage.

Terry, L. (2004) Fabricated or induced illness in children, *Paediatric Nursing,* 16(1): 14–18.

chapter **seven**

CHILD NEGLECT

Learning outcomes

This chapter will help you to:

- define and discuss child neglect;
- provide early preventative support and advice to families who are struggling to meet the needs of their children;
- debate the influence of poor socio-economic factors and other risk factors for child neglect;
- understand the potentially devastating outcomes for children and young people who are at risk of, or suffering from, neglect;
- identify and support families where there is concern about faltering growth;
- analyse the factors that may contribute to a practitioner's inability to recognise neglect;
- recognise the need for clinical supervision and support.

Introduction

The decision to devote a whole chapter of the book to issues surrounding the neglect of children and young people reflects both the complexities of definition and the importance of the roles of nurses and midwives in preventing, recognising and responding to this form of maltreatment. Universal services, such as health and education, have been acknowledged as being well placed to identify patterns of neglectful behaviour (Cantrill 2005; Daniel 2005), yet this is an area of practice that many will find especially demanding. Neglect is perhaps best viewed to be more insidious than other forms of maltreatment and it should be recognised as having the potential to lead to significant harm; as Stevenson (2005a:9) has suggested, outcomes for children who have suffered neglect may be 'grave and long lasting'. Neglect is also relatively common and is recognised to be both a predominant reason for referral to child protection agencies and to feature strongly in child fatalities and serious case reviews. Children who have been identified as at risk of, or suffering from, neglect are likely to remain under the care and supervision that is part of a child protection plan for longer than those identified as at risk of other forms of child maltreatment. According to the statistics available indicating the number of children and young people on child protection registers in England at 31 March 2006 (updated December 2006), there were a total of 13,700 registrations for neglect (this figure includes some children who were registered more than once during the preceding year). Registrations for neglect represent 43% of the total numbers of children and young people on the child protection register. See Chapter 3, pp. 61–3, for a fuller breakdown.

Health professionals need to be able to recognise that neglectful parents often have real difficulties in prioritising and meeting the health needs of their children, particularly if they have a number of small children who are close in age. Failure to meet these needs has been recognised to lead to an exacerbation of health problems, with the child subsequently becoming more unwell and difficult to manage (Stevenson 2005b). The issue of early identification and provision of support is vital.

A key challenge for nurses and midwives is the necessity to view neglect as being centred on a 'relationship' rather than an 'incident' and this can make recognition and referral difficult (Truman 2004). This is particularly so when working with children, young people and families suffering multiple deprivation. However, given that socio-economic factors are significant structural determinants of neglect, being able to distinguish between feeling sorry for struggling parent(s) and having an objective measure of the 'lived experience' of children and young people are arguably the most important skills for practitioners in ensuring their well-being and safety.

The chapter begins with a review of a 'headline' case of neglect that may be familiar to some readers. This case, involving the 'W' children from Sheffield, is important because it brings into the spotlight the care provided by midwives, the primary health care team, sexual health and mental health services. The recommendations from the subsequent serious case review (Cantrill 2005) provide important lessons for the future care of families who are experiencing multiple difficulties, especially in meeting the material, practical and emotional demands of parenting (the following chapter provides more details about the process of serious case reviews). The recommendations from the serious case review for the 'W' children are seen to build on previous work that has considered the contribution of neglect in children who have died in suspicious circumstances (Sinclair and Bullock 2002). There are clear lessons for the nursing and midwifery professions. The role of child-centred, holistic assessment in determining the need for additional support or statutory intervention is outlined with reference made to the use of formal frameworks to support decision-making and ensure that the 'lived experience' of the child is kept in focus. The roles of nurses and midwives in the prevention and early detection of neglect are crucial.

A discussion on the definition of neglect follows the case example and here we consider whether neglect should be seen as an issue of 'familial' or 'societal' causation. We then make reference to the work of Golden et al. (2003) who draw on their experience as paediatricians and argue cogently for a redefining of neglect according to intent. A section on 'faltering growth' and the growing use of this term in preference to 'failure to thrive' serves to introduce new understanding of this relatively common problem in infancy and early childhood. As practitioners who are often involved in monitoring the growth and development of children and young people, nurses and midwives need to be aware of action to be taken when normal parameters are not met. In some, but not all cases, neglect may be a contributing feature of poor growth and weight gain. A review of recent guidelines aims to help in identifying cases when early referral to other agencies is necessary. The work of O'Brien and colleagues (2004) who studied the relationship between faltering growth and postnatal depression will be of particular interest to midwives, health visitors and mental health practitioners.

The 'W' case

Case example
The 'W' family comprised young parents (both were 16 years of age when their first child was born) who at the time of the 'incident', which led to child protection and criminal proceedings, were parenting five children, including twins aged 13 months. In June 2004 ambulance and police services were called to the family home where they found all five children living in squalid and inadequate conditions (see BBC News Item 21/12/05). The physical condition of the twins was depicted as being extremely poor to the extent of being life-threatening; both were seriously malnourished and underweight. One of the twins was described as being 'moribund' and required full resuscitation and ventilation and both children spent five weeks in hospital before being taken into foster care.

Following a hearing in the Criminal Courts, the parents were both sentenced to seven years imprisonment for five counts of child cruelty. The judge at the trial concluded that the responsibility for the neglect of the children must rest with the parents.

Serious case review findings

The case of the 'W' children was subject to a serious case review (Cantrill 2005). The report of the review contains more details of the background and professional input to the family. The children's father (referred to as DA in the report) was said to have been in care from 13 to 18 years of age. He was reported as having had a poor attachment to his birth mother and experienced early loss and separation with the death of his grandmother and adoption of siblings. In January 2003 he was apparently referred to mental health services by his GP because he was said to be suffering from anxiety attacks. Although DA attended for an initial assessment, he did not attend either of two follow-up appointments. Cantrill's report is critical of the fact that the mental health services did not appear to have made any assessment of DA's ability to parent, in light of his mental health problems. Nor had they made any attempt to contact other agencies involved in the care of the family. In addition, Cantrill noted that the local care trust's mental health professionals had not undertaken any child protection training. Further concern should have been raised by the fact that domestic violence had been reported between DA and the children's mother (SJW) at this time.

Primary care, midwifery and sexual health services are also seen to have failed the family. During her four pregnancies SJW had had contact with a large number of midwives and this was seen to reduce the opportunities for offering her appropriate 'woman-centred' care. Although Cantrill (2005) deemed that the midwives' physical care to SJW had been appropriate, there was said to be little evidence that emotional, psychological and social needs were met or even assessed. The review of the case notes for the 'W' children also found that the handover from midwifery to health visiting care was inadequate. Health visiting practice itself was found to be particularly poor, and 'the little assessment undertaken was superficial' (p.14). Furthermore, the twins had notably poor attendance at routine developmental appointments, follow-up neonatal appointments and immunisation clinics. Health professionals, including the GP, apparently took few proactive steps to take any action over this important sign of neglect. Furthermore it was noted that SJW's attendance at sexual health services failed to provide her with adequate counselling and advice in relation to her pregnancies and requests for termination.

Points for reflection
Why do you think that the twins were not taken to routine developmental and immunisation appointments?

Professor Pat Cantrill, whose professional background includes nursing and health visiting, concurs with the criminal judgement. However, her report identifies many inadequacies in the practice of health and social care professionals attending the family. As with the inquiry into the death of Victoria Climbié (outlined in Chapter 1) it is important to acknowledge that the report was written with the benefit of hindsight, but that lessons for future practice are clear and valuable. The serious case review found evidence that led to a number of recommendations for improving professional practice and delivery of care to families who are experiencing multiple deprivation and complex difficulties (Cantrill 2005).

As Cantrill acknowledges, providing primary care services in areas of social deprivation is challenging, not least because the populations involved are unlikely to be able to prioritise preventative and health improvement activities. Thus it appears to be especially important to ensure that those families who are suffering from the effects of social deprivation and social exclusion are able to access and engage positively in the universal services to which they are entitled. It is crucial that nurses and midwives who practise in such areas are adequately supervised and supported in what are undoubtedly difficult roles. The political notion of 'progressive universalism' in the provision of public services seems to be entirely relevant here (see, for example, Prescott 2002; HM Government 2006e). Progressive universalism means that there should be a guaranteed minimum level of provision for everyone, with more for those who need it most. In practice this means that resources, including staff and facilities, are targeted based on assessed need. Nurses and midwives can help to ensure that public funds are used appropriately, and to their best advantage, through their contribution to timely local population-based health needs analyses, service planning and commissioning cycles.

Professor Cantrill's report on the 'W' children concluded that this was a family in which there were many indicators of potential vulnerability including the mother's obstetric history, frequent changes of address, five young children and poor engagement with services. A theme throughout the review is that the needs of the children did not take enough priority. All too often the services were focused on the needs of the adult, rather than how their (very real) needs might be impacting on the welfare and safety of the children. Certainly there would appear to have been a tolerance to sub-optimal levels of care of the children precipitated by low expectations of what parents could achieve given their social and economic circumstances. Cantrill argues that complex cases such as this demonstrate the need for practitioners to ensure that communication and information-sharing with all those involved in delivering services leads to a critical analysis of the situation in which the children find themselves and decisions on protective action that may be needed. As she notes, 'structural, cultural and individual deficiencies resulted in some services failing to have in place an effective benchmark for, or assertiveness in, the care of the 'W' children ... whilst it is right to expect parents to discharge their responsibilities, it is not good enough to assume that they will do so' (p.9). Ways in which a child-centred focus can be maintained while providing improved services to vulnerable families such as the 'W' children are reflected in the recommendations of the review, which are outlined below. The recommendations should be seen to extend beyond the circumstances of this case and judged as markers for good practice for the future.

Recommendations of the review

Cantrill's 59 recommendations go beyond important, but familiar, themes of serious case reviews (i.e. improving training, inter-agency working and record keeping) and include a recommendation that considers how extended family and communities may best be made aware of how to recognise and refer concerns about children. Specific recommendations for health services include the development of systems to follow-up children who default on appointments, improvements in the care of vulnerable women accessing sexual health services (to include a better understanding of the impact of repeated pregnancies on parenting ability), proactive holistic assessment processes to ensure maternal and child health needs are met and better inter-professional liaison. Importantly, the recommendations note that health visiting services should be promoted and their role recognised by other agencies. The health visiting service can thus provide an important channel for other health professionals' concerns. However, health visitors can only be successful in ensuring good safeguarding practice if services which focus primarily on the needs of adults (e.g. mental health) also recognise their duties in respect of children and young people where their clients are parents. Good information-sharing practice, following the principles outlined in Chapter 4, is crucial. However, above all, we return to the underlying theme of nurses and midwives undertaking holistic assessment and argue that this is essential in the early recognition and referral of neglect and provision of responsive and supportive care. This has been recognised as being good practice in recent policy documents.

The *Maternity Standard* of the National Service Framework for Children, Young People and Maternity (DH, DfES 2004b), for example, has built on earlier midwifery policy documents to encompass the importance of holistic woman-centred care. The standard is clear that maternity services should embrace the challenges of providing equitable and accessible services to those who are socially disadvantaged to improve maternal and child health outcomes. Obviously, when service design and delivery is built around an individualised approach there is more opportunity for professionals to develop a friendly and supportive relationship with those in their care, to identify wider health and social care needs and to refer appropriately where necessary. Transfer of care from midwifery to health visiting services is an important opportunity for ensuring that any additional needs have been recognised and action taken, or to be taken, is communicated and documented.

Points for reflection

Discuss with fellow students or colleagues how the NSF maternity standard may have helped to ensure more timely and appropriate care of the mother in the 'W' case.

If you are a midwife or health visitor, consider how the 'handover' and 'liaison' opportunities are utilised in your locality. How may this be improved?

One of the acknowledged difficulties for professionals caring for the 'W' family is that they were working in an area of socio-economic deprivation and that this led to lower levels of expectation as to what struggling parents might achieve for their children. However, it is important to have a benchmark for 'good enough' parenting that can be applied in any circumstance, if we are to intervene early to try and prevent poor outcomes for children and tackle the issues of inequality. The following section defines 'neglect' and offers a range of perspectives. However, ultimately, the main concern should be the impact of neglect on the safety and well-being of the child.

What constitutes child neglect?

Defining, and thus recognising, neglect is difficult. As Truman (2004) notes, neglect is complex and multidimensional and results from a number of interacting factors at an individual, familial, community and societal level. At a basic and perhaps simplistic level, neglect is often seen as a *failure* or *omission* by parents (very often the mother) in providing care for their child. This includes the failure to provide adequate food, warmth, shelter, access to health care, protection from harm and failure to meet a child's emotional needs. Thus the child becomes at risk of poor outcomes from unmet needs and the dangers associated with a lack of care and supervision (Daniel 2005). However, the issue of *persistence* of any failure to meet the needs of the child is an important dimension with the cumulative effects, rather than any 'incident' of neglect, being detrimental to the child (Truman 2004).

Case example
Joni and Troy aged 3 years and 5 years were frequently seen playing at the front of their house near a road while their parents, who were thought to drink alcohol quite heavily, were upstairs with the curtains drawn. Neighbours often gave them breakfast.

The notion of neglect as a persistent failure to meet a child's basic needs is reflected in Government guidance for England (*Working Together to Safeguard Children*, HM Government 2006a). It is notable that this edition expanded the previous categorisation of neglect to include the neglect of unborn children as a result of maternal substance abuse. As was noted earlier, the guidance also incorporated 'exclusion from home' (p.9) as a form of child neglect, this latter addition conceivably reflecting an increased political emphasis on parental responsibility and the expectation that parents provide shelter and care until their offspring reach adulthood. Many of the definitions of neglect appear to focus on physical indicators of neglect. However, emotional neglect is also an important dimension and one which arguably has a greater degree of intransigence. Emotional neglect has been reported to encompass a range of features including failure to show warmth, to provide comfort to a child who is ill or upset, to appreciate effort, to apply positive discipline and boundaries (e.g. appropriate television viewing) and to provide stimulation through outings and play opportunities. It can also relate to behaviour 'around' a child, for example allowing the child to witness parental arguments or making suicidal gestures and similar threats in front of them (Minty 2005). As Minty notes, many emotional needs are biological in origin, and meeting these needs is essential for future mental health and well-being. He suggests that it may be useful for practitioners who are concerned about the possibility of emotional neglect to ask parents some basic questions about their child, for example what they believe are their good points, or how they are getting on in school. A failure to reflect positively on aspects of their child's daily lives is seen to be indicative of an emotionally neglectful and potentially harmful relationship.

Children who are neglected are highly dependent on others to recognise and respond to their needs (Daniel 2005). Crucially however, the interpretation of the degree of failure to provide adequate care, and the judgement of an ongoing situation as being indicative of neglect (or not) rests on the assessment of the practitioner. Chester et al. (2006), for example, whose paper considers abuse and neglect in the context of children with burns and scalds, view neglect as being part of a spectrum that merges with 'pure accidents' and this raises considerable issues in relation to securing inter-professional and inter-agency agreements. Where children appear neglected because they are poorly dressed, slightly grubby, a bit underweight, missing appointments or seen to be allowed to 'run wild' objective decision-making can be extremely challenging.

Is neglect familial or societal?

Benchmarking 'good enough' parenting can be very difficult when working in an area of high material deprivation and need, yet the way in which society supports its children and families appears to be an important aspect in the epidemiology of neglect. There is wide-ranging evidence to suggest that risk factors associated with neglect include:

- poverty
- social exclusion
- family size (more than four children)

- family structure (single parenthood)
- family breakdown
- substance misuse
- domestic violence
- adult mental health problems
- adult learning disability
- maternal depression.

These factors can impact on the ability to provide for children in a variety of ways. The issue of substance misuse, for example, is seen to be important on two accounts; first because it can render parents drunk or semi-conscious and therefore unable to protect and care for their children, and second because habitual users suffer extreme financial difficulties with related issues of crime, evictions, debt and unemployment (Minty 2005). Parents with learning disabilities frequently come under the spotlight in relation to neglect and whilst they may well have difficulties in providing adequate care and control, this may be no different to those parents suffering from chronic or severe physical illness and disability (Minty 2005). The issue of ethnicity is considered by Spencer and Baldwin (2005) who note the additional stressors of stigmatisation and racism, which may co-exist with the risk factors noted above.

In other cases it is the characteristics of the children that present a risk for neglect. Kennedy and Wonnacot (2005) discuss the discrimination suffered by children who are disabled and suggests that they have a much greater risk of neglect (both familial and societal) when compared with their able-bodied peers. Whilst it would be entirely inappropriate to suggest that all families who fit into the above categories neglect their children, the central issue here is the way in which socio-economic factors can impact on the ability to parent, and this includes keeping the child safe from harm.

In an analysis of the accidental deaths of children (including those of undetermined intent), Edwards et al. (2006) found a dramatically higher death rate for children whose parents were classified as having never worked/long-term unemployed when compared with those from the higher managerial/professional occupations. Their bleak findings reflect Baldwin and Spencer's (2005) assertion that poverty and low income increases the pressure on parents (especially mothers) and makes the task of parenting much more difficult. The authors add that coping with adversity is especially difficult in the context of a consumer society where debt can be a feature of social exclusion. Golden et al. (2003: 107) suggest that 'societal neglect is as common as familial neglect' that results in, and from, poverty, and is linked to what they describe as unethical inequalities in the provision of health and social care and support for parenting. Thus, in a broad sense, society has to take some responsibility for creating the structures in which parenting happens, including the recognition that parents suffering from the effects of social deprivation and social exclusion may feel powerless and unable to meet all the competing demands of child care and family life. It is therefore not surprising that practitioners feel sympathy with these parents and conclude that they are not *deliberately* neglecting their children (Daniel 2005; Stevenson 1998). This theme has been central to recent analyses that consider the issue of intent and argue for a redefining of neglect.

Neglect versus deprivational abuse?

Golden et al. (2003) take the view that linking together 'abuse and neglect' in language and legislation has been unhelpful. They suggest that neglect is a somewhat milder term that reflects a non-deliberate failure to meet the needs of the child through stress, competing priorities, lack of education and socio-economic deprivation. Most parents, they add, would be guilty of neglect at some level as few are aware of, or able to meet, all of the needs of their children. Indeed, they go as far as suggesting that a degree of neglect is essential to normal development, as it means that children and young people will learn to understand that their needs cannot be met fully at all times and that they sometimes have to wait! The authors contrast this type of (normal) behaviour with a deliberate (intentional) or malicious failure to supply the needs of children and young people, which they call 'deprivational abuse' (p.105). The deliberateness of deprivational abuse, they suggest, makes this an act of *commission*, a view which clearly contrasts with the standard definitions of neglect.

Neglect, as described in the above paragraph, is thought to be much more common than deprivational abuse and is often directly related to the education and awareness of the parents or carers (Golden et al. 2003). Nevertheless, the authors are clear that while neglect may well be unintentional, over a period of time it is harmful for children. They remind us that children living in situations of 'low warmth, high criticism', as discussed in Chapter 3, may fair worse in the longer term than those experiencing assaults. Nurses and midwives will be very familiar with the scenario that they describe thus: young, unsupported and disorganised mothers, without 'training' (*sic*) in family life, typically with several young children, failing in the basic tasks of trying to feed, clothe and get their children to school, let alone providing the love and attention that they need. Golden et al. propose that mothers who are struggling are often aware of the fact that the care they are giving is 'not good' but are less aware of the severity of the effects of this care on their children. It is easy to question to what degree a 'child protection' route is appropriate for such families; but the serious impact of neglect on the child, whether intentional or not, does need to be acknowledged. In a related paper, Southall et al. (2003) make a very clear distinction between abuse, which they describe as being pre-meditated maltreatment perpetrated by disturbed and dangerous individuals, and mild abuse (which they see as being universal) and unintentional neglect. Daniel (2005) reminds us that while it is not necessary to establish the degree of intent to determine that a child is suffering from neglect, or to take action to safeguard their welfare, it is essential to consider intent in terms of deciding the best way to intervene.

Golden et al. (2003) also suggest that children can be neglected in an institutional setting such as a hospital. They describe the plight of 'malnourished children' who are quiet and undemanding, and who receive little attention from nursing staff. Those readers who are familiar with inpatient children's settings will be aware that such children very often do not have the benefit of a 'live-in' mother or father present with them as their parent(s) are, perhaps unwittingly, likely to be prioritising other children, or other demands. The well-being of these children is likely to be severely compromised and reminiscent of the behaviour observed so carefully by the pioneering and influential work of the Robertsons in the 1950s (Robertson 1959). More recently Kendrick and Taylor's (2000) analysis of the hidden abuse of children in hospital (including mental health facilities) reflects the continuing difficulties in ensuring care delivery that is in the best interests of children and young people. They argue that children in institutional settings need to be protected from harm, whether that is from the failures in clinical expertise and governance (Kennedy 2001), lack of appropriately trained staff who understand how to deliver child-centred care (including the need to provide adequate analgesia) or failure to protect children from physical or sexual assaults from staff, other patients or members of their family.

Despite the difficulties in defining neglect, Daniel (2005: 12), suggests that practitioners 'know a neglected child when they see one' and argues that the difficulties arise in knowing how to respond to what they see. While not everyone will agree with this view, she adds that the problems in determining intent may reflect the low rate of prosecutions or convictions. However, the case of the 'W children', discussed earlier in the chapter, reflects severe and life-threatening neglect that *did* lead to the criminal conviction of both parents. An important feature in this case, and in other 'headline' cases is the severe malnourishment of the children. Typically being underweight is seen to be an important sign of neglect, and assessment and monitoring of children's weight gain may lead to referral to the statutory agencies. However, the following section considers evidence that suggests that only a small minority of underweight children are likely to be suffering from neglect and that received wisdom and practice in cases of possible 'failure to thrive' is challenged.

Faltering growth (failure to thrive)

Adequate weight gain and growth in children is vital and it is widely recognised that the consequences for those whose weight gain is particularly poor may include some irreversible developmental delay and can result in the child being shorter as well as smaller. A recent definition of failure to thrive (FTT) is provided by Block et al. (2005) who suggest that this occurs when there is significant and prolonged failure to gain weight appropriately, usually demonstrated by a crossing of two major centiles in comparing the actual weight with expected weight for height. Nevertheless they do add that this judgement should be used with some caution as growth variants in young children are common.

Many practitioners (me included) will have been initially taught that FTT in childhood can be 'organic', i.e. due to illness, or 'inorganic' due to physical and/or emotional neglect. This latter group have been typically understood by health and social care practitioners as those children who eat, but do not grow, due to a 'syndrome' that includes emotional deprivation. Wright (2005) has cogently challenged this perception arguing that in most cases of poor weight gain or 'faltering weight' – her preferred term to FTT – the child is neither ill nor neglected. O'Brien et al. (2004) suggest that 'faltering growth' is a descriptive term that overlaps with failure to thrive, and can represent a transient, as well as a more persistent, problem with weight gain in young children. It would appear that faltering growth is a more contemporary and increasingly accepted description of problems with adequate weight gain in childhood, and that care of such children is increasingly focused within the community. However, notably, Hobbs et al. (1999a) take issue with the new terminology and argue that neglect is the most common cause of failure to thrive.

It is interesting to find that while Wright has found that faltering growth occurs across the population, she suggests that for those who are more affluent, the condition may actually go unrecognised or be labelled as 'something else'. Wright also points out that much of the early research and commentary on FTT reflected only hospitalised populations. This may have detracted from the suggestion that approximately 5% of all children show faltering weight at some point, due, in the main, to behaviour or dietary intake problems rather than illness or neglect. Wright believes that those children who have a serious medical condition will appear to be actively ill, and where weight is faltering in an otherwise well child, it may be stigmatising to suggest that they are neglected. However, she does acknowledge that in a small minority of cases the child *may well* be suffering from neglect and that this group will be the most challenging to care for. Similarly I would add that an assessment for faltering growth is an important facet of the care of children and young people who present with concerns about any form of maltreatment, as is the ongoing monitoring of weight, largely undertaken by specialist community public health nurses.

Block et al.'s (2005) analysis of failure to thrive (faltering growth) is less straightforward. These authors, who practise in North America, do recognise that the fundamental cause of FTT is nutritional deficiency, which they acknowledge can be unintentional, but suggest that it is more commonly linked with neglect. Additionally, they note that the causes may be multifactorial; for example, affecting children who typically have an organic problem (and their list includes cystic fibrosis, cerebral palsy, human immunodeficiency virus (HIV), inborn errors of metabolism, renal disease, lead poisoning and major cardiac disease) as well as subtle neurological or behavioural difficulties. In some cases they suggest that these causes of FTT are further compounded by dysfunctional parenting. Nevertheless, Block et al. do accept that under-nutrition appears to be the most common cause of faltering weight gain and that this group of children may, for whatever reason, eat less. In a paper that challenges Block et al.'s (2005) approach as being rather 'punitive' to parents, as well as inaccurate in its assertion that failure to thrive inevitably leads to developmental delay, Black et al. (2006) suggest that intellectual problems may not be as great as originally thought and remind us that many of the original studies on FTT were based on hospitalised children, who, we might assume, were both at the severe end of the spectrum and suffering the damaging effects of prolonged hospitalisation.

The issue of disability, however, is important here. Kennedy and Wonnacot (2005) make some very pertinent comments in relation to nutrition and weight gain for children with cerebral palsy. They suggest that parents may deliberately keep children and young people with cerebral palsy 'light' because this makes it easier to carry them.[1] In noting that these children may gain weight when they are cared for outside the home, they also add that where feeding difficulties are present, a parent or carer may 'give up' before a meal is completed and thus the child's growth (and development) will suffer. Nurses will also be interested in Kennedy and Wonnacot's challenge to the use of gastrostomy feeding (albeit used for supplementary feeds to ensure adequate calorific intake), arguing that whilst this makes mealtimes 'quicker', it denies the child the pleasure of taste. Their assertion that health care for these children can be 'parent-centred' (because professionals feel sorry for parents who care for disabled children) is an important one and illustrates the need for nursing staff and other health professionals to advocate wisely and judiciously to ensure that the best interests of the child are met.

Wright (2005) suggests that contributory factors to faltering weight (i.e. under-nutrition) include the high energy needs of infants and toddlers, poorer appetites in some and the fact that some children may be offered a rather limited range of foods or a 'well-meaning' but inappropriate diet. Certainly, in my practice I have come across parents who have been confused and misled by 'healthy eating' messages aimed largely at adult populations. These families have prepared high fibre or low-fat diets for their young children, for example by introducing semi-skimmed milk at too young an age. As the following section demonstrates, it is important that practitioners provide sensitive and supportive advice for parents, who may be struggling with the practical and emotional aspects of caring for a new life, and in some cases, coping with the effects of post-natal depression.

Case example
Jane, a nurse caring for her first baby, insisted on introducing skimmed milk as part of the mixed diet from 9 months of age, the age at which breast-feeding was stopped. She felt that whole milk (NB recommended from 1 year) gave her baby colic and refused to use formula. Disagreement with the health visitor led to Jane withdrawing from regular clinic contact. When she visited the health centre to ask for a weight for her daughter's first birthday there were clear signs of faltering growth.

Faltering growth and post-natal depression

A paper by O'Brien and colleagues (2004) recognises under-nutrition as a major cause of faltering growth and agrees that earlier understanding of FTT based on hospitalised populations does not reflect the issues across communities. Their work is seen to build on previous work that has recognised the adverse impact of postnatal depression on children's emotional and cognitive development. In a community-based case control study, in which specially trained health visitors undertook key data collection, they considered the relationship between faltering growth and post-natal depression. A major finding of the research was that mothers of children with faltering growth have a significant risk (almost twofold) of post-natal depression and anxiety when compared with mothers of children who are gaining weight as expected. There are important messages for practice, not least the assertion that 'The term failure to thrive may indicate to a depressed mother that she is unable to carry out one of her main responsibilities ... feeding her child adequately ...' (O'Brien and colleagues 2004: 1247). The use of a term that denotes 'failure' seems to me to be especially damaging to any mother, but especially one suffering from anxiety and/or depression. O'Brien et al. call for better collaboration between paediatricians and perinatal mental health teams, arguing that it is important to consider the 'mother-child' dyad in the management of post-natal depression and provision of advice in relation to nutrition and growth. They add that what is crucial here is a need for supervision and care that centres on ensuring adequate nutrition and reinforcement of positive parenting skills, rather than repeated measuring. The importance of the role of midwives and health visitors in the timely detection and management of both post-natal depression and faltering growth is seen to reflect, amongst other factors, the benefits of universal service provision.

Management of faltering growth

Wright (2005) suggests that in the majority of cases, faltering weight can be managed in the community and adds that health visitors are particularly well placed to lead on this due to the universality and non-stigmatising nature of the service. She believes that healthy children should be weighed every two to four weeks for the first four months of life and then every one to three months until a year old. For those whose weight appears to be faltering, an assessment, provision of dietary advice and advice on mealtime routines can lead to improved intake of food and improvement in weight gain. This can be reinforced through follow-up and the provision of written advice and through encouraging parents to keep a food diary. If progress is not maintained then referral for more specialist assessment may be necessary. However, it is important to remember that in a minority of cases, where child abuse and neglect feature, removal of the child from their family may be needed to achieve and demonstrate an improvement in weight gain. In some cases this may mean admission to hospital.

As a guide, Block et al. (2005), suggest hospitalisation for any child found to be less than 70% of their expected weight. They propose that any intervention needs to be underpinned by a careful assessment, not only of the child (and here their approach is chiefly medical) – i.e. history taking, physical and developmental assessment and systems review – but also of the parents, where a more socially based assessment including parental history of abuse, eating disorders, substance misuse, domestic violence, stressors and social skills is advocated. Concerns about child abuse or neglect should arise if there is intentional withholding of food, strong beliefs in health or nutrition regimes or resistance to multidisciplinary intervention. Block et al. suggest that failure to maintain more than 80% of expected weight post-discharge, despite aggressive intervention, should lead to consideration of child care proceedings. Although these seem to be well-founded guidelines, it is important to remember that they may not necessarily be directly applicable in the UK, where community provision (e.g. health visiting) is arguably more robust.

Assessment of neglect

In a helpful review of the complexities of identifying neglect, Truman (2004) suggests that predominance of external contributing factors make it difficult for practitioners to know whether to refer families for support or whether to make a referral to statutory agencies. Although it has been noted that neglect is a predominant reason for child protection activity, Daniel (2005) suggests that many children who are at risk of, or suffering from, neglect are still not subject to formal child protection proceedings. As we have suggested, this may be because of the difficulties associated with identifying and reporting a 'relationship' rather than an 'incident', but equally it could also relate to being drawn into the needs of parents. Holistic child-centred assessment is thus essential.

Recent evidence-based policy has promoted the need for tripartite assessments that incorporate evaluation of the developmental needs of the child, the parenting capacity to meet those needs, and the family and environmental factors which influence the ability to provide care (DH 2000b). Importantly, the assessments are very much carried out with the cooperation and input of the family, allowing strengths as well as needs to be documented and addressed. The theme of seeking out positive and protective factors as part of the child's 'lived experience' are also reflected in the Common Assessment Framework (HM Government 2006f) which has been introduced as part of the integrated service provision proposed in *Every Child Matters*. However, nurses and midwives could also consider the utility of a more detailed tool, developed specifically for use in the assessment and management of neglect. The 'graded care profile' (GCP) provides practitioners with a comprehensive bipolar measurement tool that facilitates objective assessment of parenting capacity and the means to negotiate targets for improving parenting and thus outcomes for the child. It centres on the commitment to care and, drawing on the work of Maslow, allows the practitioner to rate the care provided by parents in relation to physical care, safety, love and esteem on a scale of 1 (the best) to 5 (the worst). Those who have trialled the use of the GCP with practitioners and families argue that because it is the parents' caring instinct that protects against adverse socio-economic factors, the tool can identify good parenting in spite of poverty and hardship (Srivastava and Polnay 1997). What appears to be important here is that this is a tool to help practitioners keep focused on the needs of the child and not be distracted by their empathy and compassion for the parents. Yet it is also important to acknowledge the difficulties inherent in engaging with families who are suffering multiple disadvantages, especially in keeping a focus on the needs of the children and young people. Very often the parents who are struggling to provide 'good enough' care will be suffering from low self-esteem and believe that they neither have the ability to change nor can be helped by others to do so. Supervision for practitioners working with families in these circumstances is extremely important. As Stevenson (2005b: 110) notes: 'diffuse anxiety, confusion, hopelessness, even despair, denial and over-optimism are all linked to powerful identification with adults in the family'.

Working with families from different cultures adds further complexity to safeguarding children practice. However, as Taylor and Daniel (2005) note, factors associated with distress are very similar across all races and cultures. In some cases it may be necessary to obtain the help of outside interpreters to ensure that assessment is inclusive and meaningful. Equally, as assessment should seek out and record the views of the child (as soon as old enough to do so), specialist help may also be needed where children have communication difficulties. In all cases it is likely that practitioners will need to seek additional information from a range of sources to ensure an accurate and useful assessment. This may include gaining information from other health colleagues, education, social care, probation, police, housing and the voluntary sector. The role of the community in helping to identify and protect vulnerable children has been seen to be important (Cantrill 2005) and referrals and concerns of neighbours or extended family members should be taken seriously. The production of 'chronologies' of significant events, concerns and referral to other agencies may be extremely helpful in building a picture that reflects the ongoing parent–child relationship.

Conclusion

This chapter has focused on the issue of child neglect. We began by outlining a dramatic case of neglect that could easily have led to the death of at least one of the children. The practice of a range of health professionals, including midwives, mental health nurses, health visitors and those working in sexual health services was found to be wanting. Neglect can be both physical and emotional and there are likely to be difficulties in agreement as to thresholds for intervention. Neglect is closely related to the concept of 'good enough' parenting. While issues of possible intent or ignorance are important, the outcomes for the child or young person may be identical. As we have acknowledged, identifying neglect can be difficult, particularly for those who are faced with a caseload of families who are all experiencing multiple disadvantage. The importance of keeping the primary focus on the needs of children and young people is crucial. However, ultimately neglect may be first and foremost an issue for society and the way in which it treats, values and provides for its children and young people.

Messages for practice

- Nurses and midwives have a key role to play in the identification, prevention, recognition and response to neglect. Where the parent is the patient or client a consideration of the impact of health and social problems on the ability to parent is crucial.
- Neglect is a common reason for referral to child protection agencies and features strongly in serious case reviews.
- Poverty and social deprivation are strongly associated with neglect, but it is stigmatising to suggest that all families who live in poverty neglect their children.
- Neglect may be unintentional or intentional. In both cases, the effect on the child will be similar, but the intervention will be different.
- Neglect is a factor in some, but not all, cases of faltering growth (failure to thrive).
- Assessment should centre on the lived experience of the child. Supervision of practitioners working with families who are at risk of neglect is essential.

Recommended reading

Block, R.W., Krebs, N.F. and the Committee on Child Abuse and Neglect and the Committee on Nutrition (2005) Failure to thrive as a manifestation of child neglect, *Pediatrics*, **116**: 1234–7.

HM Government (2006) *Reaching Out: An Action Plan on Social Exclusion.* London: Cabinet Office.

Srivastava, O.P., Polnay, L., (1997) Field trial of graded care profile (GCP) scale: a new measure of care, *Archives of Disease in Childhood*, **76**: 337–40.

Taylor, J., Daniel, B. (eds) (2005) *Child Neglect: Practical Issues for Health and Social Care.* London: Jessica Kingsley.

chapter **eight**

CHILD DEATH AND CHILD MALTREATMENT

Learning outcomes

This chapter will help you to:

- understand the epidemiology of child deaths in the UK and the key factors related to fatal child maltreatment;
- examine the links between socio-economic disadvantage, child maltreatment and child death (including deaths from Sudden Infant Death Syndrome);

- explore the implications for nurses and midwives from analyses of serious case reviews;
- understand the principles and purpose of serious case review;
- be aware of the new processes for child death review;
- consider the messages for the prevention of child deaths and how these may impact on future practice.

Introduction

In the UK today the death of a child or young person is an unusual event. When death does occur, it may be expected or anticipated, for example due to a congenital abnormality or life-limiting illness. However, for a significant number of children and young people, death will be sudden and unexpected. Unexpected deaths may be due to an accident, for example a road traffic fatality, but a 'small percentage' (Kennedy et al. 2004) will be the result of intentional injury or child neglect. In all cases, whether expected, unexpected or suspicious, it is important to understand why a child or young person has died and to use this information both to gain insight into the individual death and to ensure that any messages for prevention and the future protection of children are fed into policy, legislation and practice. Nurses and midwives have an important role to play in this process.

Jenny and Isaac (2006: 265) note that 'The death of a child is a sentinel event in a community, and a defining marker of a society's policies of safety and health'. In keeping with the broad definition of safeguarding and in recognition of the need to promote the welfare of children and young people, this chapter considers the causes of death in childhood and the processes that are in place to review such deaths. Nurses and midwives may well be familiar with the 'serious case review' process in cases where a suspicious death or serious injury has been identified (sometimes referred to as a 'Part 8 Review'). However, at the time of writing there are moves in parts of the UK to introduce a more inclusive process that objectively evaluates *all* childhood deaths within a locality with a view to improving the safety and well-being of the child population. Lessons from countries that already have a child death review process (i.e. the United States, Canada and Australia) are helpful here. This chapter therefore provides an outline of both serious case review and the new child death review process. The chapter opens with an overview of childhood deaths in the UK.

Child death in the UK: an overview

There was a dramatic decline in death rates for children in the UK during the twentieth century (Office for National Statistics, ONS 2002). This was particularly so in relation to infant mortality and is linked to improvements in population health and living conditions. The majority of childhood deaths today occur in the youngest age groups, although the main causes of death vary according to different age bands. Deaths within the first month of life are linked to prematurity, congenital malformations and conditions arising in the perinatal period. These continue to be important factors in deaths that occur in the first year of life. Other major causes include infections, cancers and 'other medical diagnoses'. However, about a quarter of infant deaths are categorised as being due to external causes and those 'not elsewhere classified'. A proportion of these will be due to 'sudden infant death syndrome' (see below). In the middle childhood years natural causes of death predominate with infections, cancers and other medical causes accounting for over three-quarters of deaths. In adolescence the pattern changes, with over half of deaths during this period arising from external causes such as accidents, homicide and suicide (ONS 2006).

Links between socio-economic disadvantage and childhood death rates have been identified. These are particularly marked in relation to deaths from injury and poisoning (both accidental and of undetermined intent) in families where parents have never worked or are long-term unemployed, where rates have not fallen in line with other socio-economic groups (Edwards et al. 2006). Clearly these deaths should be viewed as potentially preventable and nurses and midwives can play a part in helping to ensure that children and young people are safe and healthy. Addressing disadvantage and targeting health care to deprived families in line with the notion of progressive universalism, as discussed in Chapter 7, should be viewed as potentially life-saving work.

Fatal child maltreatment

The true incidence of fatal child maltreatment is, not surprisingly, unknown and is hampered by difficulties in definition, recognition and reporting (Hobbs et al. 1999a; Jenny and Isaac 2006; UNICEF 2003). These difficulties include the fact that various data sources are used to derive child mortality statistics. Linked to this is the debate about the use of terminology. Child homicide is a term that is used to cover the offences of murder, manslaughter and infanticide, although there are some maltreatment deaths that will not be defined or recorded in this way. Hobbs et al. (1999a) use the terms fatal abuse and child homicide interchangeably, but recognise that some authors view child homicide as being the result of a single fatal assault and fatal child maltreatment as a consequence of assault and neglect over a longer period of time. The perpetrator is usually a parent or carer. Stranger killings of children are extremely rare (Wilczynski 1997).

Infanticide relates specifically to the death of an infant under the age of 12 months. In England and Wales this term is given legal status and relates to the killing by a mother where 'the balance of her mind was disturbed by reason of her not having fully recovered from the effects of giving birth to the child or by reason of the effects of lactation consequent upon the birth of the child'. (The Infanticide Act 1922, amended 1938). Various risk factors for infanticide are summarised by Jenny and Isaac (2006) and include: young maternal age, low level of education, unmarried, no antenatal care, low birth weight, male infant and a low Apgar score. The term 'filicide' may alternatively be applied to describe the killing of their offspring by a parent. For newborn infants the term 'neonaticide' may be used. In most cases of neonaticide the perpetrator is the mother who kills her infant on the first day of life. Common characteristics of the women in such cases are said to include: a denial of being pregnant, a claim not to experience pain during delivery, childhood physical or sexual abuse and suffering from psychotic or dissociative states (Jenny and Isaac 2006). Wilczynski (1997) notes that neonaticidal women may not seek health care for their pregnancy, but may concurrently present to professionals for other conditions.

Points for reflection
Discuss with fellow students or colleagues how your practice may contribute to identifying those who are at risk of infanticide.

Official statistics

Drawing on official homicide figures from the Home Office, the NSPCC report that, on average, every week in England and Wales one or two children under 16 years of age are killed at the hands of another person. Two-thirds of these deaths are in children aged 5 years or less, and in 60% of all cases parents are the principal suspects. Infants of under 1 year of age are most at risk of being killed and in these cases the likelihood of the parent as perpetrator is 'exceptionally high', with mothers and fathers equally likely to commit the killing (NSPCC Inform 2006). The risk of death from child maltreatment diminishes with age (Hobbs et al. 1999a).

Scotland and Northern Ireland have much smaller populations of children and young people. Figures from Children 1st (Royal Scottish Society for the Prevention of Cruelty to Children) record that 10 children under the age of 16 were victims of homicide in 2002 in Scotland (Children 1st 2006). Bunting's (2004) report on child protection statistics for Northern Ireland notes that in 2002 there were two deaths of children following assault and a further death that was classified as being caused by an event of an 'undetermined nature'.

International studies of filicide conclude that official figures may grossly under-represent the true numbers of children killed by their parents or carers (Greenland 1987; Wilczynski 1997). Fitzgerald (1998) suggests that a figure of 100 deaths per year is likely to be an underestimate. As Dale et al. (2002: 5) note:

> The process of determining the likelihood of injuries being the result of accidents or other non-abuse is a real challenge to all of the disciplines within child protection systems. The difficult task is to identify and ensure sufficient protection for children who really are in danger, whilst maintaining a fair process for parents whose children have been injured (accidentally or otherwise).

Importantly, Hobbs et al. (1999a) suggest that where there is any degree of uncertainty as to the cause of death parents are given the benefit of the doubt because of the tragedy of losing their child.

Points for reflection

Do you agree with Hobbs et al.'s analysis?

Do you think that sufficient attention is given to exploring the reasons why children die?

Causes of fatal child maltreatment

Head trauma is the most common cause of fatal child maltreatment, especially in babies and younger children. This is discussed in some depth in Chapter 4. Other presentations of deaths from child maltreatment include multiple injuries, suffocation, deliberate poisoning, sexual assault and those deaths that are associated with neglect (Hobbs et al. 1999a).

Case example

Although Jordan, aged 13 months, was pyrexial when he was put in his cot, his parents did not check him until some 15 hours later. By this time he had been dead for a number of hours. Cause of death was given as 'respiratory infection' but there were clear signs of neglect and a history of multiple house moves and domestic abuse.

Perpetrator motive

Wilczynski (1997) reviewed child homicide in England, Wales and Australia and concludes that many child killings escape detection. In her analysis of perpetrator motive, she found a range of factors linked to the killings that include: retaliation against a background of domestic violence; jealousy of, or rejection by the child; unwanted children (especially in neonaticide); physical punishment; altruistic (mercy) killing; induced illness; psychosis and ritual abuse. In relation to filicide as a result of physical punishment, Wilczynski found that parents had typically admitted to assaulting their child in a fit of temper and had not meant to inflict serious harm. One of her key recommendations for reducing child deaths from filicide is the banning of corporal punishment and the introduction of more positive means of enforcing discipline. She notes that 'The social and legal approval of corporal punishment needs to be seen in the context of children's powerlessness, as does child abuse and filicide more generally' (p.54).

Risk factors for fatal child maltreatment

Family composition appears to be an important risk factor for fatal child maltreatment. One study, published in the United States, found that children living in a household with an unrelated adult were 27 times more likely to die of inflicted injury than of natural causes when compared with children living with one or both biological parents, with most of these deaths related to the presence of unrelated males and 'mother's boyfriends' (Stiffman et al. 2002). The authors also found a link between greater risk of fatal child maltreatment in families where there are adoptive, foster or step-parents. However, Dale and colleagues' study in the UK found that only one of a series of 17 serious case reviews they examined had a natural parent/step-parent combination. Key to their findings was that it was generally an only child or the youngest child that suffered the fatal or serious injury that had led to the review.

Parental mental health problems were found in 32 of 100 serious case reviews examined by Falkov (1996), in 18 of the 38 cases reviewed by Dale et al. (2002) and 18 of the 40 cases reviewed by Sinclair and Bullock (2002) suggesting that this too may be an important risk factor. As they and others (e.g. Sanders et al. 1999) have commented, child health services and mental health services should work more closely together and each should consider and understand the needs of all those in the family.

In their study of 19 serious case reviews undertaken in Wales between 1991 and 1996, Sanders et al. (1999) found material problems such as financial and housing concerns to be a very common characteristic, although relationship problems between parents also featured prominently. This was also the case in Sinclair and Bullock's (2002) sample where the 'norm' was said to be frequent arguments. Other important patterns of concern that emerge from the serious case review literature include the risk factors that are well recognised in relation to child maltreatment generally, such as parents' past history of childhood abuse, previous suspicious injuries in the child, escalation of threat and harm, domestic violence and parental substance misuse.

Presentation

Wilczynski (1997) reviewed the presentations of child homicide cases and concluded that filicidal parents often initially deny killing their child. They may claim that their child died from accidental or natural causes. Examples include parents who say that they were carrying the child and tripped or slipped, that the child fell from a low height and struck their head on the floor or a hard object, or choked, turned blue or had a fit, or were unexpectedly found dead. Furthermore, the difficulties in obtaining evidence and the reluctance of professionals to either suspect or to act on suspicions because of what Wilczynski describes as the 'abhorrent nature' of the topic means that cases will be missed.

The notion of 'discrepant explanations' proposed by Dale et al. (2002) is important here. These authors reviewed the case management and/or serious case reviews (Part 8 Reviews) of a number of seriously or fatally injured infants and toddlers under the age of 24 months, where the parent(s) had given either no explanations or explanations that were inconsistent, conflicting or considered implausible by expert medical opinion. Here a common explanation, if one was given at all, was that the baby had suddenly become seriously unwell. Parents had also reported inadvertently hurting the baby whilst, for example, holding them to administer eye drops (this was in the case of an 8-week-old baby with multiple rib fractures). Others claimed that the injuries were self-inflicted, for example trapping their leg whilst sleeping (in the case of a 6-week-old baby with a spiral fracture of the tibia). Another common explanation was where one parent accused the other or reported that a boisterous elder sibling may have caused the injuries.

Dale et al. (2002) recognise that the diagnosis of abuse (or non-abuse) often rests on uncertainty and that this can raise conflict amongst professionals and unimaginable anguish for parents. They draw on US studies undertaken in emergency departments that have demonstrated that babies and young children, like anyone else, can present with accidental injuries. Nevertheless, they do suggest that approximately one-quarter of injury presentations in babies and young children are likely to be as a result of maltreatment. The literature also suggests that in contrast to intentional injuries, accidental injuries are likely to be less serious or complex and rarely result in permanent disability. Parents of babies and children who present following accidents are also more likely to provide an explanation that fits the presentation and the developmental stage of the child.

Where cases are brought before the court, the criminal justice system is generally more compassionate in its treatment of mothers who kill in comparison with that of fathers. Mothers are more likely to get a probation order alongside a recommendation for mental health treatment and fathers given a custodial sentence (Hobbs et al. 1999a). Wilczynski (1997) summarises these differences as 'mothers mad' and 'fathers bad' and suggests that narrow conformity to gender types may actually lead to filicide with mothers being overburdened with child care and domestic responsibilities and fathers' exclusion leading to jealousy and retaliation.

Points for reflection

In July 2004 a father smothered his 10-year-old son who was suffering from Hunter's Syndrome. The subsequent court case and sympathetic treatment of the father received widespread publicity.

How should such a death be classified?

Fall-out deaths

Jenny and Isaac (2006) note that child deaths that result from emotional abuse or neglect are rarely identified or classified as child maltreatment deaths. Their examples of deaths from neglect suggest parental failure to respond appropriately to the health and developmental needs of children, and this includes providing measures for their safety. Deaths from neglect may include those from starvation, neglect in providing life-saving medical care (including the use of faith healers), inadequate supervision and exposure to extreme heat or cold. Furthermore, they found that children and young people who have been victims of child maltreatment, especially physical abuse, face a much greater risk of dying before their 18th birthday when compared to their non-abused peers. Causes of such deaths are said to include suicide linked to depression, the increased likelihood of fatal substance misuse and deaths from other risk-taking behaviour. There are important opportunities for nurses and midwives to take preventative action to prevent these so called 'fall-out' deaths.

Points for reflection
Could failure to ensure that a child is safely restrained when travelling in a vehicle be construed as child neglect?

Despite the individual tragedies that the fatal child maltreatment figures represent, it is important to remember that these deaths are a rare and often unpredictable event (Falkov 1996; Axford and Bullock 2005). This latter point is important in the context of the 'blame culture' when deaths from maltreatment become headline news. As Sanders et al. (1999: 257) note, this 'can create an unhelpful "witch hunt" scenario in which the process is directed as much at targeting blame as avoiding recurrences'. The following section discusses the ways in which cases of fatal or serious child maltreatment are reviewed in an effort to learn from what happened and to improve practice for the future.

Serious case review

When a child dies and maltreatment is known or suspected, a local case review will be undertaken to consider lessons to be learned about the ways in which organisations work together to safeguard and promote the welfare of children, and to help to prevent similar tragedies in the future. Sanders et al. (1999) discuss the trend in the UK to replace high profile inquiries of previous times, for example the public inquiry into the death of Maria Colwell (DHSS 1974), with an internal review process. Although the findings of such reviews are sometimes made public, the names of the children and family are generally not. Nurses, midwives and other health professionals have an important contribution to make to serious case reviews, both in terms of making available details of clinical care provided to the child and their family, and also in taking forward recommendations for future delivery of services across local populations.

At the time of writing the procedures are similar for England, Wales and Northern Ireland, whereas Scotland is consulting on a single approach to 'significant incident review' (see below). In England, LSCBs are responsible for ensuring that 'serious case reviews' are undertaken in line with the government guidance in Chapter 8[1] of

Working Together (HM Government 2006a). In addition to reviewing cases when a child dies in suspicious circumstances (including death by suicide), serious case reviews may also take place when a child: sustains a potentially life-threatening or permanent injury; has been subjected to particularly serious sexual abuse; has lost a parent through murder; has been killed by a parent with a mental illness; or the case gives concern as to inter-agency working to protect children from harm. Any other cases that are likely to be of public interest can also be subject to a serious case review. This may include concerns about maltreatment in institutional settings such as nurseries, schools, young offender institutions or Armed Services training establishments. Any professional can refer a case to the LSCB for a serious case review if it is believed that there are important lessons to be learned about inter-agency working. The Secretary of State for the DfES also has the legal powers to ask for a review.

The purpose of serious case reviews is to:

- 'establish whether there are lessons to be learned from the case about the way in which local professionals and organisations work together to safeguard and promote the welfare of children;
- identify clearly what those lessons are, how they will be acted upon, and what is expected to change as a result; and
- as a consequence, to improve inter-agency working and better safeguard and promote the welfare of children.'

(HM Government 2006a: 142–3)

LSCBs are expected to establish a 'Serious Case Review Panel' to consider the evidence for a review. This should include representatives from health alongside those from the local authority children's social care, education and the police. The ultimate decision on whether or not a serious case review should take place rests with the Chair of the LSCB. Health professionals from the PCT are expected to inform the Strategic Health Authority (SHA) of any case which becomes subject to a serious case review. The review panel will consider the scope of the review and draw up clear terms of reference. This will include deciding how and what information will be obtained, to appoint an author to write an independent overview report (see below) and to make a decision as to whether outside expertise, including legal advice, will be required. It is important that any lessons learned from serious case reviews are acted upon as quickly as possible. Although reviews will vary in their complexity, tight timescales are set. Decisions whether or not to hold a review are expected to be made within one month of a case coming to the attention of the LSCB Chair and the overview report would normally be completed within four months. This means that individual agencies are expected to secure records at the earliest opportunity in order to begin work on a chronology of their involvement with the child and family. In some cases there will be concurrent criminal proceedings, and while this may affect completion or publication of serious case review findings, it should not stop early lessons from being implemented (HM Government 2006a).

Each organisation is responsible for undertaking a management review of its involvement with the child and family, which will be considered in the development of the overview report. Designated and named health professionals will normally lead on this process unless either they have had direct involvement with the case or are the immediate line manager of the practitioner(s) involved. Feedback and de-brief is especially important as the process can be extremely stressful for staff. Although serious case reviews are not part of any disciplinary proceedings, if information that arises suggests malpractice then disciplinary action may be needed. The *Working Together* guidance on serious case reviews provides a useful outline, together with prompts, to assist in the analysis of agency involvement and in the making of recommendations for action (p.149). Copies of the overview report, action plan and individual management reports are sent to the Commission for Social Care Inspection (CSCI) and to the DfES. The DfES, in keeping with the tradition of the DH who previously held responsibility for safeguarding children policy and practice, will continue to commission overview studies of serious case reviews on at least a two-yearly basis, drawing out key findings and considering the wider implications for policy and practice.

In Wales, at the time of writing, the 'all Wales procedures' highlighted in Chapter 4 currently follow the guidance on serious case reviews from the 1999 edition of *Working Together.* In essence this is very similar to the 2006 guidance, although guidance specifically for Wales is pending. In Scotland, there has been no standard approach to reviewing fatal and serious child maltreatment. However, the Scottish Executive (2006b) is currently consulting on the processes for what is labelled as 'significant incident review'. There are parallels with the other systems in the UK, and the suggestion is that a serious incident review takes place when:

- 'abuse or neglect is known or suspected to be a factor in the child's death;
- the child is on, or has been on, the child protection register (CPR) or a sibling is on the CPR ... regardless of whether or not abuse or neglect is known or suspected to be a factor in the child's death unless it is absolutely clear that having been on the CPR has no bearing on the case;
- the death is by suicide;
- the death is by murder;
- the child was being "looked after" by the local authority.'

Scottish Executive (2006b: 7)

The consultation document also suggests that a significant incident review should take place when an abused or neglected child has not died, but whose maltreatment gives rise to concerns about professional or service involvement. The proposal for carrying out a significant incident review rests on the actions of involved agencies working in liaison with the Chair of the Child Protection Committee (CPC). After completing an 'initial review' a decision will be made by the CPC as to the need for a further review, if necessary by commissioning an external agency to undertake the work. A key theme from the consultation document is one of consistency in process, structure and content of reports. As with other UK systems, action-oriented recommendations for practice and plans as to the implementation of any changes form an important part of the process. Families and carers of the child or young person involved should be kept fully informed of the process, where appropriate (with regard to any concurrent criminal investigations). A final version of an anonymised report will be published and copies sent to the Scottish Executive.

In Northern Ireland, when a child dies and abuse or neglect are known or suspected to be a factor in the death, procedures for a 'Case Management Review' as laid out in Chapter 10 of *Co-operating to Safeguard Children* (DHSSPS 2003) should be followed. This states that Health and Social Services Trusts should inform the Chair of the Area Child Protection Committee (ACPC) and the Director of Social Services of the circumstances of the case. In addition to deaths from possible child maltreatment, case management reviews may also be undertaken where there has been potentially life-threatening injury, permanent impairment of health and concerns about the way in which local professionals and services have worked together to safeguard children.

Lessons to be learned

Axford and Bullock (2005), who were commissioned by the Scottish Executive to explore the ways in which other countries conducted 'significant case reviews', suggest that the recommendations from reviews of child deaths and serious injuries could be somewhat cumbersome and expensive. They add that the process may also reinforce an adversarial and forensic approach that may not reflect the bulk of safeguarding children work, where children and young people who are 'at risk' are protected within their own homes with the help of family support services. However, they did note that all of the 16 countries that they studied (their list includes England, Wales and Northern Ireland) had, in recent times, strengthened their child protection policies and sought to enhance children's rights, although arguably the contribution of the serious case review process to this is difficult to gauge. In an earlier paper, Sinclair and Bullock (2002) noted that death and serious injuries may not tell us about child maltreatment in general and that a wider monitoring of successful intervention would be helpful. Corby (2006) comments that fatal maltreatment is extremely rare and that underlying rates should not be used to gauge or monitor the success or otherwise of child protection systems.

Nevertheless, the serious case review process lays claim to being chiefly about learning lessons locally and to providing an opportunity to share good practice rather than being a 'trial or ordeal' (HM Government 2006a). The suggestion here is that recommendations should be focused on a few key areas with specific and achievable proposals for change. The guidance adds that PCTs should seek feedback on their reviews and action plans from their SHA and that this process is embedded in the SHA's performance management role. Clearly, to be useful, it is important that serious case reviews lead to improvements in practice that better protect children and young people in the future. Sanders et al. (1999) are critical of the fact that serious case reviews do not attempt to address the causes of child maltreatment fatalities, but rather concentrate on whether procedures have been followed or should be amended. However, one of the key features of both individual serious case reviews and various analyses of series of reports is that similar messages for practice are evident.

In their study of 17 serious case reviews undertaken in the South of England, Dale et al. (2002: 37) discuss problems with 'health management and misjudgements'. For example, in almost half of the cases they noted that serious antenatal concerns had been recorded, but that the level of concern appeared to evaporate as responsibility shifted between professionals. This has important ramifications for the transfer of care from midwife to health visitor, as well as the need to ensure that a plan is in place to ensure the safety and well-being of the baby once born. They also suggest that inadequate health provision and medical mismanagement were apparent in seven of the 17 cases. In these cases the infants had been seen by health professionals for routine checks but general practitioners, health visitors and, in some cases paediatricians, had not detected or suspected serious injuries that were later apparent at post-mortem examination. These old injuries include healing rib fractures, skull fractures, limb fractures and brain damage from subdural haematoma. Whilst they recognise that these were 'hidden' injuries they comment that contextual concerns, including distress in the infant, should have led to further urgent medical investigations.

Case example

Unusually, Charlie's father stayed with him during a hospital stay for investigations of vomiting and sleepiness. He had been referred by the GP following consultation with the health visitor. Nursing staff found

Charlie's father most protective of his son and happy to undertake all the routine care. One week following discharge Charlie was rushed to the emergency department in a moribund condition. The post-mortem found evidence of old and new head injuries and three healing rib fractures.

In their study, which was commissioned by the DH, Sinclair and Bullock (2002) analysed the findings of 40 serious case reviews of children who were 'all born in the UK', 31 of whom had died. It is, perhaps, remarkable that one of the children was physically disabled, four had special educational needs and five had what were described as 'significant health problems'. Two specific background factors were mentioned as possible indicators of inadequate parenting; these were poor antenatal care in eight cases and irregular attendance at playgroup or school in 11 cases. A further significant finding was that the families had generally been involved with a large number of both child- and adult-oriented services in the two years leading up to the incident.

In their Welsh study, Sanders et al. (1999) used a framework for analysis that captured both quantitative and qualitative data. This framework enabled a consideration of the frequency of agency contact and pattern of inter-agency communication. Seven key themes emerged from the analysis. These were:

- an unstructured approach to assessment;
- poor inter-agency communication;
- failure to accept responsibility;
- involvement of a large number of professionals;
- general practitioners who were 'peripheral' to the child protection process;
- insufficient training for paediatricians/radiologists;
- parents being given too much 'choice'.

Sanders et al. discuss each of these factors and make links with similar findings from previous inquiries and reviews. The issue of 'parental choice' appears to be a more recent concern compared to the others and one that the authors link to notions of 'partnership' and 'closure'. Whilst health and social care policy has embraced 'choice' as its watchword – see, for example, *The National Service Framework for Children, Young People and Maternity* (DH, DfES 2004) – it will be important to ensure that new approaches to maternal and child health care delivery recognise that the welfare of the child is paramount. This means that there may be situations where practitioners have to go against parents' wishes to ensure the safety and well-being of the child, and such an action is clearly supported by the 'paramountcy principle' of the Children Act 1989. Although their research uncovered a somewhat *traditional* pattern of concerns about professional knowledge and practice, especially that concerning inter-agency communication, Sanders et al. conclude that it is very difficult to make any connection between poor practice and a fatal outcome, because much of what happens in every day safeguarding children work is not routinely monitored or scrutinised. Furthermore, they pick up on the issue of the unpredictable nature of the deaths and serious injuries captured in their review. This can be illustrated by one of their cases: 'The tragic event that occurred although suggestive of being premeditated was not predictable [*sic*] by staff. The committee does not believe that any inaction on the part of the staff led directly to the child's death' (Sanders et al. 1999: 263). Even so, it is likely that a front-line practitioner who has a child on their caseload who dies in suspicious circumstances will need a great deal of help and support in making their contribution to the serious case review.

The importance of health services

Axford and Bullock (2005) comment that although social workers are often seen to have the remit for child care, most front-line workers in serious case reviews are health professionals, closely followed by police and teachers. Thus, they argue, the problem is not one of incompetent social workers (as so often portrayed in the press) but of identification, assessment and action by others. Sinclair and Bullock (2002: 33) describe the contribution of health as 'very substantial', and highlight the roles of GPs and health visitors in particular. Good safeguarding practice must reflect an ability to communicate and work with other services. As highlighted in Chapter 1, nurses' and midwives' success in safeguarding children is dependent on a sound knowledge base, accessibility of supportive advice and clinical supervision, and engagement in integrated working with other children's services. Failings in these three areas are perhaps epitomised by some of the past findings of serious case reviews, although the views of those who have questioned the authority of such reports are noted.

Sudden Unexpected Death in Infancy

Sudden Unexpected Death in Infancy (SUDI) is the term applied when an infant dies unexpectedly and may be caused by a 'myriad' of conditions that include organ-specific disorders, metabolic diseases, infectious diseases, genetic diseases, accidents and homicide (Jenny and Isaac 2006). Most SUDI deaths, however, are unexplained and thus meet the definition of Sudden Infant Death Syndrome (SIDs). This is now discussed.

SIDS

SIDS is defined as the sudden unexpected death of an infant (aged younger than 1 year) for which a detailed post-mortem examination and a review of clinical history and the circumstances of the death, fail to find an explanation. SIDS is likely to occur as a result of a variety of factors, rather than having a single cause (Jenny and Isaac 2006). It is sometimes referred to as 'cot death'. Most SIDS deaths occur during the first eight months of life, with a peak incidence at two to four months. Although the syndrome is seen across all social groups, it is much more prevalent in socially disadvantaged groups where mothers are more likely to be young, single, to smoke, or to live in a household with smokers, and to formula feed, rather than breast feed their babies. Other important risk factors include prematurity and multiple births, prone sleeping and possibly bed-sharing (Hobbs et al. 1999a; Blair et al. 2006; Jenny and Isaac 2006). The number of deaths from SIDS has fallen dramatically in the UK and elsewhere since the 'Back to Sleep' campaign promoted the evidence for placing babies to sleep on their back, rather than prone (i.e. on their front). Craft and Hall (2004) suggest that, as the rates have fallen, the social class gradient has become steeper.

Importantly, Blair et al. (2006) note that side-sleeping is unsuitable for small infants who could roll onto their front, yet find that it is still recommended by some midwives and neonatal nurses, despite the lack of any firm evidence that supine sleeping leads to the risk of aspiration of vomit. They also recommend that parents should be advised not to co-sleep with their infants on a sofa, as they found evidence to suggest that this appears to be associated with a greater risk of SIDS.

Points for reflection
What advice is given locally to new parents in relation to sleeping arrangements for their baby? Is this different for those infants who are being discharged from a neonatal unit?

Essentially, SIDS is a diagnosis of exclusion, although it is recognised that for a small percentage of deaths that are initially labelled as SIDS, maltreatment or 'covert homicide' (Levene and Bacon, 2004) may be a factor. Hobbs et al. (1999a) highlight research that has found an association between cot death and child abuse by comparing rates of SIDS for families with siblings of children on child protection registers with national and local rates. Yet, given the association of both SIDS and child maltreatment with social deprivation, the issue is far from clear cut. The work of Reece (1993), in the United States, has been widely promoted in helping to differentiate between SIDS and fatal child abuse and other medical conditions. Factors that Reece finds suggestive of maltreatment include: age outside of the norm for SIDS; discrepant or unclear history; prolonged interval between bedtime and death; skin injuries; malnutrition; physical signs of neglect; unwanted pregnancy; little or no antenatal care; no immunisations or well-baby checks; use of drugs/alcohol and tobacco during and after pregnancy; unusual feeding practices; hostility and discord in caretakers; more than one previous unexplained death; and involvement of police or child protection services on more than two occasions. In the UK, Craft and Hall (2004) draw together the evidence on a 'substantial relationship' between unexplained death and social background: social chaos; poverty; parental mental illness; prematurity; parental smoking and substance misuse; and pre-existing symptoms of illness in the baby. However, such a relationship is not by any means diagnostic of child maltreatment.

While the fall in the number of SIDS deaths is to be celebrated, there is now speculation that the proportion of such deaths which may in fact be due to homicide (child maltreatment) has risen. As Jenny and Isaac (2006: 267) note: 'suffocation of an infant with a plastic bag or a soft item such as a pillow can be indistinguishable from SIDS in a post mortem examination. This leaves investigators in a terrible dilemma, particularly if more than one infant dies unexpectedly in a family.' Certainly there has been a recent spate of cases in the UK where suspicion has fallen on families that have suffered more than one apparent SIDS death. However, the literature suggests that because the same genetic factors and environmental risk factors that predispose to a first SIDS death can persist in families, each case of multiple infant deaths must be objectively and carefully evaluated (Levene and Bacon 2004; Jenny and Isaac 2006).

Despite the concerns, especially where more than one SIDS death has occurred in the same family, a minority of unexpected deaths will be as a result of, or associated with, child maltreatment. It is anticipated that the development of protocols that support a systematic and evidence-based process for obtaining the history and examining the baby, paediatric forensic autopsy, death scene investigation and multi-professional review should not only lead to a greater chance of avoiding criminal proceedings for innocent parents, but also offer a better chance of identifying cases of child homicide (Ward Platt 2005). These factors have been instrumental in the development of new child death review processes in the UK.

Child death review processes

Child death review processes, such as those developed in the United States, Canada and Australia, aim to prevent child death or serious injury through the formation of multidisciplinary panels or teams who enquire into deaths of children in a given locality and recommend strategies for prevention. While such teams initially focused on unexpected deaths (especially where there were features suggestive of child maltreatment) most now consider all deaths of children and young people up to the age of 18 years (Durfee et al. 2002). Stillbirths are normally excluded.

Drawing from the literature, Bunting and Reid (2003) provide a useful review of the benefits of child death review teams that include:

- improved multi-agency working and communication;
- more effective identification of suspicious cases;
- a decrease in inadequate death certificates;
- better understanding of the causes of child death;
- a move towards a public health approach to the prevention of all child deaths, including those from maltreatment;
- targeting of prevention strategies at specific communities.

Durfee et al. (2002) summarise the achievements of teams throughout North America to include advocacy and programme development in relation to: 'abandoned infants; SIDS; Shaken Baby Syndrome; day care licensure; smoke detectors; child passenger, bicycle, water and boating, hunting and firearm safety; graduated driver's licensing; truancy and youth homicide; faith based services and grief and mourning services.' (p.626). They give a concrete example as to how the sharing of information in individual cases can lead to better protection of other children:

> Five children died, all on a Sunday, after ingesting doses of their parents' methadone. Apparently, the methadone clinics were not opened on Sundays and the clients had to bring home their Sunday doses on Saturday. Had the drug not come in the form of a pink liquid with a sweet taste that was attractive to children it may not have been ingested. (p.627)

Points for reflection
Should the deaths of children from accidental overdoses be classified as neglect? Do your views change if the medication is not prescribed or illegal?

On a visit to the Center on Child Abuse and Neglect in Oklahoma, I was able to see for myself the impressive work of a local child death review team. The team, which is health-led, have been able to influence state regulations in relation to motor vehicles, bicycles and pedestrian safety and to promote safe-sleep campaigns, pool and hot tub safety and the provision of smoke detectors. Their recommendations have also influenced the provision of primary and secondary child maltreatment prevention programmes.

In an article reviewing the work of the Arizona Child Fatality Review Program, Rimza et al. (2002) discuss the lessons learnt in relation to the prevention of childhood deaths including those attributable to medical conditions. Deaths that were considered preventable in this category include those: following inadequate paediatric emergency care; receiving a poor continuity of care; or receiving inadequate antenatal care; and deaths from vaccine preventable infections in non-immunised children. Deaths of children thought to be due to a delay in seeking medical care because of a lack of health insurance seemed especially poignant.

Child death review processes in the UK

At the time of writing, child death review teams are being established in parts of the UK. In England, Chapter 7 of *Working Together* (HM Government 2006a) sets out the procedures to be followed by LSCBs when any child dies. There are two elements to these; first, to offer a multi-disciplinary 'rapid response' to evaluate all unexpected deaths and second, to provide an overview of all child deaths (under the age of 18 years) in a locality, including those of children with known medical conditions or disabilities. Child death review functions will become compulsory in all English local authority areas on 1 April 2008. LSCBs are expected to develop Child Death Overview Panels to undertake this role (which may be shared across neighbouring LSCBs where the population is less than 500,000). The work of these teams should be coordinated and they are normally led by a lead paediatrician. The professionals involved in a Rapid Response Team will include a paediatrician, GP, health visitor, midwife (if still involved), mental health professional, social worker and a probation or police officer. Their joint responsibilities in relation to a rapid response to unexpected deaths include:

- 'making immediate enquiries into and evaluating the reasons for and circumstances of the death, in agreement with the coroner;
- undertaking the types of enquiries/investigations that relate to the current responsibilities of their respective organisations when a child dies unexpectedly. This includes liaising with those who have ongoing responsibilities for other family members;

- collecting information in a standard, nationally agreed manner;
- following the death through and maintaining contact at regular intervals with family members to ensure they are informed and kept up to date with information about the child's death.'

(HM Government 2006a: 132)

Collaboration with a range of professionals and agencies is at the heart of the child death review processes and will involve, among others, midwives, health visitors, school nurses, emergency department nurses and adult and child and adolescent mental health professionals. Case discussions will take place after the initial and final results of post-mortem examinations become available. The main aim of the case discussion is to share information and to identify the cause of death and any factors that may have contributed to it. Care of the family should also be planned. Child maltreatment should be explicitly discussed and the outcome of the discussion recorded, even where abuse or neglect are not suspected as a causal factor.

The second process that is being introduced, that of the Child Death Overview Panel (CDOP), is also the responsibility of the LSCB. This group, which also has responsibility for the implementation of local procedures and protocols, will meet on a regular basis to evaluate the deaths of all children in their area. The CDOP will consider professional responses and identify patterns, trends and lessons to be learnt, especially those that inform effective inter-agency working to safeguard and promote the welfare of children and young people. If the panel considers that there is a need for further enquiries or investigations or a serious case review they can refer the case to the LSCB chair.

In Northern Ireland at the time of writing, the DHSSPS are consulting on a regional multi-agency procedure to be followed in cases of sudden or unexpected child deaths in under-18-year-olds (DHSSPS 2006b). The aim is to set up Child Death Review Meetings (CDRM) to enable agencies to 'enquire into and evaluate whether and how the death may have been prevented' (p.1). The purpose of the CDRM is broadly similar to the process for reviewing deaths in England, although, at the time of writing, there are no proposals to cover all childhood deaths. The consultation document provides a detailed and helpful overview of the expectations and roles of those likely to be involved in the sudden or unexpected death of a child, which nurses and midwives from other UK countries may find helpful.

Summary

In summary, child death review processes appear to be a positive move and one that will help to ensure the health and safety of child populations. As Covington et al. (2005) have argued, reviews bring a broad ecological perspective to childhood deaths, thus medical, social, behavioural and environmental risks can be identified and addressed. They add that while the processes may help to identify cases where child maltreatment may have been missed, and to ensure programmes for the prevention of other unnatural deaths, there are preventable elements in many natural deaths, for example in pre-term infants and those of a low birth weight or where better management of conditions such as asthma may have led to a different outcome. Where deaths are considered non-preventable or expected, for example those from cancers or congenital malformations, the review process may identify important patterns or clusters, as well as the opportunity to consider the geography and availability of health services. Finally, a further benefit of a nationally recognised child death review protocol is that parents are not singled out or stigmatised by the process, but perhaps reassured that lessons to prevent further childhood deaths will be learnt from their own personal tragedy.

Conclusion

This chapter has considered child death and child maltreatment. Whilst fatal child maltreatment is rare, there may be occasions where covert homicide is otherwise classified. The relationship between SIDS and child maltreatment suggests some common pathways, particularly in relation to social deprivation. The likelihood that an increased proportion of deaths recorded as SIDS are due to maltreatment is recognised in tandem with the overall decline in cases. The well-established serious case review and the development of a significant incident review in Scotland (Scottish Executive 2006b) scrutinise professional practice in cases where there has been fatal or serious child maltreatment, but they may be somewhat limited in their scope. Child death review processes, on the other hand, take a broader perspective and have the potential to contribute much to the prevention of all deaths in childhood and to ensure the wider health and safety of whole populations of children and young people.

Messages for practice

- Death in childhood is a rare and sentinel event.
- When a child dies it is important to understand why, and to ensure that any messages for prevention and the future protection of children are fed into policy, legislation and practice.

- The majority of childhood deaths today occur in the youngest age groups, although the main causes of death vary according to different age bands.
- Addressing disadvantage and targeting health care to deprived families should be viewed as potentially life-saving work.
- SIDS is a diagnosis of exclusion, although it is recognised that for a small percentage of deaths that are initially labelled as SIDS, maltreatment may be a factor. All young infants should be placed 'Back to Sleep'.
- Health professionals have a very substantial role to play in serious case reviews and the new child death review processes.

Recommended reading

Durfee, M., Tilton Durfee, D., West, P.M. (2002) Child fatality review: an international movement, *Child Abuse and Neglect*, **26**: 619–36.

HM Government (2006a) *Working Together to Safeguard Children: A Guide to Inter-agency Working to Safeguard and Promote the Welfare of Children.* London: Department for Education and Skills (Chapters 7 and 8).

Rimza, M.E., Schackner, R.A., Bowen, K.A., Marshall, W. (2002) Can child deaths be prevented? The Arizona Child Fatality Review Programme Experience, *Paediatrics* http://pediatrics.aapublications.org/cgi/reprint/110/1/e11 (accessed 25/02/07)

Royal College of Pathologists, Royal College of Paediatrics and Child Health (2004) *Sudden Unexpected Death in Infancy: A Multi-agency Protocol for Care and Investigation. The Report of a Working Group Convened by the Royal College of Pathologists, Royal College of Paediatrics and Child Health.* London: Royal College of Pathologists, Royal College of Paediatrics and Child Health.

chapter **nine**

CONCLUSION: KNOWLEDGE FOR PRACTICE

This book began and will conclude on a positive note. It has, nevertheless, tackled an extremely difficult and challenging aspect of nursing and midwifery practice; that of preventing, recognising and responding to child maltreatment. This important aspect of practice has been set in the contemporary context of 'safeguarding' which can broadly be seen to embrace the actions that can be taken to ensure that all children and young people are able to reach their potential and enter adulthood successfully. The book celebrates the contribution that nurses and midwives can make to the safeguarding agenda by virtue of the universality of their services, their professional accountability and the shared core attributes of safeguarding and professional practice. Importantly, this book has been written for *all* nurses and midwives who work with children, young people and their families. Whilst acknowledging that this is a disparate group, the unifying attributes of modern nursing and midwifery have much in common with safeguarding, i.e. assessing need, working in partnership with individual children and young people, their families and multidisciplinary teams to promote physical and emotional well-being and to ensure safety.

The book recognises the fact that safeguarding is primarily accomplished through good parenting. Nurses and midwives can make a major contribution to better supporting parents, particularly those who have very little experience, knowledge or resources. This includes promoting 'positive parenting'. As universal service providers, nurses and midwives have a key role to play in early intervention and support for families facing difficulties. This work rests on an underpinning philosophy of children's rights and child-centredness. The

United Nations Convention on the Rights of the Child 1989, to which all four countries of the UK are signatories, provides the framework for legislation and practice and encourages us to consider children and young people's needs as unique, discrete and important. Maintaining a child-centred focus not only helps in identifying concerns about possible maltreatment, but also reflects the need to consult with children and young people on all aspects of their daily lives.

We have shown that child maltreatment is a complex construct that has been (and will probably always be) interpreted in many different ways. The fact that all children and young people, whoever their parents are, are potentially 'at risk' of child maltreatment is an important one; however, the correlation between poverty and a greater risk of a range of poorer outcomes has to be acknowledged. Approximately one in ten of all children and young people will experience maltreatment at some point in their childhood. Child maltreatment has many guises and our understanding of the problem has developed over time. We have seen that there are wide-ranging professional and academic perspectives on the problem, which may contribute to a variety of discourses and approaches. The policy definitions of physical abuse, emotional abuse, sexual abuse and neglect have some merit in classifying the presentations and effects, but contextual factors may be more important than any 'signs or symptoms'.

The role of nurses and midwives goes further than being able to recognise child maltreatment. This book provides the knowledge to help practitioners to take forward their concerns, even where these are not shared by others. It is always important to take a team approach and systems of (child protection) clinical supervision are vital in working through concerns about families and ensuring that practitioners are appropriately supported. At times it may be possible, and indeed preferable, to facilitate a timely response through working within the framework of service provision for 'additional needs' rather than child protection. Whether a 'child in need' or 'child protection' referral has been made to children's social care, it is they who will lead any enquiry, undertake specialist assessments and engage health professionals and others to work together to ensure the future safety and protection of the child or young person. The wider team includes professionals from a range of agencies; although the centrality of the child and their family should be the focus of all joint working to safeguard and promote their welfare.

The book has highlighted the needs of children, young people and families who are at a greater risk of child maltreatment. These groups are likely to have high levels of contact with a variety of health services and include families where there is domestic abuse, disabled children and young people, children who are at risk of sexual exploitation and children who are refugees or asylum seekers. It is important that children in these special groups are recognised as 'children first'. The risk to children whose parents or carers fabricate or induce illness and the primacy of a multi-agency child protection response to such concerns have also been outlined. Cases of fabricated or induced illness challenge the well-established contemporary practice of working in partnership with parents in the delivery of care and treatment.

A separate chapter on neglect recognised that nurses and midwives have a key role to play in its identification, prevention, recognition and response. Where the parent is the patient or client a consideration of the impact of their health and social problems on the ability to parent is crucial. Finally, we considered the rare and sentinel event of child deaths and recognised that when a child dies it is important to understand why, and to ensure that any messages for prevention and the future protection of children are fed into policy, legislation and practice.

Messages for the future

At the beginning of this book I noted that as child health continues to improve and new treatments are developed for previously fatal or life-limiting conditions, the morbidity and mortality from child maltreatment, an essentially *preventable* event, begin to take on an ever greater significance. This may have been the first time that readers had come across such a contention. Greater knowledge and understanding of the theory and practice of safeguarding children will help to ensure that the impact of child maltreatment fails to become the major public health issue that it is threatening to be. Prevention is uppermost, but where this is not possible a timely and appropriate response to suspected child maltreatment can have a major, even life-saving, outcome. Nursing and midwifery are an enviable force and the potential to make a greater contribution to safeguarding children and young people needs to be recognised and promoted. The professions are changing and will continue to change to meet the health care challenges of tomorrow. Above all we must remember that whatever the future holds for the practice of nursing and midwifery, the best interests, welfare and safety of the child or young person should always come first. They are our future too.

APPENDIX

Websites

www.everychildmatters.gov.uk

This website, hosted by the DfES, provides links to information and publications related to the *Every Child Matters: Change for Children* programme in England.

www.dfes.gov.uk

This is the main DfES website.

www.wales.gov.uk/organipo/index.htm

Information about the work of the Welsh Assembly Government.

www.scotland.gov.uk/childprotection

Information about the work the Scottish Executive is doing to improve the protection of children and young people in Scotland.

www.dhsspsni.gov.uk/

Information about the work of the Department of Health, Social Services and Public Safety in Northern Ireland.

www.nspcc.org.uk

Links to a wealth of information on safeguarding children and young people. NSPCC Inform provides a good resource for professionals.

www.childfriendlyhealthcare.org

The CFHI is a health care project concerned with the physical, psychological and emotional needs of children and their families and aims to make visits to health care settings 'child friendly'. One of its standards relates to protection from maltreatment.

www.childreninwales.org.uk/index.html

Children in Wales is the national umbrella organisation for those working with children and young people in Wales.

www.victoria-climbie-inquiry.org.uk

This site provides access to the main report and work of the inquiry team.

www.safeguardingchildren.org.uk

Links to inspection reports and other publications relating to safeguarding issues undertaken since the first Joint Chief Inspectors' Review of Children's safeguards was published in 2002.

www.childrenscommissioner.org/

The Office of the Children's Commissioner for England.

www.childcom.org.uk/

The Office of the Children's Commissioner for Wales.

http://www.sccyp.org.uk/

The Office of the Children's Commissioner for Scotland.

www.niccy.org/

The Office of the Children's Commissioner for Northern Ireland.

www.childrenareunbeatable.org.uk/

The Children Are Unbeatable! Alliance campaigns for the UK to satisfy human rights obligations by modernising the law on assault to afford children the same protection as adults.

www.childline.org.uk

Help for children and young people.

www.bullying.co.uk

Gives help and advice for those dealing with the effects of bullying.

www.parentlineplus.org.uk

Help with parenting.

www.core-info.cardiff.ac.uk/

A valuable source of information on systematic reviews of published literature on aspects of physical child abuse.

www.womensaid.org.uk/

www.welshwomensaid.org

www.scottishwomensaid.co.uk

www.niwaf.org

and

www.refuge.org.uk

Domestic violence support.

www.thehideout.org.uk

An online resource for children and young people who are witnessing or experiencing domestic violence.

www.childrenslegalcentre.com

Free legal advice on law and policy affecting children.

www.ceop.gov.uk

The Child Exploitation and Online Protection (CEOP) Centre works across the UK maximising international links and combines police powers with the expertise of business, government, specialist charities and other organisations focusing on tackling child sexual abuse. It also hosts www.thinkuknow.co.uk which is a dedicated educational programme for children and young people and helps them to use the internet and other new technology safely.

www.kidscape.org.uk

A charity that offers help and advice to protect children from harm from peers, adults they know or strangers.

http://www.harpweb.org.uk/

HARPWEB consists of three websites, each developed in collaboration with health professionals working with asylum seekers and refugees in the UK. They are designed to enable easy access to the wealth of information, practical tools, and articles that have been written by health care professionals, NGOs, academics and research bodies with expert knowledge of working with asylum seekers and refugees, both in the UK and other countries.

http://www.refugee-action.org.uk/about/default.aspx

Refugee Action is an independent national charity working with refugees to build new lives in the UK. They are a source of practical advice and assistance for newly arrived asylum seekers and have a long-term commitment to their settlement through community development work.

Helplines

Childline 0800 1111
Childline Wales 0800 1111
National Society for the Prevention of Cruelty to Children 0808 800 5000
National Domestic Violence Helpline 0808 2000 247
Wales Domestic Abuse Helpline 0808 80 10 800
Scottish Domestic Abuse Helpline 0800 027 1234
Northern Ireland Women's Aid 0800 917 1414
Parentline Plus 0808 800 2222

NOTES

Preface

1 The term 'child abuse and neglect' and 'child maltreatment' are used interchangeably throughout the text, although it should be noted that 'child maltreatment' is increasingly dominating the literature.

Chapter 1 Introduction: why a safeguarding children guide for nurses and midwives?

1 At the time of writing, all countries in the world with the exception of the United States and Somalia have ratified the Convention.

Chapter 2 Why every child matters

1 I use this term in preference to the customary 'family-centred care' (see for example Smith et al. 2006) in recognition that while the majority of parents are loving and caring and will always act in their child's best interests, in some instances the actions of parents (or carers) are detrimental to the health and well-being of their child, and that in all cases the needs of the child are paramount (Children Act 1989).
2 Children (under 18) may be 'looked after' by local authorities under a number of legal arrangements including care orders and (criminal) supervision orders.
3 Children Act 1989; The Children (Northern Ireland) Order 1995; Children

(Scotland) Act 1995. (The Children Act 1989 is applicable in England and Wales.)

Chapter 4 Safeguarding children: professional roles and responsibilities

1 The Sexual Offences Act 2003 does not affect the duty of care and confidentiality of health professionals to young people under 16 years of age.
2 Connexions partnerships offer advice on education, careers, housing, money, health and relationships for 13–19-year-olds in the UK.

Chapter 7 Child neglect

1 Readers may also be aware of a headline case regarding a disabled child in the US who had invasive medical treatment to prevent her physical growth and development. http://ashleytreatment.spaces.live.com/

Chapter 8 Child death and child maltreatment

1 The tradition of placing the guidance on serious case reviews in Chapter 8 of each edition of *Working Together* led to these reviews formerly being referred to as 'Part 8 Reviews'.

REFERENCES

Abbs, P. and colleagues (2006) 'Modern life leads to more depression among children' (letter to the *Daily Telegraph*). http://www.telegraph.co.uk/core/Content/displayPrintable.jhtml?xml=/news/2006/09/12/njunk112.xml (accessed 18/09/06).

Alderson, P. (1993) *Children's Consent to Surgery.* Buckingham: Open University Press.

All Wales Area Child Protection Committees (2004) *Safeguarding Children in Whom Illness is Fabricated or Induced.* Cardiff: All Wales Child Protection Review Group.

All Wales Area Child Protection Committees (2005a) *All* Wales *Child Protection Procedures (amended).* Cardiff: Wales Child Protection Review Group.

All Wales Child Protection Review Group (2005b) *Female Genital Mutilation Protocol.* Cardiff: All Wales Child Protection Review Group.

Alper, J. (2005) Retrospectoscopy, *UK Casebook,* 13: 3. http://www.medicalprotection.org/medical/united_kingdom/publications/casebook/2005_3_retro.aspx (accessed 7/6/06).

Amnesty International (2006) *Making the Grade?* London: Amnesty International UK.

Archard, D. (1993) *Children: Rights and Childhood.* London: Routledge.

Archard, D.W. (2003) *Children, Family and the State.* Aldershot: Ashgate.

Avon and Somerset Joint Area Protocol for the Management of Suspected Fabricated or Induced Illness in Children (2005). http://www.bathnes.gov.uk/NR/rdonlyres/38FCE5B7-263C-4F10-A0FB-7D04046A7A65/0/BANESJointAgencyProtocol.pdf (accessed 28/01/07).

Axford, N. and Bullock, R. (2005) Child Death and Significant Case Reviews: International Approaches. http://www.scotland.gov.uk/publications/2005/07/1485820/58341 (accessed 13/10/06).

Baird, K. and Salmon, D. (2006) Identifying domestic abuse against women and children, *Primary Health Care,* 16(5): 27–31.

Bajaj, M., Mease, R.G., Allen, K. and Dryburgh, E.H. (2006) Safeguarding children – is there a role for a coordinator? *Child Abuse Review,* 15: 127–37.

Baldwin, N. and Spencer, N. (2005) Economic, social and cultural contexts of neglect, in J. Taylor and B. Daniel (eds) *Child Neglect: Practical Issues for Health and Social Care.* London: Jessica Kingsley.

Bannon, M. and Carter, Y. (eds) (2003) *Protecting Children from Abuse and Neglect in Primary Care.* Oxford: Oxford University Press.

BBC News Item (2005) *System 'failed starving children',* 21 December. http://news.bbc.co.uk/1/hi/england/south_yorkshire/4546736.stm (accessed 19/07/06).

Beckett, C. (2003) *Child Protection: An introduction.* London: Sage Publications.

Belsky, J. (1993) Etiology of child maltreatment: a developmental-ecological analysis, *Psychological Bulletin*, 114(3): 413–34.

Bishop, N. (2006) Don't ignore vitamin D, *Archives of Disease in Childhood*, 91: 549–50.

Black, M.B., Dubowitz, H., Casey, P.H., Cutts, D. et al. (2006) Failure to thrive as distinct from child neglect, *Pediatrics*, 117: 1456–8.

Blair, P.S., Sidebotham, P., Berry, P.J., Evans, M. and Fleming, P.J. (2006) Major epidemiological changes in sudden infant death syndrome: a 20-year population-based study in the UK, *Lancet*, 367: 314–19.

Block, R.W., Krebs, N.F. and the Committee on Child Abuse and Neglect and the Committee on Nutrition (2005) Failure to thrive as a manifestation of child neglect, *Pediatrics*, 116: 1234–7.

Blumenthal, I. (2002) Shaken baby syndrome, *Postgraduate Medicine*, 78: 732–5.

BMA (British Medical Association) (2006a) Parental Responsibility: Guidance from the Ethics Department. http://www.bma.org.uk/ap.nsf/Content/Parental (accessed 01/09/06).

BMA (British Medical Association) (2006b) A BMA statement on information sharing in relation to sexually active young people. http://www.bma.org.uk/ap.nsf/Content/childrensexualhealth (accessed 23/09/06).

Bowlby, J. (1969) *Attachment and Loss*. London: Hogarth.

Brooks, L. (2006) *The Story of Childhood: Growing Up in Modern Britain*. London: Bloomsbury.

Browne, K., Davies, C. and Stratton, P. (eds) (1988) *Early Prediction and Prevention of Child Abuse*. Chichester: John Wiley.

Browne, K. and Hamilton, C. (2003) Prevention: current and future trends, in M. Bannon and Y. Carter (eds) *Protecting Children from Abuse and Neglect in Primary Care*. Oxford: Oxford University Press.

Bunting, L. and Reid, C. (2003) *Reviewing Child Deaths in Northern Ireland*. Belfast: NSPCC Northern Ireland Policy and Research Unit.

Bunting, L. (2004) *Key Child Protection Statistics in Northern Ireland*. Belfast: NSPCC Northern Ireland Policy and Research Unit. http://www.nspcc.org.uk/Inform/OnlineResources/Statistics/KeyCPStatsNI/KeyChildProtectionStatisticsInNI_pdf_gf25471.pdf (accessed 18/10/06).

Butler-Sloss, E. (1988) *Report of Inquiry into Child Abuse in Cleveland 1987*. London: HMSO.

Cantrill, P. (2005) *Sheffield Area Child Protection Committee, Executive Summary re: JWW, CLW, SW, NW, JDW*. Sheffield: ACPC.

Caplan, G. (1964) *Principles of Preventative Psychiatry*. New York: Basic Books.

Carter, B. (1994) *Child and Infant Pain: Principles of Nursing Care and Management*. London: Chapman and Hall.

Case, M.E., Graham, M.A., Handy, T.C., Jentzen, J.M. and Monteleone, J.A. (2001) Position paper on fatal abusive head injuries in infants and young children, *American Journal of Forensic Medical Pathology*, 22(2): 112–22.

Cawson, P., Wattam, C., Brooker, S. and Kelly, G. (2000) *Child Maltreatment in the United Kingdom: A Study of the Prevalence of Child Abuse and Neglect*. London: NSPCC.

Cawson, P. (2002) *Child Maltreatment in the Family: The Experience of a National Sample of Young People*. London: NSPCC.

Chantler, K., Burman, E., Batsleer, J. and Bashir, C. (2001) *Attempted Suicide and Selfharm: South Asian Women*. Manchester Metropolitan University Women's Studies Research Centre in Department of Health (2005).

Chester, D.L., Rajive, M.J., Aldlyami, E., King, H. and Moiemen, N.S. (2006) Non-accidental burns in children – are we neglecting neglect? *Burns*, 32: 222–8.

Children are Unbeatable! Alliance (2006) *Equal Protection from Assault is Every Child's Human Right*. http://www.childrenareunbeatable.org.uk (accessed 04/07/06).

Children 1st (2006) *Child Abuse* fact-sheet. http://www.children1st.org.uk/pdfs/factsheet2.pdf (accessed 18/10/06).

Children's Commissioner for Wales (2006) Annual Report 2005–2006. http://www.childcom.org.uk/publications/CCFW_ann_review_eng.pdf (accessed 20/01/07).

Children's Rights Alliance for England (2005) *State of Children's Rights in England: Annual Review of UK Government Action on 2002 Concluding Observations of the United Nations Committee on the Rights of the Child*. London: CRA.

Clarke, A. and Nicholson, S. (2001) How 'child friendly' are you? *Paediatric Nursing*, 13(5): 12–15.

Clift, F. (2003) Legal aspects of child abuse in M. Bannon and Y. Carter (eds) *Protecting Children from Abuse and Neglect in Primary Care*. Oxford: Oxford University Press.

Clothier, C. (1994) *The Allitt Inquiry*. London: HMSO.

Commission on Families and the Well-being of Children (2005) *Families and the State*. http://www.nfpi.org.uk/data/research/docs/family-commission-exec-summary-31.doc (accessed 4/07/06).

Commission for Social Care Inspection, Her Majesty's Chief Inspector of Schools, Her Majesty's Chief Inspector of Court Administration, Her Majesty's Chief Inspector of Probation, Her Majesty's Chief Inspector of Constabulary, Her Majesty's Chief Inspector of Prisons, Healthcare Commission, Her Majesty's Chief Inspector of the Crown Prosecution Service (2005) *Safeguarding Children: The Second Joint Chief Inspectors' Report on Arrangements to Safeguard Children*. www.safeguardingchildren.org.uk

Corby, B. (2006) *Child Abuse: Towards a Knowledge Base*, 3rd edition. Maidenhead: Open University Press.

Covington, T., Foster, V. and Rich, S. (2005) *A Program Manual for Child Death Review*. Okemos, MI: The National Center for Child Death Review.

Craft, A.W. and Hall, D.M.B. (2004) Munchausen syndrome by proxy and sudden infant death, *British Medical Journal*, 328: 1309–12.

Croke, R. and Crowley, A. (eds) (2006) *Righting the Wrongs: The Reality of Children's Rights in Wales*. Cardiff: Save the Children Wales/Achub y Plant.

Dale, P., Green, R. and Fellows, R. (2002) *What Really Happened? Child Protection Case Management of Infants with Serious Injuries and Discrepant Parental Explanations*. London: NSPCC.

Daniel, B. (2005) Introduction to issues for health and social care in neglect, in J. Taylor, B. Daniel (eds) *Child Neglect: Practical Issues for Health and Social Care*. London: Jessica Kingsley.

David, T. (1999) Shaken baby (shaken impact) syndrome: non-accidental head injury in infancy, *Journal of the Royal Society of Medicine*, 92(11): 556–61.

Davidson, L. and Lynch, M. (2003) Domestic violence and child protection, in M. Bannon and Y. Carter (eds) *Protecting Children from Abuse and Neglect in Primary Care*. Oxford: Oxford University Press.

Debelle, G. (2003) Child protection in a multicultural society, in M. Bannon and Y. Carter (eds) *Protecting Children from Abuse and Neglect in Primary Care*. Oxford: Oxford University Press.

Dent, R.J. (1998) (ed.) *Dangerous Care: Working to Protect Children*. London: The Bridge Child Care Development Service.

DfES (Department for Education and Skills) (2006) *Referrals, Assessments and Children and Young People on Child Protection Registers, England – Year Ending 31 March 2006*. London: The Stationery Office.

DH (Department of Health) (1995) *Child Protection: Messages from Research*. London: HMSO.

DH (Department of Health) (2000a) *The NHS Plan*. London: Department of Health.

DH (Department of Health) (2000b) *Framework for the Assessment of Children in Need and Their Families* London: The Stationery Office.

DH (Department of Health) (2003) *Getting the Right Start: National Service Framework for Children: Standard for Hospital Services*. London: Department of Health.

DH (Department of Health) (2004) *Best Practice Guidance for Doctors and Other health Professionals on the Provision of Advice and Treatment to Young People under 16 on Contraception, Sexual and Reproductive Health*. London: Department of Health.

DH (Department of Health) (2005) *Responding to Domestic Abuse: A Handbook for Health Professionals*. London: Department of Health.

DH (Department of Health), Home Office, DfEE (Department for Education and Employment), Welsh Office (2000) *Safeguarding Children Involved in Prostitution*. London: Department of Health.

DH (Department of Health), Home Office, Department for Education and Skills, Welsh Assembly Government (2002) *Safeguarding Children in Whom Illness is Fabricated or Induced*. London: Department of Health.

DH (Department of Health), DfES (Department for Education and Skills) (2004a) *The Chief Nursing Officer's Review into the Nursing, Midwifery and Health Visiting Contribution to Vulnerable Children*. London: Department of Health.

DH (Department of Health), DfES (Department for Education and Skills) (2004b) *National Service Framework for Children, Young People and Maternity Services: Core Standards*. London: Department of Health.

DH (Department of Health), DfES (Department for Education and Skills) (2004c) *National Service Framework for Children, Young People and Maternity Services: Maternity Standard*. London: Department of Health.

DHSS (Department of Health and Social Security) (1974) *Report of the Inquiry into the Care and Supervision Provided in Relation to Maria Colwell*. London: HMSO.

DHSSPS (Department of Health, Social Services and Public Safety) (2003) *Co-operating to Safeguard Children*. Belfast, Northern Ireland: DHSSPS.

DHSSPS (Department of Health, Social Services and Public Safety) (2006a) *Community Statistics: 1 April 2004–31 March 2005*. Belfast: Northern Ireland, DHSSPS. http://www.dhsspsni.gov.uk/master_community_statistics_(2004-05).pdf (accessed 2/10/06).

DHSSPS (Department of Health, Social Services and Public Safety) (2006b) *Regional Multi-Agency Procedure to be Followed in Cases of Sudden or Unexpected Child Deaths from Birth to 18 Years: A Consultation Document*. Belfast: Northern Ireland, DHSSPS.

Domestic Violence, Crime and Victims Act 2004. http://www.opsi.gov.uk/ACTS/acts2004/20040028.htm (accessed 28/01/07).

Dubowitz, H. and King, H. (1995) Family violence: a child centred, family focused approach, *Pediatric Clinics of North America*, 42: 1: 153–66.

Durfee, M., Tilton Durfee, D. and West, P.M. (2002) Child fatality review: an international movement, *Child Abuse and Neglect*, 26: 619–36.

Edwards, P., Green, J., Roberts, I. and Lutchmun, S. (2006) Deaths from injury in children and employment status in family: analysis of trends in class specific death rates, *BMJ, doi:10.1136/bmj.38875,757488.4F* (published 7 July)

Falkov, A. (1996) *Study of Working Together Part 8 Reports: Fatal Child Abuse and Parental Psychiatric Disorder – An Analysis of 100 ACPC Case Reviews Conducted under the Terms of Part 8 of Working Together Under the Children Act 1989: A Guide to Arrangements for Interagency Co-operation for the Protection of Children from Abuse*. London: Department of Health.

Felitti V.J., Anda, R.F., Nordenberg, D. et al. (1998) Relationship of childhood abuse and household dysfunction to many of the leading cause of death in adults. The Adverse Childhood Experiences (ACE) Study, *American Journal of Preventative Medicine*, 14: 4: 245–58.

Firestone, S. (1970) *The Dialectic of Sex*. London: Cape.

Fitzgerald, J. (1998) Policy and practice in child protection, in R.J. Dent (ed.) *Dangerous Care: Working to Protect Children*. London: The Bridge Child Care Development Service.

Fitzgerald, M. (2002) Meeting the needs of individuals, in J. Daly, S. Speedy, D. Jackson, P. Darbyshire (eds) *Contexts of Nursing: An Introduction*. Oxford: Blackwell.

Franklin, B. (1995) *The Handbook of Children's Rights*. London: Routledge.

Fulton, D.R. (2000) Shaken baby syndrome, *Critical Care Nursing Quarterly*, 23(2): 43–50.

Glasper, E.A. and Powell, C. (2000) First do no harm: parental exclusion from the anaesthetic room, *Paediatric Nursing*, 12(4): 14–17.

Golden, M., Samuels, M.P. and Southall, D.P. (2003) How to distinguish between neglect and deprivational abuse, *Archives of Disease in Childhood*, 88: 105–7.

Greenland, C. (1987) *Preventing Child Abuse and Neglect Deaths: An International Study of Deaths Due to Child Abuse and Neglect*. London: Tavistock.

Hall, A. (2003) Emotional abuse, in M. Bannon and Y. Carter (eds) *Protecting Children from Abuse and Neglect in Primary Care*. Oxford: Oxford University Press.

Hall, D. (2003) Protecting children, supporting Professionals, *Archives of Disease in Childhood*, 88: 557–9.

Hall, D. and Sowden, D. (2005) Primary Care for Children in the 21st Century, *British Medical Journal*, 330: 430–1.

Hammarburg, T. (2006) Children and corporal punishment: 'The right not to be hit, also a children's right'. http://crin.org/violence/search/closeup.asp?infoID=8562 (accessed 01/09/06).

Hammond, H. (2001) *Child Protection Inquiry into the Circumstances Surrounding the Death of Kennedy McFarlane, d.o.b. 17 April 1997*. Dumfries and Galloway Child Protection Committee.

Hart, R. (1992) *Children's Participation: From Tokenism to Citizenship*. Florence: UNICEF Innocenti Research Centre.

Hay, T. and Jones, L. (1994) Societal interventions to prevent child abuse and neglect, *Child Welfare*, 73(5): 379–403.

Hayes, E. (2002) *Encouraging Better Behaviour: A Practical Guide to Positive Parenting*. London: NSPCC. http://www.nspcc.org.uk/documents/encouraging.pdf (accessed 26/09/05).

HM Government (2004) *Every Child Matters: Change for Children*. London: Department for Education and Skills.

HM Government (2006a) *Working Together to Safeguard Children: A Guide to Inter-agency Working to Safeguard and Promote the Welfare of Children*. London: Department for Education and Skills.

HM Government (2006b) *Information Sharing: Practitioners' Guide*. London: Department for Education and Skills.

HM Government (2006c) *Information Sharing: Further Guidance on Legal Issues*. London: Department for Education and Skills.

HM Government (2006d) *Information Sharing: Case Examples*. London: Department for Education and Skills.

HM Government (2006e) *Reaching Out: An Action Plan on Social Exclusion*. London: Cabinet Office.

HM Government (2006f) *Common Assessment Framework: Practitioners' Guide*. London: Department for Education and Skills.

Hobbs, C. (2003) Physical abuse, in M. Bannon and Y. Carter (eds) *Protecting Children from Abuse and Neglect in Primary Care*. Oxford: Oxford University Press.

Hobbs, C., Hanks, H. and Wynne, J. (1999a) *Child Abuse and Neglect: A Clinician's Handbook*, 2nd edn. London: Churchill Livingstone.

Hobbs, G.F., Hobbs, C.J. and Wynne, J. (1999b) Abuse of children in foster and residential care, *Child Abuse and Neglect*, 23(12): 1239–52.

Holt, J. (1975) *Escape from Childhood: The Needs and Rights of Children*. Harmondsworth: Penguin.

Home Office, Lord Chancellor's Department, Crown Prosecution Service, Department of Health and National Assembly for Wales (2002) *Achieving Best Evidence in Criminal Proceedings: Guidance for Vulnerable or Intimidated Witnesses Including Children*. London: Home Office.

Horner, G. (2005) Physical abuse: recognition and reporting, *Journal of Pediatric Health Care*, 19: 4–11.

Horwath, J. (2003) Developing good practice in cases of fabricated and induced illness by carers: new guidance and the training implications, *Child Abuse Review*, 12: 58–63.

House of Commons Hansard Debate 25 October 1996 at: http://www.publications.parliament.uk/pa/cm199697/cmhansrd/vo961025/debtext/61025-08.htm (accessed 27/01/07).

Humphreys, C. and Mullender, A. (1999) *Children and Domestic Violence: A Research Overview of the Impact on Children.* http://www.rip.org.uk/publications/documents/researchreviews/mullendar.pdf (accessed 14/11/06).

Jayawant, S., Rawlinson, A., Gibbon, F., Price, J., Schulte, J., Sharples, P., Sibert, R. and Kemp, A.M. (1998) Subdural haemorrhages in infants: population based study, *British Medical Journal*, 317: 1558–61.

Jenny, C. and Isaac, R. (2006) The relationship between child death and child maltreatment, *Archives of Disease in Childhood*, 91: 265–9.

Jose, N. (2005) Child poverty: is it child abuse? *Paediatric Nursing*, 17(8): 20–3.

Kemp, A., Stoodley, N., Cobley, C., Coles, L. and Kemp, K.W. (2003) Apnoea and brain swelling in non-accidental head injury, *Archives of Disease in Childhood*, 88: 472–6.

Kempe, CH., Silverman, F., Steele, B., Droegemuller, W. and Silver, H. (1962) The battered child syndrome, *Journal of the American Medical Association*, 181(1): 17–24.

Kendrick, A. and Taylor, J. (2000) Hidden on the ward: the abuse of children in hospital, *Journal of Advanced Nursing*, 31: 565–673.

Kennedy, H., Epstein, J., Fleming P.J. et al. (2004) *Sudden Unexpected Death in Infancy: A Multi-agency Protocol for Care and Investigation. The Report of a Working Group Convened by the Royal College of Pathologists, Royal College of Paediatrics and Child Health.* London: Royal College of Pathologists, Royal College of Paediatrics and Child Health.

Kennedy, I. (2001) *The Report of the Public Inquiry into Children's Heart Surgery at the Bristol Royal Infirmary 1984–1995: Learning from Bristol.* CM5207(1). London: The Stationery Office.

Kennedy, M. and Wonnacot, J. (2005) Neglect of disabled children, in J. Taylor and B. Daniel, *Child Neglect: Practical Issues for Health and Social Care*, London: Jessica Kingsley.

Kipps, S. (2005) Sexual health needs of women in violent relationships, *Primary Health Care*, 15(8): 27–32.

Kydd, J.W. (2003) Preventing child maltreatment: an integrated, multisectoral approach, *Health and Human Rights*, 6(2): 34–65.

Laming, Lord (2003) *The Victoria Climbié Inquiry: Report of an Inquiry by Lord Laming*, CM 5730. London: The Stationery Office.

Lansdown, G. (1995) Children's rights to participation and protection: a critique, in C. Cloke and M. Davies (eds) *Participation and Empowerment in Child Protection.* Chichester: NSPCC/Wiley and Sons.

Larcher, V. (2005) Consent, competence and confidentiality, *British Medical Journal*, 330: 353–6.

Lawrence, A. (2004) *Principles of Child Protection: Management and Practice.* Maidenhead: Open University Press.

Lee, N. (2001) *Childhood and Society*. Buckingham: Open University Press.

Levene, S. and Bacon, C.J. (2004) Sudden unexpected death and covert homicide in infancy, *Archives of Disease in Childhood*, 89: 443–7.

Levy, A. (2004) *Stigmatised, Marginalised and Criminalised.* London: NSPCC.

LGA (Local Government Association) (2006) *Vision for Services for Children and Young People Affected by Domestic Violence.* London: Local Government Association.

Lister, P. and Crisp, B. (2005) Clinical supervision in child protection for community nurses, *Child Abuse Review*, 14: 57–72.

London Borough of Brent (1985) *A Child in Trust: The Report of the Panel of Inquiry into the Circumstances Surrounding the Death of Jasmine Beckford.* London: London Borough of Brent.

Marchant, R. (1991) Myths and facts about sexual abuse and children with disabilities, *Child Abuse Review*, 5(2): 22.

Mayer, B.W., Burns, P. (2000) Differential diagnosis of abuse injuries in infants and young children, *American Journal of Primary Health Care (Nurse Practitioner)*, 25: 15–37.

Mayor, S. (2006) Guidance does not require mandatory reporting of underage sex, *British Medical Journal*, 332: 872.

Mayor of London (2004) *Offering More than they Borrow: Refugee Children in London.* London: Greater London Authority.

McEvoy, R. (2006) Nursery workers (letter) *Children Now*, 30th August–5th September, p.14.

McNeish, D. (1998) An overview of agency views and service provision for young people abused through prostitution, in *Whose Daughter Next? Children Abused through Prostitution.* Ilford: Barnardo's.

Meadow, R. (1977) Munchausen Syndrome by Proxy: the hinterland of child abuse, *Lancet*, ii: 343–5.

Meadow, R. (1995) What is and what is not Munchausen Syndrome by Proxy? *Archives of Disease in Childhood*, 72: 534–8.

Meadow, R. (1999) Mothering to death, *Archives of Disease in Childhood*, 80: 359–62.

Midgley, C. (2006) Our cotton wool kids. http://women.timesonline.co.uk/article/0,,27869-2275465,00.html (accessed 24/08/06).

Miller, A. (1987) *The Drama of Being a Child*. London: Virago.

Ministry of Health (1959) *The Report of the Committee on the Welfare of Children in Hospital (The Platt Report)*. London: HMSO.

Minty, B. (2005) The nature of emotional child neglect and abuse, in J. Taylor, B. Daniel (eds) *Child Neglect: Practical Issues for Health and Social Care*. London: Jessica Kingsley.

Morgan, C. (2006) Archbishop warns of dysfunctional 'infant adults'. http://www.timesonline.-co.uk/article/0,,2087-2361466,00.html (accessed 23/09/06).

Mott, A. (2003) Child sexual abuse, in M. Bannon and Y. Carter *Protecting Children from Abuse and Neglect in Primary Care*. Oxford: Oxford University Press.

National Assembly for Wales (2006) SSDA 908.1: Children and Young People on the Child Protection Register 2005–2006: Additions and removals. http://www.lgdu-wales.gov.uk/Documents/Data_-Set/PSS/2005_06/lgd01096_ssda908_table_1_2005_06_v1_bi.xls (accessed 2/10/06).

Nayda, R. (2004) Registered nurses communication about abused children: rules, responsibilities and resistance, *Child Abuse Review*, 13: 188–99.

NCIPCA (National Commission of Inquiry into the Prevention of Child Abuse) (1996) *Childhood Matters* Volumes I and II. London: The Stationery Office.

Newell, P. (1989) *Children are People Too: The Case Against Physical Punishment*. London: Bedford Square Press.

Newell, P. (2006) Corporal punishment beats a retreat, *Child Rights Information Network*, 19: 13–15.

Newham Area Child Protection Committee (2002) *Ainlee*. Newham: ACPC.

Newman, M., Otvos, B. and Harris-Hendriks, J. (1998) Evaluating the risks to children, in R.J. Dent (ed.) *Dangerous Care: Working to Protect Children*. London: The Bridge Child Care Development Service.

NICE (National Institute for Clinical Excellence) (2003) *Antenatal Care: Routine Care for the Healthy Pregnant Woman*. London: National Institute for Clinical Excellence.

NMC (Nursing and Midwifery Council) (2004a) *The NMC Code of Professional Conduct: Standards for Conduct, Performance and Ethics*. London: Nursing and Midwifery Council.

NMC (Nursing and Midwifery Council) (2004b) *Standards of Proficiency for Specialist Community Public Health Nurses*. London: Nursing and Midwifery Council.

Norfolk Health Authority (2002) *Summary Report of the Independent Health Review (Lauren Wright)*. Norfolk: NHA.

Northern Ireland Commissioner for Children and Young People (2006) Priorities. http://www.niccy.org/priorities.aspx?menuId=6 (accessed 20/01/07).

NSCAN (National Safeguarding Children Association for Nurses) (2006) *Professional Core Competencies for Nurses Specialising in Safeguarding Children*. Huddersfield: NSCAN.

NSPCC Inform (2006) Child Homicides. http://www.nspcc.org.uk/inform/onlineresources/statistics/KeyCPstats/ (accessed 18/10/06).

NWGCPD (National Working Group on Child Protection and Disability) (2003) *It Doesn't Happen to Disabled Children*. London: NSPCC.

O'Brien, L.M., Heycock, E.G. and Hanna, M. et al. (2004) Postnatal depression and faltering growth: a community study, *Pediatrics*, 113: 1242–7.
Office of the Children's Commissioner (2006) *Annual Report 2005/06*. London: The Stationery Office.
ONS (Office for National Statistics) (2002) *Social Focus in Brief: Children*. London: ONS.
ONS (Office for National Statistics) (2004) *The Health of Children and Young People*. London: ONS.
ONS (Office for National Statistics) (2006) *Mortality Statistics: Childhood, Infant and Perinatal* (Series DH3 No. 37). London: ONS.
Paavonen, J. and Eggert-Kruse, W. (1999) Chlamydia trachomatis: impact on human reproduction, *Human Reproduction Update*, 5(5): 433–47.
Pace, M. (2003) The child protection process, in M. Bannon and Y. Carter (eds) *Protecting Children from Abuse and Neglect in Primary Care*. Oxford: Oxford University Press.
Parse, R. (1992) Human becoming: Parse's theory of nursing, *Nursing Science Quarterly*, 5(1): 35–42.
Parton N., Thorpe D. and Wattam C. (1997) *Child Protection, Risk and the Moral Order*. Basingstoke: Macmillan.
Pearce, J. (2006) Who needs to be involved in safeguarding sexually exploited young people? *Child Abuse Review*, 15: 326–40.
Pearch, J. (2005) Restraining children for clinical procedures, *Paediatric Nursing*, 17(9): 36–8.
Perry, B. (2002) Childhood experience and the expression of genetic potential: what child neglect tells us about nature and nurture, *Brain and Mind*, 3: 79–100.
Poblete, X. (2003) Overview of child abuse and neglect, in M. Bannon and Y. Carter *Protecting Children from Abuse and Neglect in Primary Care*. Oxford: Oxford University Press.
Powell, C. (1997) Protecting children: the crucial role of the children's nurse, *Paediatric Nursing*, 9(9): 13–16.
Powell, C. (2002) There is no such thing as a child receiving 'a good smack', *British Journal of Nursing*, 11(22): 1425.
Powell, C. (2003a) Early indicators of child abuse and neglect: a multi-professional Delphi study, *Child Abuse Review*, 12: 25–40.
Powell, C. (2003b) The Delphi technique: myths and realities, *Journal of Advanced Nursing*, 41(4): 376–82.
Powell, C. (2004) Why nurses should support the 'Children are unbeatable!' Alliance, *Paediatric Nursing*, 16(8): 29.
Powell, C. (2006) Children as individuals (letter), *Children Now*, 12th July, p.14.
Prescott, J. (2002) Speech by the Deputy Prime Minister on mainstreaming social justice for the 21st Century, to the Fabian Society. See: http://www.socialexclusionunit.gov.uk/news.asp?id=397 (accessed 21/07/06).
Qvortrup, J. (1994) Introduction, in J. Qvortrup, M. Bardy, G. Sgritta and H. Wintersberger (eds) *Childhood Matters: Social Theory, Practice and Politics*. Aldershot: Avebury.
Radbill, S. (1968) A history of child abuse and infanticide, in R.A. Helfer, C.H. Kempe (eds) *The Battered Child*. Chicago and London: The University of Chicago Press.
Ramchandani, P. and McConachie, H. (2005) Editorial: mothers, fathers and their children's health, *Child: Care, Health and Development*, 31(1): 5–6.
RCN (Royal College of Nursing) (2003) *Defining Nursing*. London: Royal College of Nursing.
RCN (Royal College of Nursing) (2006) *Female Genital Mutilation: An RCN Educational Resource for Nursing and Midwifery Staff*. London: Royal College of Nursing.
RCPCH (Royal College of Paediatrics and Child Health) (2002) *Fabricated or Induced Illness by Carers*. London: Royal College of Paediatrics and Child Health.
Reder, P., Duncan S. and Gray M. (1993) *Beyond Blame: Child Abuse Tragedies Revisited*. London: Routledge.
Reder, P. and Duncan, S. (1999) *Lost Innocents*. London: Routledge.

Reece, R.M. (1993) Fatal child abuse and sudden infant death syndrome: a critical diagnostic decision, *Pediatrics*, 91: 423–9.

Reece, R.M. and Sege, R. (2000) Childhood head injuries: accidental or inflicted? *Archives of Pediatrics and Adolescent Medicine*, 154: 11–15.

Regan, L., Lovett, J. and Kelly, L. (2004) *Forensic Nursing: An Option for Improving Responses to Reported Rape and Sexual Assault*. London: Home Office.

Rimza, M.E., Schackner, R.A., Bowen, K.A. and Marshall, W. (2002) Can child deaths be prevented? The Arizona Child Fatality Review Programme Experience. http://www.pediatrics.org./cgi/content/full/110/1/e11 (accessed 5/10/06).

Roberts, J. (1988) Why are some families more vulnerable to child abuse?, in K. Browne, C. Davies and P. Stratton (eds) *Early Prediction and Prevention of Child Abuse*. Chichester: Wiley.

Robertson, J. (1959) *Young Children in Hospital*. London: Tavistock Publications.

Royal College of Midwives, Royal College of Paediatricians and Child Health, Royal College of General Practitioners, Royal College of Nursing, Community Practitioner and Health Visitor Association (2006) *Safeguarding Children and Young People: Roles and Competences for Health Care Staff – Intercollegiate Document*. London: Royal College of Paediatrics and Child Health.

Royal College of Psychiatrists (2003) *Child Abuse and Neglect: The Role of Mental Health Services*. London: Royal College of Psychiatrists.

Sanders, M. (1999) Triple P-Positive Parenting Program: towards an empirically validated multi-level parenting and family support strategy for the prevention of behaviour and emotional problems in children, *Clinical Child and Family Psychology Review*, 2(2): 71–90.

Sanders, R., Colton, M. and Roberts, S. (1999) Child abuse fatalities and cases of extreme concern: lessons from reviews, *Child Abuse and Neglect*, 23(3): 257–68.

Sanders, T. and Cobley, C. (2005) Identifying non-accidental injury in children presenting to A&E departments: an overview of the literature, *Accident and Emergency Nursing*, 13(2): 130–6.

Scotland's Commissioner for Children and Young People (2006) *Second Annual Report 05/06*. Edinburgh: SCCYP.

Scott, S. and Skidmore, P. (2006) *Reducing the Risk: Barnardo's Support for Sexually Exploited Young People*. Ilford: Barnardo's.

Scottish Executive (2002) *It's Everyone's Job to Make Sure I'm Alright: Report of the Child Protection Audit and Review*. Edinburgh: Scottish Executive.

Scottish Executive (2004) *Protecting Children and Young People: Framework for Standards*. Edinburgh: Scottish Executive.

Scottish Executive (2006) *Protecting Children and Young People: Significant Incident Review, Draft for Consultation*. Edinburgh: Scottish Executive.

Seibel, M. and Parnell, T.F. (1998) The physician's role in confirming the diagnosis, in T.F. Parnell and O. Day (eds) *Munchausen Syndrome by Proxy: Misunderstood Child Abuse*. London: Sage.

Sidebotham, P. (2003) Red skies, risk factors and early indicators, *Child Abuse Review*, 12: 41–5.

Sinclair, R. and Bullock, R. (2002) *Learning from Past Experience: A Review of Serious Case Reviews*. London: Department of Health.

Smith, L., Colman, V. and Bradshaw, M. (2006) Family-centred Care, in E.A. Glasper and J. Richardson (eds) *A Textbook of Children's and Young People's Nursing*. Edinburgh: Churchill Livingstone.

Sobley, D. (2006) Special cases, not double standards, please, *Child Rights Information Network Newsletter*, 19: 30–3.

Southall, D.P., Samuels, M.P. and Golden, M.H. (2003) Classification of child abuse by motive and degree rather than type of injury, *Archives of Disease in Childhood*, 88: 101–4.

Speight, N. and Wynne, J. (2000) Is the Children Act failing severely abused and neglected children? *Archive of Diseases in Childhood*, 82: 192–6.

Spencer, N. and Baldwin, N. (2005) Economic, cultural and social contexts of Neglect, in J. Taylor and B. Daniel, *Child Neglect: Practical Issues for Health and Social Care*. London: Jessica Kingsley.

Srivastava, O.P. and Polnay, L. (1997) Field trial of graded care profile (GCP) scale: a new measure of care, *Archives of Disease in Childhood*, 76: 337–40.
Stevenson, O. (1998) *Neglected Children Issues and Dilemmas*. Oxford: Blackwell Science.
Stevenson, O. (2005a) Foreword, in J. Taylor and B. Daniel (eds) *Child Neglect: Practical Issues for Health and Social Care*. London: Jessica Kingsley.
Stevenson, O. (2005b) Working together in cases of neglect, in J. Taylor and B. Daniel (eds) *Child Neglect: Practical Issues for Health and Social Care*. London: Jessica Kingsley.
Stiffman, M.N., Schnitzer, P.G., Adam, P., Kruse, R.L. and Ewigman, B.G. (2002) Household composition and risk of fatal child maltreatment, *Pediatrics*, 109(4): 615–21.
Taylor, J. and Daniel, B. (eds) (2005) *Child Neglect: Practical Issues for Health and Social Care*. London: Jessica Kingsley.
Taylor, V. (2003) Female genital mutilation: cultural practice or child abuse? *Paediatric Nursing*, 15(1): 31–3.
Terry, L. (2004) Fabricated or induced illness in children, *Paediatric Nursing*, 16(1): 14–18.
Thomas, A.E. (2004) The bleeding child: is it NAI? *Archives of Disease in Childhood*, 89: 1163–7.
Thyen, U., Thiessen, R. and Heinsohn-Krug, M. (1995) Secondary prevention: serving families at risk, *Child Abuse and Neglect*, 19(11): 1337–47.
Truman, P. (2004) Problems in identifying cases of child neglect, *Nursing Standard*, 18(29): 33–8.
UNICEF (The United Nations Children's Fund) (2003) *A League Table of Child Maltreatment Deaths in Rich Nations - Innocenti Report Card No. 5*. Florence: UNICEF.
Utting, W. (1997) *People Like Us: The Report on the Review of Safeguards for Children Living Away from Home*. London: The Stationery Office.
Walker, M. (1992) *Surviving Secrets*. Buckingham: Open University Press.
Walker, M. and Glasgow, M (2005) Parental substance misuse and the implications for children, in J. Taylor and B. Daniel, *Child Neglect: Practical Issues for Health and Social Care*. London: Jessica Kingsley.
Walker, S., Shemmings, D. and Cleaver, H. (2003) *Write Enough*. London: HMSO. http://www.writeenough.org.uk/formats_genogram.htm (accessed 10/11/06).
Ward Platt, M. (2005) Investigating infant deaths, *British Medical Journal*, 330: 206–7.
Wattam, C. and Woodward, C. (1996) And do I abuse my children? NO! in NCIPCA *Childhood Matters*, volume II, Part 3. London: The Stationery Office
WCPSRG (Welsh Child Protection Systematic Review Group) (2005a) *CORE-INFO: Bruises on Children*. London: NSPCC.
WCPSRG (Welsh Child Protection Systematic Review Group) (2005b) *CORE-INFO: Fractures in Children*. London: NSPCC.
Webb, E. (2002) Health services: who are the best advocates for children? *Archives of Disease in Childhood*, 87: 175–7.
Webb, E. (2004) Discrimination against children, *Archives of Disease in Childhood*, 89: 804–8.
Welsh Assembly Government (2005) *National Service Framework for Children, Young People and Maternity Services*. Cardiff: Welsh Assembly Government.
WHO (World Health Organisation) (2003–4a) Child abuse and neglect UK Collaborating Centre. www.iop.kcl.ac.uk/who (accessed 24/04/06).
WHO (World Health Organisation) (2003–4b) *Bullying*. Collaborating Centre. www.iop.kcl.ac.uk/who (accessed 24/04/06).
Wilczynski, A. (1997) *Child Homicide*. London: Greenwich Medical Media Ltd.
Wolke, D., Woods, L., Bloomfield, L. and Karstadt, L. (2001) Bullying involvement in primary school and common health problems, *Archives of Disease in Childhood*, 85: 197–201.
Wright, C.M. (2005) What is weight faltering (failure to thrive) and when does it become a child protection issue?, in J. Taylor and B. Daniel, *Child Neglect: Practical Issues for Health and Social Care*. London: Jessica Kingsley.

INDEX